Notes from the Dream House

Philip French was born in Liverpool in 1933. He did his national service in the Parachute Regiment and was educated at Exeter College, Oxford and in the United States at Indiana University, Bloomington. He spent most of his career as a talks producer for BBC Radio.

He wrote movie essays and reviews from the early 1960s onwards for a variety of magazines and newspapers. Between 1973 and 2013 he was film critic for the *Observer*. In 1986 he was on the jury of the Cannes Film Festival, and in 1988 was a member of the Booker Prize jury. He was the Critics Circle Critic of the Year in 2003 and the British Press Awards Critic of the Year in 2009. He became an Honorary Member of BAFTA in 2008 and a Fellow of the British Film Institute in 2013. In 2013 he was awarded an OBE.

He wrote or edited numerous books including *The Movie Moguls* (1969), *Westerns: Aspects of a Movie Genre* (1974) and *The Faber Book of Movie Verse* (co-edited with Ken Wlaschin, 1993). A husband and father of three sons, French died in 2015. In 2016 the Critics Circle established the Philip French Award for outstanding breakthrough filmmaker of the year. In 2016 the Watershed arts venue in Bristol established the annual Philip French Lecture.

Enter the dream-house, brothers and sisters, leaving
Your debts asleep, your history at the door:
This is the home for heroes, and this loving
Darkness a fur you can afford.

C. Day Lewis, 'Newsreel'

Philip French

Notes from the Dream House
Selected Film Reviews
1963–2013

Edited by
Kersti, Karl, Patrick and Sean French

CARCANET

First published in Great Britain in 2018 by
Carcanet Press Limited
Alliance House, 30 Cross Street,
Manchester, M2 7AQ
www.carcanet.co.uk

A CIP catalogue record for this book is available from the British Library,
ISBN 978 1 78410 602 7

The publisher acknowledges financial assistance from Arts Council England.

Supported by
ARTS COUNCIL
ENGLAND

Typeset in Great Britain by XL Publishing Services, Exmouth, Devon
Printed in Great Britain by SRP Ltd., Exeter, Devon

Contents

2012

2013

Introduction

After Philip French's funeral in November 2015, the mourners came back for drinks at his house. A couple of younger film critics asked, a little nervously, if they might visit his 'cinema' which they'd heard talk about. It was worth seeing. There's a large screen, which descends with a buzz at the touch of a button in front of the windows, cutting out the daylight. The walls and the ceiling are painted a matt dark blue, the ceiling lights create a starlight effect, and there are old-fashioned lamps on either side of the screen. The walls are lined with shelves of videos, DVDs and Blu-rays. The videos are relics of a near-defunct technology, but Philip was reluctant to dispose of them. Many were otherwise unobtainable rarities taped at strange times of the night from obscure broadcasts.

Of course, most of Philip's movie-watching took place in Soho viewing theatres. He tended to use his home cinema for checking details or to revisit old movies he had first seen as a child at matinees in Liverpool, as a schoolboy in Bristol, in troop screenings in the Canal Zone, at Oxford, or in long-closed or long-demolished cinemas like the Academy on Oxford Street, the Tolmer in Camden, or the Astoria in Finsbury Park.

He wrote his reviews in a back room of his house crammed with movie reference books and also, oddly enough, a large collection of poetry. In the 1960s his working desk accommodated a portable Olivetti typewriter, an ashtray, a packet of cigarettes, and, as often as not, a gin and tonic. For the French family the early articles in this book will always be seen through a blue haze of smoke accompanied by the clacking of two-finger typing. By the early seventies, the gin and tonic had gone. By the mid-seventies the cigarettes had gone as well. And by the late-ish 1980s the Olivetti had, finally, joined them. But Philip was never entirely comfortable in the world of the Amstrad 8256, the MacBook and the Internet Movie Database. For him, journalism should be something in the style of Cary Grant and Rosalind Russell in *His Girl Friday*. And what need of the IMDb when you have Philip French's brain?

He wrote his first film reviews as an Oxford undergraduate in 1953. He filed his final one – a DVD re-issue of *The Ladykillers* – on the evening of Monday 26 October 2015, the day before he died. From 1959, his day job was producing radio programmes at the BBC, but during the 1960s and 1970s he regularly reviewed films, mostly for the *Times* and the *Observer*. He was more than once offered the job of *Observer* film critic, but the BBC management frowned on extra-curricular employment. Finally, in 1978, they relented, and he wrote for the *Observer* regularly until his eightieth birthday in summer 2013.

As *Observer* film critic, Philip reviewed the weekly releases as well as screenings of films on TV and, in later years, video and then DVD re-issues. He also wrote obituaries, thematic articles, book reviews and interviews. His writings for the *Observer* during this period amounted to well over three million words. His reviews from the previous couple of decades come to another few hundred thousand. So the selection in this book – about 120,000 words – represents a small fraction of his output.

What to include? What to leave out? We could easily have compiled an anthology entirely of his essays on westerns to accompany his 1974 book on the genre. 'There is no such thing as an uninteresting western,' was one of his dicta, and there was certainly never a Philip French review of a western that wasn't engaged, and few that were not combative. He felt a particular pleasure (one might almost say duty) in defending maligned, commercially challenged westerns like *Heaven's Gate* or, more recently, the Gore Verbinski-Johnny Depp version of *The Lone Ranger*. His reviews of the movies of Woody Allen, Clint Eastwood, the Coen brothers, Walter Hill, John Boorman, Ken Loach, Mike Leigh and many others are like extended works of reflection, dialogues with both his own past views and the filmmakers' developing careers. Only some of this can be suggested in an anthology of this scope.

Could there be room for some of his exchanges with his readers, not always amicable? He began his review of Richard Lester's 1979 movie *Butch and Sundance: The Early Days*, by lamenting the term 'prequel' that was used to describe it, concluding, 'Hopefully only those not dis-interested in language will be offended.' A schoolteacher wrote to point out that while correcting someone else's poor English, Philip had made two mistakes himself, and the teacher was using this in his class as an example of illiteracy. Philip wrote back: 'Not to worry. You can use it in your class – but as an example of misunderstood irony.'

Philip had made a tentative start at preparing an anthology of his reviews and had thought of organising the material thematically. Reluctantly we decided against this. It is our view that this book shows Philip developing as a critic. The thirty-something writer of the earlier articles was very different, we feel – more polemical perhaps) – from the Philip French of the 2000s, with a thirty-year relationship with his readers and almost a lifetime of films, not to mention the decades of voracious reading and theatre-going and absorption in the visual arts.

This is not a potted history of the cinema. It is not an anthology of masterpieces. There are masterpieces reviewed here, but also minor films. We tried to choose films that covered the range of Philip's interests and the scope of his life. Faced with the choice between two equally good reviews, we chose the more important film. But each review we picked struck us as in some way revealing, enticing, entertaining in itself.

This is not a systematic account of the cinema. But even so we hope that a particular idea of the movies emerges from these pages, and also the idea of a man. Robert Warshow, an American critic Philip much admired, once wrote: 'A man watches a movie, and the critic must acknowledge that he is that man.' The reader of these reviews will come to know and recognise a man who grew up in provincial England, served in the army, studied at Oxford and in the United States, married a Swedish woman, had three sons, and spent his working life mainly at the BBC and the *Observer*. He was an old-fashioned liberal, a Labour supporter in the Clement Attlee/Nye Bevan tradition, a critical friend of America and an opponent of totalitarianism in all its forms. Among many other things – and, we hope, many other pleasures – this collection may serve as the memoir Philip French never quite got around to writing.

Kersti, Karl, Patrick and Sean French

The Damned (Joseph Losey)

The Times, 19 May 1963

'WARNING – don't go alone, take a brave, nerve-less friend with you', the advertisements advise would-be patrons of a new Hammer double bill. The main feature is *Maniac,* accompanied however by Joseph Losey's *The Damned,* to which 'In the Picture' drew attention last week.

Losey, an American who has worked in this country since the early fifties, has directed a film that would have been a credit to Britain if shown at Cannes – as it is, it hasn't even been shown to the British press.

The Damned is set on the Dorset coast between Weymouth and Portland and involves five main characters – Bernard (Alexander Knox), the Scots head of a top secret Government research establishment, Freya Nilsson (Viveca Lindfors), a Swedish sculptress who rents a cottage from him, King (Oliver Reed), the leader of a teenage motorcycle gang, his sister (Shirley Anne Field) and an American visitor (Macdonald Carey).

In the first five minutes Losey links their fate. The American is led into the gang's trap by the girl, robbed by them, then assisted back to his hotel by two of Bernard's military aides, where he meets Bernard and the sculptress. Every movement of the camera, every frame, each line of dialogue plays its part in establishing Losey's picture of the town, his characters and their troubled world.

'I never expected something like this to happen to me in England,' says the American. 'The age of senseless violence has caught up with us too,' Bernard tells him. We are gradually introduced to Bernard's answer to this age – his elaborate sterile establishment, where nine children are incarcerated in an underground classroom. He addresses them only via TV, and their every move is watched on monitor screens. (Images of spying and surveillance recur throughout the film.)

These children are being trained by Bernard to inherit a contaminated earth. Discovering Bernard's secret costs the other four their lives.

The Damned belongs with Franju's *The Keepers* and Rivette's *Paris nous appartient,* to the cinema of Angst; it captures and projects the anxiety of a world trying to live with the threat of a nuclear holocaust. It is necessarily schematic, depending less on the direct representation of everyday life than on the reorganisation of reality to present a coherent personal vision. It is a highly complex film, the best sequences have a peculiar density, the images a rare impact and memorability – a ton-up around a quiet harbour, a rubber-gloved hand turning a globe, a helicopter pursuing a speeding sports car.

One example of the careful overall conception is the use made of Elizabeth Frink's sculptures of menacing birds and liberating bird-like men. Their ambiguous symbolism – suggesting freedom and activity, anxiety and peace – is used to define the protagonists' attitudes to society both verbally and pictorially. (At the end this motif is ironically extended in the grim inhuman harbingers of death, the helicopters which fly at Bernard's will.) The sculptures are a major unifying element and ultimately give an indefinable poetic quality to this superbly photographed and designed film.

It is not without flaws. Macdonald Carey is stolid and negative, Shirley Anne Field indifferent, several sequences are plainly inadequate. Nevertheless it is one of the most significant recent British movies, a disturbing work of real importance.

After the publication of the above review, Philip received the following letter. Having been blacklisted by House Un-American Activities Committee (HUAC), Losey had been forced to move his filmmaking across the Atlantic. The response from this iconic figure to one of his very earliest reviews touched Philip deeply.

London, 6 June 1963

Dear Mr French,

I don't normally write to critics, but since it was made so difficult for the press to see 'The Damned', and since your thoughtful review was so very helpful both to the picture and to myself, I should like to make this exception, and thank you for your trouble, and your perceptiveness in praising it and not over-praising it.

The review meant a great deal to the situation of the film, and to my own practical working situation at the moment, and I much appreciate your interest and effort.

Sincerely,

Joseph Losey

In 'my own working situation at the moment' Losey was referring to
the easing of the pressure on him during the production of The Servant,
which remained one of Philip's favourite films, a work that he regarded
as one of the towering achievements of British film-making.

Cul-de-sac (Roman Polanski)

The Times, 5 June 1966

By temperament and lately by necessity many Central European artists
have been drawn to allegorical forms, and it was in this vein that Roman
Polanski made his name with *Two Men and a Wardrobe* in 1958 while
still a student at the Polish film school. He followed it up with another
allegorical short, *Le Gros et le maigre*, made in France in 1960.

His three feature films, the Polish *Knife in the Water*, the British
Repulsion and now his second British movie, *Cul-de-sac* (Cameo-Poly),
are also allegories of sorts, but so fully realised in terms of character and
situations as to defy any one simple explanation. Underpinned with a
mythic force, they work on a surface level, both realistically and within
their particular dramatic conventions – respectively, psychological
drama, psychiatric horror story and black comedy.

Cul-de-sac, I'd say, owes a little to Harold Pinter (it has something in
common with Albee and a few others as well). The wounded gangsters,
who first appear pushing a stolen taxi along the causeway leading to an
island off the Northumberland coast, are somewhat reminiscent of
Goldberg and McCann in *The Birthday Party*; equally, however, they
recall Polanski's men with a wardrobe. These two thugs have come to
menace the already disturbed existence of a middle-aged businessman,
George (a shaven-headed Donald Pleasence), who has retired to an
eleventh-century castle to nurse his ulcers, his illusions and his sluttish
young French wife, Teresa (Françoise Dorléac). After the rapid demise
of his Irish partner (Jack McGowran), the American thug, Richard
(gravel-voiced Lionel Stander), stays on to terrorise George and Teresa,
becoming the confessor of one and the butt of the other. When guests
arrive unexpectedly, he is forced into the role of butler.

As in the earlier pictures, Polanski's characters play games, the deadly kind described by Eric Berne in his book *Games People Play*, and exploit one another with a cruelty ranging from the childlike to the calculatedly sadistic. Each one is alone but can define himself only in relation to other people. George actually obtains a kind of release through Richard's persecution and humiliation – from his inhibitions (he can insult his so-called friends), from his wife and eventually from his mind. At the end he slays his intruder as the girl did in *Repulsion* and the husband *thought* he did in *Knife in the Water*.

Like the Polish lakes in *Knife in the Water* and the South Kensington of *Repulsion*, the setting of *Cul-de-sac* is integral to the overall conception, as is the capturing of the precise mood induced by the time of day and the weather. In this Polanski has been helped by one of the finest black-and-white cameramen around, Gilbert Taylor, who also photographed *Repulsion* (as well as *Dr Strangelove* and *A Hard Day's Night*).

Polanski directs with the sort of unobtrusive skill and economy we associate with Renoir and Hitchcock. The latter, after his experiments in the forties with the ten-minute take, would be particularly impressed with the brilliance of a virtuoso single-take sequence in *Cul-de-sac*. It is a complicated scene that starts with the wife running down to bathe in the distant sea and concludes with her returning to Richard and George and the three of them disappearing over the sand dunes back to the castle. In the middle of the sequence a low-flying coastal patrol plane passes over, and throughout the camera moves back and forth between close-up and long-shot, following the subtly changing relationship of the two men in the brooding pre-dawn light. It's a remarkable seven or eight minutes of filmmaking, yet handled in so reserved a way that only on a second viewing did I become aware of it being done without a single cut.

It is not a pleasant world Polanski creates, the images are intense and disturbing, but it is compellingly presented, with a personal, obsessive undercurrent. For all that, the film is frequently very funny and it is beautifully acted. The pathetic trio are viewed objectively but not heartlessly.

The Round-Up (Miklos Jancso)

The Observer, 6 November 1966

It is rarely advisable to describe a film as a masterpiece on the strength of a single viewing, especially if one has emerged from it physically and mentally limp. But this is what I consider Miklos Jancso's *The Round-Up* to be.

The setting is a prison camp on the Hungarian plains in the 1860s, where the sorry remnants of Kossuth's revolutionary forces have been interned in a general round-up of outlaws. Operating like chessmasters, the police play off the prisoners against one another, manipulating them by complicated manoeuvres into revealing themselves and betraying their comrades. From our very first sight, at the beginning, of a man being silently selected from the anonymous crowd of abject captives, we are drawn into this terrible one-sided game in which every move turns out to be part of an overall scheme. Our minds are simultaneously fascinated and horrified by the skill of the exploiters; our emotions alternate between pity and contempt for their victims.

The whole film, informed by a ferocious intelligence and a rigorous economy, is directed towards the creation of a single image. It is austerely shot in hard black on bleached white. The prison is bare and clean like a model farm, standing in the middle of a flat, seemingly unending plain that continually invites escape while denying all possibility of its success. There is little physical violence apart from a harrowing sequence of a girl being beaten to death – and this, to the persecutors, is only part of a larger psychological pattern. There is no comment on the events or their implications; everyone is too intent upon his business of pursuit or evasion.

Until the last twenty seconds, when a few bars of 'Deutschland über Alles' accompany the final turn of the screw, there is no music, only a background of natural sounds: the chirping of unseen birds, the wind, the crunch of boots on gravel, the creaking of doors. Totally realised within its time and place, completely self-contained artistically by its own ruthless logic, *The Round-Up* can be both accepted for what it is and, like the best work in the tradition of Kafka, interpreted in ways limited and universal.

The Gospel According to St Matthew (Pier Paolo Pasolini)

The Times, 4 June 1967

When the subject of religion and the cinema is raised it's usually the unforgettably bad films that come first to mind rather than the memorably good ones. But though there have been a number of outstanding movies on religious themes, only one film of distinction, D.W. Griffith's *Intolerance*, has dealt with the life of Christ and that only in the least developed of its episodes. At least until Pier Paolo Pasolini's *The Gospel According to St Matthew*.

There have been in the sixties two major American treatments of the same subject by directors of some standing: Nicholas Ray's *King of Kings* and George Stevens's *The Greatest Story Ever Told*. Both of them were rightly accorded short shrift by critics, whatever merit they may have had in the eyes of 'the Divine Projectionist', to use the phrase of His lifelong servant Cecil B. DeMille. These films have been forgotten but their malodorous publicity lingers on to be cherished by connoisseurs of that Hollywood rhetoric from which the pictures are inseparable.

Jeffrey Hunter was chosen to play the King of Kings 'because of his rugged strength, sincerity and personal integrity', and 'the dedicated dream of Samuel Bronston' was realised by a director 'whose envisionment of the herculean task reflected a deeply reverent, personal dedication.' *The Greatest Story Ever Told*, as befits the humility of its title, was 'envisioned as the American motion-picture industry's first definitive answer to the almost universal quest for peace of mind and hope, in a troubled and confused world', and so 'religious leaders of every leading faith – Protestant, Catholic, Jewish, Islamic, Hindu and Buddhist' were consulted before Stevens could set about 'the exhausting, man-killing job of beginning the actual production'.

It is easy and necessary to make fun of these pictures, and no one has done so better than Pasolini himself in his savage contribution to the four-part film *Rogopag* in which he satirises the shooting of a biblical extravaganza. But having done this he then proceeds to demonstrate exactly how such a picture should be made. He does not, like Stevens, examine 'thirty different editions of the Bible', nor 'study the most up-to-date opinions' of theologians. What he does is something so simple that at this stage in the evolution of the cinema it has about it the mark of genius. He takes St Matthew's Gospel as the sole basis of his screenplay, casts his film from non-professionals who seem to him to have the right kind of faces (his Christ was a Spanish architectural student) and makes the picture entirely in Southern Italy.

Where Stevens's rationalising liberalism (altogether too flabby to be called demythologisation) drove him to conceal the miracles and bring on Satan as 'the dark hermit', the rigorous Italian Marxist Pasolini dodges nothing; the angels, the miracles, the temptation, the walking on the water, St Matthew described them and they are there. We see the loaves and the fishes suddenly appear, but the instant they do a swarm of flies descends to cover them.

The brisk, choppy style of the picture reflects the style of the Gospel, and the stern, rapidly striding Christ matches the urgent figure who is its hero. No scene is given more or less weight than in the original, and the barren impoverished regions in which the film was shot frame the events with total conviction. Pasolini's John the Baptist is a scrawny fellow, balding and undernourished, with a mouthful of bad teeth and the radiance of a true believer. The disciples look like men who do the jobs from which they are called, and one can believe that they dropped their nets instantly to follow this man of unwavering conviction. Their clothes, like their master's, are threadbare and torn. When Christ is put on the cross we see that he is a man of unimpressive physique. His power resides in his will and is expressed in his face, gesture and words. We also sense the crucifixion as occurring on the fringe of Roman imperial history, of immediate significance only to a handful of devoted followers.

Apart from the eclectic score, which works admirably as an unobtrusive modern commentary on the film's simplicity, Pasolini never forces any attitude upon the audience. What he does is to present a society and a man who arose in it as contemporaries recorded it. In the case of the Sermon on the Mount he avoids a built-in impact by shooting it in a series of terse close-ups against different backgrounds of sky and scenery, thus eliminating any distraction from the uncompromising word.

The Gospel According to St Matthew is a noble film of which one can say nothing higher in praise than that Pasolini has fully earned the right to dedicate it to the memory of Pope John XXIII.

1967   7

My Children's Taste in Films

The Times, 16 July 1967

I know a lot about my children, but I'm not really sure what they like. So I can't predict just how they (or anyone else's children) will respond to the three films this week that seem to be directed principally at them: the comedy western *Texas Across the River*, the cod science fiction *Jules Verne's Rocket to the Moon* and the Hollywood fairy tale *Jack the Giant Killer*.

My eight-year-old will happily sit through any kind of rubbish, though his favourite movies are *Easy Street*, *The Red Badge of Courage* and *The War Lord*, which he liked for the battles and the whiff of historical authenticity without worrying too much about the intricacies of *droit du seigneur*. My six-year-old can take them or leave them; told that *The Sound of Music* was going to be a long film, he stood up, a relieved expression on his face, at the end of the pre-credit sequence, only to be clamped down in his seat for a further three hours. (Neither of them is much impressed, incidentally, by Julie Andrews. They belong, I think, to a generation that will prefer the au pair across the street to the girl next door.) My three-year-old hasn't been initiated yet, and there's no knowing how a child brought up to believe that there are Daleks at the bottom of the garden is going to react.

Point Blank (John Boorman)

Sight & Sound, Spring 1968

During the last couple of years the character of Hollywood movies has been affected by the popularity of free-style films from Europe and the altered attitude at home of the industry's own censorship requirements and those of the National Catholic Office for Motion Pictures, which is now giving awards to pictures that once would have received its 'Condemned' rating. Both the 'C' change and the sea-change are to be seen at their most extreme in *Point Blank*, a film that is interesting for a variety of reasons, quite apart from the reflection that it would make the late Louis Mayer spin in his tomb – a thought that occurred to me during the picture when the central character visits his wife's grave in a Los Angeles cemetery and passes a yellow mechanical digger coolly excavating a hole for another anonymous corpse.

It is interesting as a first-class thick-ear thriller that grips from beginning to end; as a dazzling American debut by John Boorman; as an even more remarkable case than *Bonnie and Clyde* of the imaginative feedback into Hollywood of New Wave borrowings; and as the latest film starring Lee Marvin, whose place alongside Julie Andrews as the biggest box-office draw of the moment is both a tribute to his impressive screen presence and some sort of comment on our times.

Without Marvin the film would probably never have been made, or, having been made, achieved its popular success; for to a large extent the aggressive, forward-thrusting, impassive Marvin contains the meaning of the picture. At only one point does he smile, and that is when his wife, just before her suicide, recalls an unregainable past happiness: in a dreamy silent flashback he registers this brief show of emotion. Marvin's current position deserves an essay in itself, inasmuch as he has shifted to the centre of movies without substantially changing the nature or depth of his roles. Briefly one might say that Julie Andrews is the hawks' favourite dove and Marvin the doves' favourite hawk.

The movement of *Point Blank* is circular. The film begins at the deserted Alcatraz federal prison in San Francisco Bay, where a middle-aged thug called Walker (Marvin) has been left for dead by his wife and partner, who have cheated him out of his share of a hi-jacking operation. It ends after Walker has gone, rung by murderous rung, up a criminal syndicate's chain of command to regain his $93,000, only to find himself back at Alcatraz facing the syndicate's boss Fairfax, who under an alias has been offering advice and assistance throughout the pursuit. The baffled Walker withdraws impotently into an abandoned cell, and the film closes with a desolating long shot of a mist-shrouded Alcatraz.

The outline of this plot comes from Richard Stark's novel *The Hunter*, as does the idea of the freelance crook up against the faceless syndicate which his treacherous ex-partner has joined. But whereas Godard used Stark's *Série noire* novel *The Jugger* merely as a springboard for *Made in U.S.A.*, Boorman and his scriptwriters (Alexander Jacobs, David Newhouse and Rafe Newhouse) use *The Hunter* as a trampoline. They transform the story by leaving out all but the barest suggestion of motivation, by introducing Fairfax as a mysteriously ubiquitous figure like Arkadin in *Confidential Report*, and by the movie's style, which owes a good deal to Welles, Truffaut, Godard and above all Resnais. They have also changed the setting from New York to California, and mostly Los Angeles, where the syndicate becomes as much a part of what Alison Lurie called *The Nowhere City* as the characters of *Muriel* are of Resnais's 'Nowhere City', Boulogne. And for all the occasional artiness of *Point Blank*, its self-consciousness is less an inclination of self-indulgence than of a director and writers supremely confident of what they are doing.

Like Lang and Hitchcock before him, Boorman has found in California a resonant reality to be manipulated instead of one to be created, as in his first film *Catch Us If You Can*. In his first feature, where he was gravely handicapped by the obligatory presence of the Dave Clark Five, Boorman was forcing his material, imposing a burden upon his London and West Country locations that they could scarcely bear, though the underlying theme of a disillusioning quest where nothing turns out to be as it seems – and even the conclusion on a deserted island with an ambiguous meeting between pursuer and pursued – is much the same.

But the quest in *Point Blank* is quite unlike that in say *Moving Target*, or *Tony Rome* and the other attempts to revive the private-eye genre of the forties. Walker is no knight errant; the complexity of *Point Blank* lies in the style, in the omission of motivation and explanation, the flashbacks, flash-forwards and repetition, not in a tortuous story; and it does not provide an excuse for a galaxy of stars to give cameo performances with a perverse eccentricity that the new permissiveness allows. There are no false trails, few intrusions by outsiders whether ordinary citizens or police, and the syndicate is run by colourless figures with respectable names like Carter, Brewster and Fairfax who inhabit smart offices atop elegant concrete slabs or live in suburban houses redolent of gracious living.

When Walker confronts Carter the scene is an upper-class charity drive meeting; when Brewster returns home to find a vengeful Walker waiting, his first remark is that no one has watered the plants in his absence. They view Walker's vulgar demand for cash with contempt: Brewster carries a mere eleven dollars and the dead Carter's wallet unfolds into a string of credit cards. Against their tenuous order, Walker's weapons are the forces of disruption at his disposal – his own controlled, unpredictable psychopathic violence, and sex. His break-through into the syndicate hierarchy is achieved by using his wife's sister (Angie Dickinson), who has become his ex-partner's mistress.

Ultimately this superficially amoral little fable has many of the quali-ties of a dream – there are in fact close resemblances between *Point Blank* and Norman Mailer's fantasy of sex and violence *An American Dream*. Herein I think lies much of its power and the key to its form as a bleak, deadly and often grimly funny allegory of contemporary American life, which while falling some way short of *Bonnie and Clyde* is incomparably superior to *The Happening*. With or without irony, the picture is genu-inely Made in U.S.A.

Tell Them Willie Boy Is Here (Abraham Polonsky)

The Financial Times, 12 April 1969

In 1948 the screenwriter Abraham Polonsky made an auspicious direc-torial debut with *Force of Evil*, a gangster film suffused with bitter social criticism and a sort of tragic poetry. It still ranks among the most pene-trating studies that Hollywood has given us of the underworld's relationship to the larger American society. Shortly after making this picture Polonsky fell victim to the House Un-American Activities Committee investigations and found himself on the blacklist where he remained, writing pseudonymous screenplays, for twenty years. He has now emerged from oblivion to write and direct *Tell Them Willie Boy Is Here*, a western that uses its chosen genre as powerfully as did *Force of Evil* the crime picture.

Like most of the more interesting recent westerns, *Willie Boy* is con-cerned not with the heroic struggles of the early pioneers but with the social and psychological problems posed at the turn of the century during the difficult transition from rough frontier life to an apparently more settled existence. The film asks questions about the legacy of the frontier experience and the Western myth to modern America; it is also, and pretty obviously, an allegory of universal and local application that can be interpreted in several mutually supporting ways. The plot is based fairly closely on a true incident that occurred in southern California in 1909. A young Paiute Indian called Willie Boy accidentally shot his prospective father-in-law and took off across the Mojave Desert with his girl. According to tribal custom he had committed no offence, and the initial pursuit by a local posse was half-hearted. The demise of an Indian was a relatively unimportant matter and the deputy-sheriff in charge of the case had more important things to do that week, for he had been appointed as personal bodyguard to President Taft, who was to stop over in a local town during a cross-country tour. Unfortunately the news-hungry press contingent accompanying the President seized on various rumours surrounding Willie's pathetic flight to whip up a scare story about a possible Indian uprising and a threatened Presidential assassination. The chase thus turned into a full-scale manhunt that culminated in the deaths of the two fugitives.

Polonsky doesn't build up Willie into a simple, sympathetic, noble savage. In the end perhaps he takes on a tragic stature, but the film has no obvious heroes or villains and has few touches of sentimentality. As played by Robert Blake, Willie's a tough, glowering, intransigent figure, aware of the helplessness of himself and his people, and incapable of either adjusting to this situation or doing anything to change it. 'You walk around as if you still own this country,' a bar-room lout unjustly tells him, and he himself remarks that, 'nobody gives a damn what Indians do.' On the other side of the racial fence from Willie and his girl are the young deputy sheriff Cooper (Robert Redford) and his mistress, Dr Elizabeth Arnold (Susan Clark), a Boston-educated Reservation Superintendent. Cooper, the coarse, ill-educated son of an Indian fighter ('Your daddy was lucky, he died when it was still good to live,' a nostalgic old-timer remarks), is conscious of deeper affinities with Willie than the burgeoning, self-important twentieth-century community that sends him out to capture the young Indian. Dr Arnold is a well-meaning, rather neurotic liberal who wishes to integrate the Indians by converting them into model American citizens; she wants Willie's girl brought back to continue her training as a teacher. But she blinds herself both to the implications of destroying the autonomous Indian culture and to the obvious reluctance of her fellow citizens to accept Indians on equal terms. These relationships are not quite as schematic as this description implies.

Except for a few intrusive lines of rhetoric, Polonsky tells his story modestly and economically, without rancour or resort to caricature. And he is well served by his admirable cast and his photographer Conrad Hall, whose bleached colour images of the autumn journey through the scorching desert and the parched mountain trails provide at every stage an exact pictorial equivalent of the film's dramatic movement. Particularly telling is the cross-cutting between Willie's desperate flight and the flag-bedecked hotel where local dignitaries are gathering to greet the President for whom a special outsize chair has been made. Remarkable too is the gunfight in which Willie shoots not at his pursuers but at their horses; the result is a confused, painful spectacle, drained of the usual audience-pleasing excitement.

Yet for all the closely observed detail, what remains in the mind is the total firm-boned structure of the narrative development that takes Willie inexorably from the opening scene as a primitive car rattles past him on a dusty road to the final shot of the funeral pyre in the mountains. That Polonsky, nearly sixty, should have been able to return to Hollywood and make such a personal, deeply felt movie is indeed extraordinary. While nothing can make up for those lost years when he was denied the means of practising his art, it is to be hoped that he will now have the opportunity of creating that significant body of work that not so long ago seemed out of the question.

Last Tango in Paris (Bernardo Bertolucci)

The Times, 16 March 1973

Two things need to be said straight away about Bernardo Bertolucci's *Last Tango in Paris*. First, it is almost totally unerotic, and the sex scenes are briefer, less explicit than in many commercial movies nowadays. I found it a good deal less shocking than Bergman's *The Silence* ten years ago, a film which in many ways it resembles. Second, the film falls some way short of greatness, though this is due more to the limitations of its vision than to any technical or aesthetic imperfections. Except perhaps for some rather heavy-handed cinéaste's homages (particularly one to Vigo's *L'Atalante* which is maybe intentionally clumsy) and a few crudely observed sequences involving a television film unit, the picture is masterly, as one might expect from the director of *Before the Revolution* and *The Conformist*.

Bertolucci establishes the mood and theme by placing beside the credit titles two Francis Bacon portraits of a man and a woman, each isolated and hideously distorted by some unnameable agony. His film might be seen as a commentary on these paintings made through the central character, Paul (Marlon Brando), a desperate, middle-aged figure at the end of his tether whose unfaithful wife has just committed suicide in the cheap hotel they ran together.

Paul meets a twenty-year-old girl, Jeanne (Maria Schneider), while inspecting an apartment in Passy, where the film opens with a stunningly photographed sequence on the double-level Bir-Hakeim bridge. Their initial encounter culminates in a violent sexual act, semi-rape, semi-mutual seduction, ending with them stretched out on the floor in tormented Baconian postures. Thereafter they meet daily in the half-furnished flat on a no-name basis to engage in what is supposed to be an exclusively carnal relationship, during which they indulge in reminiscence and cruel and playful banter. She makes gestures of tenderness, and he subjects her to gross humiliation and degradation.

Meanwhile they go about their lives. She lives with her mother, a colonel's widow, and is the subject of a smart, self-indulgent cinema-vérité film being made by her boyfriend, a TV director played by Jean-Pierre Léaud, a presence invoking the Paris of Godard and Truffaut. Paul slouches around his sordid hotel, arranging his wife's funeral, coping with his distraught mother-in-law ('You're not alone, I'm here,' she says with unconscious irony), talking to his wife's lover (Massimo Girotti) who lives at the hotel.

At the very moment that Paul comes to terms with his wife's death and seeks to re-enter the so-called real world, Jeanne has prepared herself to marry her fiancé. He pursues her through the streets, and there is a brilliantly staged and bitterly comic interlude when they intrude upon a highly symbolic tango contest. Then they reach her home where, in a melodramatic anti-climax to which Bertolucci has been building in a variety of subtle ways, she kills him with her father's service revolver.

As Paul, Brando gives a performance of shattering intensity that draws the whole film together, lifting it above the schematic intellectualised level it might have remained on with a lesser actor (or an actor giving less of himself) in the role. He transforms *Last Tango* into an emotional experience that leaves one both totally exhausted and yet eager to see it again as soon as possible. Several interpretations of the picture will be obvious from the foregoing account, but this is a work from which everyone will extract his own personal meaning. What we see on the screen is a truthful image of life today, the ways in which we try to make contact with each other and the world around us. It is not the total truth, or everybody's truth, but like a Beckett play or a Bacon painting it is a sufficiently large and resonant segment of the whole to give us a new perspective on ourselves.

Two-Lane Blacktop (Monte Hellman)
The Times, 23 March 1973

During the sixties an informal school of young filmmakers sprang up in Hollywood around that prolific producer-director of low-budget movies, Roger Corman. His generous encouragement and assistance initiated the careers of some and re-directed those of others, among them actors Jack Nicholson, Peter Fonda and Dennis Hopper, the cameraman Laszlo Kovacs and the directors Peter Bogdanovich, Francis Ford Coppola and Monte Hellman. The least known of this important group is Hellman, whose remarkable western, *The Shooting*, Corman financed back in 1965, though it wasn't shown here until the end of 1971 at the Screen on Islington Green. The same cinema is to be congratulated on exhibiting his latest picture, *Two-Lane Blacktop* (1971), one of the best movies to come out of America in the past few years.

The film's structure is simple and linear, its varied resonances complex, even mystical. Two long-haired young car freaks head east from California, going nowhere in particular in the souped-up 1955 Chevrolet they race for small bets. In Arizona they take aboard a hippie girl, as laconic, disaffiliated and cool as themselves. From time to time they are overtaken by the grinning middle-aged driver of a gleaming orange Pontiac GTO, and half-way across New Mexico this random rivalry becomes a race to Washington DC, the winner to take the loser's car. Known simply as GTO (the other characters are similarly identified on the cast list as 'The Driver', 'The Mechanic' and 'The Girl'), the Pontiac driver changes his identity with every situation, turns a new face to each hitchhiker he picks up. He becomes among other things a test pilot, a TV producer with a broken family, a man with sinister 'connections' in Chicago. To a bereaved mother and granddaughter he is on his way to Florida to fix a house for his old mum. At the end, when the race has been casually abandoned, he tells his latest passengers that he has just won the Pontiac in a contest with the '55 Chevy he had built up from scratch to confound Detroit; 'those satisfactions are permanent', he says with the same conviction he brings to every role he assumes.

GTO is a familiar figure in American life and literature, from the nineteenth-century novel up to Barth, Pynchon and Nabokov. The relationship between the boys and him is similar to that described by Tony Tanner in *City of Words*: 'In many recent American novels we will find the hero in quest of identity confronting a Protean figure whose quick metamorphoses seem to make him enviably well adapted to reality; but the hero seldom takes him for a model, no matter how much he will learn from him, for that way lies chaos, the nightmare jelly, the ultimate dissolution of self.'

With unobtrusive precision Hellman captures the feeling of the vastness of American space, its variety and monotony, and the eternal restlessness of its nomadic people. 'The thing is you've got to keep moving.... You can never go too fast,' say the boys, and a Kris Kristofferson song (heard from a car radio, as is the rest of the film's music) comments on their situation: 'Freedom's just another word for nothing left to lose.' Any tug towards easy romanticism is undercut by Hellman's consistent detachment. He refuses to take sides, or present a situation through the main character's eyes, or to view the often bizarre and hostile scenes maliciously or satirically. In this the film differs significantly from the much inferior *Easy Rider* with its postcard scenery and paranoid vision.

The performances all round are excellent, especially Warren Oates as GTO, who has now joined that rank of semi-ugly stars led by Lee Marvin. If the rise of the powerful, menacing Marvin, the doves' favourite hawk, paralleled interestingly the build-up of the Vietnam War, then Oates, the tough, vulnerable, optimistic loser, might be considered the Lee Marvin of de-escalation.

Day for Night (François Truffaut)

The Times, 16 November 1973

Back in 1920, D.W. Griffith laughed when Scott Fitzgerald suggested that one of the best subjects for a movie was the filmmaking business itself, and twenty years later the novelist died halfway through proving that it was also a fitting subject for a major novel. David O. Selznick took the same view. 'I believed,' he said, 'that the whole world was interested in Hollywood, and that the trouble with most films about Hollywood was that they gave a false picture, that they burlesqued it, or they over-sentimentalised it.' Selznick made one of the best examples of what has now become almost a genre (*A Star Is Born* in 1937), and was himself the model for another (Minnelli's *The Bad and the Beautiful*, 1952).

The movie about the movies offers rich opportunities for comedy (exploited by Chaplin in *Behind the Screen* as early as 1915), for tragedy, for exercises in illusion, disillusion and instant Pirandello, for the confrontation of commerce and culture, for observing a microcosm of contemporary society, for looking at the real tinsel behind the false tinsel and so on. And Selznick's strictures still apply to the majority of them.

Perhaps the finest examples of the genre are *Singin' in the Rain*, *8½*, and Godard's *Contempt*. They are now joined by François Truffaut's *Day for Night*, which is the technical term for shooting night scenes in daylight using a filter, what is known among French filmmakers as 'la nuit américaine', the film's resonant original title. *Day for Night* is a celebration of Truffaut's love of moviegoing and moviemaking and expresses his warm Renoiresque feeling for mankind; it might also be seen as a belated answer to his friend's bitter *Contempt* of ten years ago that so angrily assaulted the movie industry and which the new film closely parallels.

The picture-within-the-picture is called *Meet Pamela*, an unpromising international drama being shot at the Victorine Studio in Nice, though the setting is Paris, starring a nerve-shattered English actress (Jacqueline Bisset), a callow juvenile lead (Jean-Pierre Léaud), an ageing near-alcoholic Italian star (Valentina Cortese) and a homosexual matinée idol (Jean-Pierre Aumont, once known in Hollywood as 'the Continental lover'). At the centre of the hurricane is Truffaut himself as a director coping hour by hour for seven weeks with what must be his own lifetime of experiences (and several other people's) of what can go wrong while making a picture. 'Shooting a movie,' he muses, 'is like taking a stage-coach journey through the Wild West – first you hope for a good trip and then you finish up just thinking about reaching the destination.'

There are running jokes, reversals of roles, rapid changes of mood, a tangling and unravelling of life and art, layers and layers of allusion and implication. We are shown how the magician prepares his tricks and are then lured into applauding them when they are next performed. For instance, early on we are instructed in how a fake candle is illuminated from within and hear the theme music from a key fancy dress scene played over the telephone; later we watch a most affecting sequence featuring the candle and the music – but what we are responding to is the 'real-life' situation of the actors who are performing it in *Meet Pamela*. Again, a complicatedly set up scene, in which a cat is supposed to lap up some milk, goes comically wrong several times and a new cat has to be found – and we appreciate that for the 'real' Truffaut it must have been more difficult to get this scene 'wrong' than 'right'.

Each night during shooting the director has a recurrent dream, which is shot expressionistically like a dream from a forties *film noir*. As he tosses and turns, the echoing voices of people who have troubled him on the set during the day give way to a black-and-white sequence of a boy (who must be the young Truffaut) progressing down an empty night street carrying a hooked walking stick. Each time we see it he gets farther towards his objective – which turns out to be not something sinister, not a nightmare at all, but the deserted cinema showing *Citizen Kane*, from the foyer of which, with the aid of the stick, he steals a batch of cherished stills from Welles's film.

Day for Night is a beautifully acted, funny, thoughtful, oddly elegiac film. It may be a trifle self-indulgent, but never slips over into sentimentality or caricature. There's also the added bonus of spotting Graham Greene in a walk-on part as the studio's British insurance adviser. Altogether it is the most enjoyable picture I've seen this year and one of the few recent occasions when I've emerged from the cinema feeling better than when I went in.

Aguirre, Wrath of God (Werner Herzog)

The Times, 15 November 1974

There are few good historical films and even fewer intelligent epics, so for this reason Werner Herzog's *Aguirre, Wrath of God* is doubly welcome. This West German film is based on a little-known event during the Spanish conquest of Peru, an incident so relatively minor that John Hemming accords it a brief footnote, and Prescott doesn't mention it at all. In late 1560, Gonzalo Pizarro (Francisco's brother) led an 11,000-strong expedition across the Andes in search of the golden city of El Dorado. Bogged down in the swamps of the Upper Amazon, he sent a small advance party down the river under Don Pedro de Ursúa with the ambitious Don Lope de Aguirre as second in command. Rather than turn back and give up all that wealth and all those souls beckoning from the illusory city of gold, Aguirre with clerical support led a successful revolt and pressed on with Ursúa and his beautiful wife as prisoners. Fever, hunger, exposure, execution and the poisoned arrows of an unseen enemy did for the party one by one, and only the diary of the monk Brother de Carvajal was left to record what had happened.

From this story Herzog has forged a film of great beauty and considerable power that has all the ingredients of a colourful movie epic together with the attributes of an austere Brechtian epic. Aguirre is played with great presence by Klaus Kinski (an actor known to me hitherto only for his heavies in German gangster pictures and spaghetti westerns), but Herzog is interested neither in his protagonist's individual psychology nor in Aguirre's relationship with the fifteen-year-old daughter who accompanies the expedition. He intends us to be engaged with Aguirre and his comrades only in so far as they embody their rapacious society. Unlike *The Royal Hunt of the Sun*, which in several obvious ways it resembles, Herzog's picture is not concerned with the clash of cultures, though we do see the horrible treatment of the manacled native bearers. Rather, it is about the self-destructive character of a society as it faces a wilderness, tearing itself apart with its lust for wealth, power, glory and possessions – whether it be the acquisition of souls or of unusable land.

The picture concludes with a devastating metaphor for a civilisation gone mad or for a colonial impulse gone wildly astray. The demented

Aguirre roams over his drifting, water-logged raft, his dead followers slumped around a decaying sedan chair and a useless cannon, and he rants away about his grandiose plans to possess the world, with no one to listen but the hundreds of little monkeys that swarm about him. This is the key image, but it is only the finest of many, for which considerable credit must go to the director of photography Thomas Mauch, whose task the film's remote Latin-American locations must have made very difficult. The opening five minutes, for example, are breathtaking: we see the vast expedition in the far distance winding down an almost vertical mountainside like a knotted ribbon in the mist; then suddenly the camera draws back to reveal that the head of the column is climbing out of a precipitous valley to pass immediately across the foreground in close-up.

Dog Day Afternoon (Sidney Lumet)

The Observer, 21 December 1975

In his 20 years behind the camera, the prolific Sidney Lumet has turned his hand to almost everything from Eugene O'Neill to Agatha Christie, but he's at his most effective when putting his cast through their paces on the streets of New York as in *The Anderson Tapes*, *Serpico* and his latest picture, *Dog Day Afternoon*. Appropriately enough, Lumet began his stage career forty years ago as a child actor in a Broadway production of *Dead End*.

Closely based on a true incident of 1972, his new film recounts the fantastic events that ensue when three incompetent young criminals hold up a Brooklyn bank one hot summer afternoon. The first thing that happens is that the leader, Sonny (Al Pacino), an unemployed Vietnam vet with a wife and two children, has trouble removing his rifle from the fancy package it's concealed in; the second is that the youngest crook backs out and is allowed to slip away from the scene of the crime, provided he doesn't take the getaway car. Soon 250 cops are on the spot with helicopters circling overhead, the street is sealed off, partisan crowds are seething behind barriers. Everyone – the law, the seven female hostages, sundry members of the public, and the likeable, feckless Sonny himself – seems to be onstage in some absurd tragi-comedy, performing for the others and to the television cameras.

The robbery has opened a fissure in the city's thin surface and strange ugly things come bubbling through. Lives converge and vague hatreds, resentments and fears find points of focus. Yet in the midst of the hysteria, odd sympathies and a weird camaraderie develop too. And when it transpires that Sonny has recently 'married' a homosexual in a full-dress gay wedding and that one aim of the robbery is to raise money for his boyfriend's sex change operation, the revelation seems no more bizarre than much of what has gone before.

Dog Day Afternoon is funny, moving and sad, often at the same time, and it's beautifully acted by everyone concerned, especially Pacino and John Cazale as his loyal, dim-witted born loser of an accomplice. It is also a modest film that tells us a lot about the ineluctable despair of modern city life, while refusing to compose itself into a pretentious metaphor.

A Bridge Too Far (Richard Attenborough)

The Times, 24 June 1977

For many of us, our vicarious experience of warfare over the past thirty-odd years has been closely associated with the career of Richard Attenborough as he has climbed from the boiler room of *HMS Torrin* to the sergeants' mess, the ward room, a general's staff car and finally the director's chair on big budget films. *A Bridge Too Far*, which he and scriptwriter William Goldman have carved from Cornelius Ryan's painstakingly researched account of the Arnhem affair, is like an anthology of his life's work, with a bit of everything from Cockney good humour under gunfire to Whitehall insensitivity.

What we in Britain call 'Arnhem' was 'Operation Market Garden', the September 1944 airborne assault behind the German lines in Holland that might have ended the war before Christmas had not intelligence and logistical failures conspired with fate, hubris and military politics to bring about one of the costliest disasters of World War II. The full extent of the debacle of Market Garden and the American participation in the operation were not generally appreciated before Ryan's book appeared (not even, let it be said, by those like myself who served with Airborne Forces in the postwar years). Given the immense complexity of the subject and the necessity of cutting from headquarters to front line and between dishevelled allied invaders and immaculate German defenders, Attenborough has produced a coherent if necessarily somewhat simplified movie that only occasionally puzzles. The chief and least justified simplification resides in making General Browning bear the brunt of the responsibility for the operation's failure, a decision reinforced by a twitchily neurotic performance by Dirk Bogarde at his most uningratiating.

All war movies nowadays are professedly anti-war, and their makers routinely inject the message that war is absurd, brutal and hellish. Attenborough wisely avoids any explicit statements, but apart from laying on the gore, his feelings are made pretty apparent – including having the informational prologue delivered by our current elected voice of civilised feminine reason, Liv Ullmann (who later appears as a Dutch housewife comforting dying paratroopers in her living room) and closing with a silhouette of an uprooted Arnhem family trudging Mother Courage-like along the horizon, a young boy at the rear falling into a military arms-bearing stride.

Audiences, however, do not flock to big-budget combat pictures to be revaccinated against the virus of Mars; they go to exult in scenes of battle, to identify with acts of courage and vicariously share in military glory, and *A Bridge Too Far* is scarcely designed to send them home dissatisfied. If one accepts that the martial blockbuster is a movie genre with its own conventions like the western and the gangster film, then this is a superior example of it, better written, acted and directed than *The Longest Day* and *The Battle of the Bulge*, less pretentious than the bogus *Bridge on the River Kwai*, and matched only by *Patton*, which is psychologically more interesting but has far inferior battle sequences.

Although the film has been financed and scripted by Americans, they come less well out of it than the British. Americans participate in the scenes of greatest beauty – the mass parachute drop, the erection of a Bailey bridge at night – but the episodes of derring-do starring James Caan, Elliott Gould and Robert Redford, for all their verified factual basis, ring embarrassingly false, and other American actors seem equally ill-at-ease. Perhaps it is because they cannot take quite the same pride that we do in defeat and failure. The Americans had to wait after all for an Irish journalist to inform them of their involvement in this story. The finest, and bloodiest, action sequences involve the British, most notably the fighting around Arnhem Bridge, which is among the best re-created movie combat footage I have ever seen and far more authentically ferocious than anything in Peckinpah's *Cross of Iron*. The British stars also get the better acting opportunities, and two are particularly splendid, Anthony Hopkins as Colonel John Frost, one of the Parachute Regiment's most characteristically colourful figures, and Edward Fox, whose uncannily accurate impersonation of General Brian Horrocks catches precisely his histrionic quality and that distinctive mixture of concerned bonhomie and steely detachment.

Welcome to LA (Alan Rudolph)

The Times, 11 November 1977

Welcome to LA is doubly welcome to London, first because it inaugurates a new cinema that has risen Phoenix-like on the site of the old Haverstock Hill Odeon (opposite Belsize Park Station). This attractive small cinema with its elegant foyer and austere auditorium is to be run by Romaine Hart, who over the past eight years has made such a good job of managing Islington's Screen-on-the-Green. Second, because it is a remarkable movie, but like much recent work from America (Monte Hellman's pictures, for instance, which Ms Hart has so noticeably championed) it isn't immediately commercial here at a time when British audiences have become astonishingly insular.

Three extraordinary films this year carry Robert Altman's name – *Three Women*, which he wrote and directed, and a pair of pictures about Los Angeles that he produced, Robert Benton's splendid but formally pretty orthodox private-eye movie *The Late Show* and Alan Rudolph's bold directorial debut *Welcome to LA*. Rudolph was assistant director on *The Long Goodbye*, *Nashville*, and (what is possibly Altman's masterwork) *California Split*, and co-scripted *Buffalo Bill and the Indians*. *Welcome to LA* is strung along songs composed by *Nashville*'s musical director Richard Baskin, and virtually the whole cast are members of that informal Altman repertory company that has been growing since *M*A*S*H**, but while it owes a lot to Altman (including its budget), the picture is very much Rudolph's own, both its virtues and its flaws.

Like *Nashville*, it is about a town and a group of people, whose elaborately patterned associations constitute the film's plot and morality. The central thread here is the folk rock composer Carroll Barber (Keith Carradine) returning home from a three-year absence in London to hear a daemonic singer record an album featuring his songs. The time is Christmas in LA, a city without seasons or significant changes in weather, and Carroll floats as if in a dream, testing his identity against six women, his middle-aged agent (Viveca Lindfors), his realtor (Sally Kellerman), his father's black secretary (Diahnne Abbott), his topless housekeeper (Sissy Spacek), the wife (Geraldine Chaplin) of his father's lieutenant, and finally his father's photographer mistress (Lauren Hutton). All these people and their various husbands and lovers (most memorably Harvey Keitel's brilliant, self-abnegating performance as Chaplin's husband) drift into one another's lives like bumper cars in slow motion. The effect is like a curious cross between the wild contrivance of a Feydeau farce and that stately Continental ebb-and-flow that unites and separates characters in *Dr Zhivago*.

Eventually it is revealed that Carroll's father, a multimillionaire dairyman, had rigged the recording session to lure his son home, partly just to meet him, partly to try to get him to take over the business. Some very obvious mythological connexions about musicians and fathers lurk here, and it is scarcely fortuitous that the son finds his own voice only after the conquest of his father's mistress.

Welcome to LA, witty and perceptive as it is (and the constantly reiterated title, suggesting that everyone there has just arrived, is a controlling irony), lacks the energy of *Nashville*. But the ebullience, the vivacity that Altman manages to project at his very bleakest, is often bought at the expense of his characters. Unlike *Nashville*, *Welcome to LA* does not invite one to feel superior to its characters or to the town they live in. Rudolph's film is in fact much more tightly structured than Altman's and indeed a closer comparison stylistically and thematically would be with Antonioni's *La Notte* and its equivocal welcome to Milan.

Quite deliberately Rudolph denies us any grandly objective long-shots of his people or tours of their city, that compel us to judge it harshly, as, say, Woody Allen does in *Annie Hall*. Mostly we see them in interiors, and when alone always examining themselves in mirrors, forever seeking confirmation of their identity and justification for the exercise of their unimpeded will. Their most relaxed form of intercourse is the telephone. Panoramic views invariably involve some occluded, out-of-focus foreground, as when shots across Los Angeles include leaves or eaves, and subjective shots from cars are distorted by tinted glass. There are two exceptions to this. The first is the overhead views of the LA freeway which present the central and perhaps commonplace image of people isolated in their vehicles, liberated captives of modern society. At one point Sally Kellerman challenges this by asserting that she retains her personal autonomy by keeping off the freeways in the city of 'day-dreams and traffic'.

At another point, and more ambivalently, Geraldine Chaplin appears beside the road in Beverly Hills, waif-like and importuning the passing composer. She drifts around Los Angeles in taxi cabs, jotting down her sentimental aperçus, dropping into empty cinemas showing Garbo in *Camille*, the role she identifies with. But if she reminds us of the heroine of Joan Didion's *Play It As It Lays*, she also brings to mind another, earlier British exile in California, her father.

That Obscure Object of Desire (Luis Buñuel)

The Observer, 2 April 1978

The seventy-eight-year-old Buñuel continues his gleeful dance beside the still empty grave of Western civilisation. His latest movie is in the glossy style initiated ten years ago by *Belle de jour*, when his belated acceptance by the very bourgeois audience he affects to despise brought him the large budgets he'd been denied in his rough and ready (and many would argue tougher, more rebarbative) Mexican pictures.

That Obscure Object of Desire is based on a turn-of-the-century novel by Pierre Louÿs, filmed four times before, most recently starring Bardot, most notably directed by Von Sternberg in 1935 as *The Devil Is a Woman*, a lugubriously stylish piece where Marlene Dietrich played the elusive Spanish temptress and Lionel Atwill the aristocrat who ruins himself in vain pursuit of her dubious virginity.

Buñuel has brought it up to the present and transformed it into a brisk black comedy starring the superb Fernando Rey as the rich gull Mathieu, who tells his story in a first-class compartment of a Spanish train to a quartet of prurient French fellow travellers, one of them a bland freelance psychologist played by a solemn dwarf.

In this hilarious send-up of traditional flashback narration, Mathieu explains why he has just thrown a bucket of water over a handsome girl attempting to board the train at Seville station. She is his former Spanish maid, Conchita, whom he has pursued from Paris to Lausanne and on to Spain, forever being deserted, humiliated and confronted with fantastic chastity belts and unlikely excuses.

Conchita (christened Concepción and daughter of the sly Annunciación) is played by two actresses, Carole Bouquet to represent her cool northern side, Angela Molina her earthy Mediterranean aspect, and it is a tribute to the old surrealist Buñuel that after a mere couple of appearances we have come to accept the capricious duo as a single person.

Miss Bouquet is the one that gets the water over her, Miss Molina the Conchita who returns the compliment or insult. While the affair goes on, terrorist outrages occur all around them – bombings, kidnappings, assassinations – masterminded by the so-called 'Revolutionary Army of the Infant Jesus'. The world is falling apart, and Mathieu's mad obsessions are as absurd, irrelevant and obscure as the activities of the urban guerrillas, and the expression of similar repressions. This is hardly a profound statement, but the film that contains it is an undeniably attractive little artefact – cold, glittering and deadly, like a Fabergé hand grenade.

NOTES FROM THE DREAM HOUSE

The Chess Players (Satyajit Ray)

The Observer, 21 January 1979

Satyajit Ray's first movie outside his native Bengal, *The Chess Players* takes place in Lucknow in 1856 on the eve of the East India Company's annexation of Oudh, and uses chess as its central metaphor. For this, his first period movie, and the first in Hindi, Ray has developed a short story about two wealthy, chess-obsessed nabobs written fifty years ago by Premchand, the father of modern Hindi fiction, a tough ironic Marxist (whose real name incidentally was Rai). The hen-pecked Mirza (Sanjeev Kumar) and the cuckolded Mir (Saeed Jaffrey) are the decadent descendants of mogul warriors, feckless sybarites living only for chess. A visit to a dying friend is a pretext to use his chess board; with naïve fascination they learn that the English, having taken over India's national game, have changed the moves in the interests of speed. This sublimely blinkered pair recall the cricket-obsessed Charters and Caldicott played by Basil Radford and Naunton Wayne in Hitchcock's *The Lady Vanishes*.

Meanwhile a larger game of chess is being played around them as the British Resident, General Outram (Richard Attenborough) moves in on the frivolous King Wajd and thus completes Lord Dalhousie's scheme for the total subjugation of the subcontinent. The confrontation between Outram and the King is history as macrocosmic energy, the story of Mirza and Mir history as microcosmic farce. Ironically the only bloodshed from the only shot fired occurs when Mir wounds Mirza as they quarrel at the deserted spot outside town where they have repaired to continue their game untroubled by the threat from the English invasion. The occupying force, which marches past their sanctuary into Lucknow, takes over the state unopposed.

The Chess Players is a brilliant piece of Brechtian epic theatre, with every scene carefully calculated to make a specific dramatic point. An ironic narrator links the two strands, and an elegant montage of engravings, documents and animated cartoons establishes the larger political context. But this is epic theatre irradiated by Ray's richly humanistic sensibility. There are no caricatures in the picture, and everyone, whatever role he appears to have on the board, is being manipulated by some unseen player. If Ray does favour anyone it is the women, who as usual in his pictures have a strength of character and purchase on reality their men lack. The beautiful Shabana Azmi as Mirza's neglected wife denounces the chess board, and with it the world of power struggles, as 'that stupid piece of cloth'.

Richard Attenborough's Outram, a thoughtful Scots puritan with a pawky sense of humour and an unassuageable conscience, ranks among the best things he has given us. The Hindi matinee idol Kumar and the London-based character actor Jaffrey (best known here for TV's *Gangsters*) act as if they've been playing together for years. The music (by Ray himself) and the classical dancing are splendid, and despite a print of variable quality, the images are fastidiously composed and consistently striking. *The Chess Players* is one of Ray's finest achievements, the work of a master filmmaker in easy, often playful, command of his craft.

The Tree of Wooden Clogs (Ermanno Olmi)

The Observer, 29 April 1979

During the 1960s the humanist spirit of Italian neo-realism was kept alive by Ermanno Olmi in such low-key studies of modern urban Italians as *The Job*, *The Engagement* and *One Fine Day*.

Now, after too long an absence from our screens, he has returned with a three-hour evocation of peasant life in late nineteenth-century Lombardy, performed by a cast of non-professionals recruited from around his native Bergamo. This masterwork, *The Tree of Wooden Clogs*, won the main prize at the 1978 Cannes Festival.

The picture focuses on five families working for the same landlord, and Olmi patiently observes them over the course of a year in the fields, at church, killing a pig, attending a fair, getting married, giving birth. It is a harsh life in which a broken clog can be a disaster, the death of a cow a tragedy. Yet though these peasants are exploited, they are not downtrodden. They have dignity, a sense of community, strong family ties and a sustaining religion. 'Only by loving our neighbours can we deserve God's love,' the sympathetic priest tells them.

This is a marvellous film. Bold in conception, rich in detail, unsentimental and ultimately affirmative. In tone and treatment it is far removed from Bertolucci's polemical, operatic *1900*. It's much closer to Ray's *Pather Panchali*, the National Theatre's recent *Lark Rise* or the paintings of Millet.

Olmi draws our attention to a wider social context – a radical speaker appears among the mountebanks and entertainers at a village festival, a honeymoon couple sees soldiers driving a column of manacled anarchists through the streets of Milan – but his characters are quite unaware of these currents of impending change. They are indeed living in a kind of Eden, innocent though not idyllic, and buried within the complex fabric of the film is a fable about the tree of knowledge to which the title refers.

The movie begins with a couple being advised to send their son to school and have him become the first literate member of the little community. When the boy splits one of the clogs he needs to walk the six kilometres to his classroom, the father cuts down a poplar tree to carve a new pair. For this offence the family is expelled from their home by the landlord's bailiff, and the picture ends as they drive away, their silent, unprotesting neighbours gathering sadly to watch the tiny light on the car disappear in the night. Olmi leaves us in no doubt that the system under which they live is manifestly unjust, yet he clearly implies that its passing will involve irreplaceable losses.

The Warriors (Walter Hill)

The Observer, 13 May 1979

Walter Hill's new film, *The Warriors*, confirms his reputation as the American cinema's leading fabulist. Like his study of bare-knuckle boxers during the Depression, *The Streetfighter*, and his existential crime picture, *The Driver*, it takes place in the mythical interstices of urban life.

A dynamically edited opening sequence shows New York's bizarre teenage gangs emerging into the streets and subway stations that ordinary citizens have abandoned to them for the night. They're heading for a park in the Bronx where Cyrus, a charismatic leader of the Riffs, has summoned delegations from a hundred neighbourhood gangs to plan an armistice and take over the city. When, at the height of his address, Cyrus is assassinated, the Warriors from Coney Island are unjustly accused of the murder, and their eight survivors have to reach home twenty miles away through the turf of hostile tribes.

The complicated subway map of New York suggests a hazardous version of some board game like Monopoly. The name Cyrus for the dead leader and Swan for the *ad hoc* commander on the return journey suggests something else – a parodic (or anti-) epic. Based on a novel by Sol Yurick, the film is a transposition of Xenophon's *Anabasis* from 400 BC Persia to present-day Manhattan.

Through empty subway stations and gleaming night streets, the unarmed eight make their way, encountering weird gangs like the Baseball Furies, a mob in clown make-up wielding bats, and harassed by cops. A Circe figure tempts the licentious Ajax only to reveal herself as a plainclothes policewoman and handcuff him to a park bench. Sirens in the form of a gang called The Lizzies lure three warriors to their den. A female disc jockey on the airwaves acts as chorus and tribal messenger.

Eventually in the pre-dawn, Swan (the angular Michael Beck) arrives home with his depleted force to view the dismal roofscape of his neighbourhood and ask, as many a returning warrior has, 'This is what we fought all night to get back to?'

The Warriors is a graceful, irreverent film, uninterested – as all Hill's work is – in individual psychology and conventional morality. In what sense, it asks, are Ulysses and his crew, Jason and the Argonauts, Xenophon and his ten thousand Greeks, superior to any New York street gang, save in the way their deeds are commemorated? Hill celebrates the vigour, comradeship and shared danger of gang life, and he does it in a stylised, almost balletic fashion, though one far removed from the sentimentalities of *West Side Story*.

For this is also a brutal picture about desperate marginal characters, and the visual style is calculatedly garish, full of startling blues and reds that sometimes look like neon, and sometimes as if they've soaked into the cheap pulp paper of a comic book. There is undoubtedly something perverse about Hill, but he is a minor master. I'd now like to see him tackle a western.

Manhattan (Woody Allen)

The Observer, 26 August 1979

The first thing to be said about Woody Allen's new movie, *Manhattan*, is that it's one of the two most visually entrancing films of the year, the other being Coppola's *Apocalypse Now*.

The second is that it's a happy example of a self-conscious artist progressing through a rigorous examination of his own work. The determinedly comic *Annie Hall* and its determinedly lugubrious successor, *Interiors*, have been brought together, shorn of their formal contrivance and turned into a sharp, wonderfully observant romantic comedy.

Manhattan is the subtly nuanced tale of the relationships within a group of wilful middle-class New Yorkers, centring on the successful, angst-ridden TV writer Isaac Davis (Woody Allen). The principal figures are Isaac's best friend, a glib Wasp academic called Yale (Michael Murphy), and Yale's tough, willowy wife (Anne Byrne); Isaac's current lover Tracy (Mariel Hemingway), an emotionally precocious seventeen-year-old high-school girl; Yale's lover, Mary (Diane Keaton), a pretentious journalist who becomes Isaac's obscure object of desire; and Isaac's second ex-wife (Meryl Streep), a handsome bi-sexual who has gone off with another woman and is writing a frank account of her marriage.

Noting the relationship between Tracy (a beautifully assured performance from Papa Hemingway's granddaughter) and the philosophical middle-aged clown, American critics have compared *Manhattan* with Chaplin's *Limelight*. A closer comparison, I think, would be with Bergman's early comedies *A Lesson in Love* and *Smiles of a Summer Night*. There's the same feel for shifting relationships, a similar melancholy.

The movie is not set in the world of the true New York intelligentsia, but rather in that of those well-heeled consumers of ideas and cultural artefacts, the people who flick through the *New Yorker* and subscribe to *New York Magazine* to discover what they should be wearing, thinking, worrying about and sneering at. They use the names of fashionable authors (Kafka, Borges, Kierkegaard) and the titles of books as social counters and talismans but rarely come to grips with matters of substance.

Isaac characterises his friends as people who elevate minor personal problems in order to keep at bay the universal, eternal questions of life and death. He of course underrates the artistic uses of their problems, just as he overestimates their capacity to grapple with the larger metaphysical issues. Allen is particularly telling about their talent for self-deception, their ability to disguise selfishness as honesty, and not least in the character that he and his co-scriptwriter Marshall Brickman have written for Woody himself to play.

Manhattan is packed with quotable lines. Isaac has written a story about his mother called 'The Castrating Zionist'; he suggests dryly to some friends that 'physical force is always better than satire when dealing with Nazis'; his son plays sand-lot baseball in Central Park sporting a T-shirt emblazoned with the words 'Divorced Fathers' Sons All-Stars'. But they arise naturally from the dramatic context and mostly derive from Isaac's role as compulsive funny-man.

Photographed in black-and-white Panavision by the brilliant Gordon Willis, the film opens on a montage of nocturnal widescreen images of New York: the skyline; a floodlit Yankee stadium with an elevated train snaking past; Sixth Avenue looking north to Radio City Music Hall; Park Avenue in winter. They're shot in that gleaming monochrome one associates with the great *Life* cameramen of the thirties and forties who shaped the enduring, magical vision of Manhattan for my generation. This is the New York of our dreams, before the worm penetrated the heart of the Big Apple; it's not the New York of *Taxi Driver*.

This initial sequence is underscored by Gershwin's *Rhapsody in Blue* performed by the New York Philharmonic under Zubin Mehta, and it is counterpointed by an anxious commentator constantly rewriting the first chapter of an autobiographical novel that tries on a variety of literary styles in the course of proposing New York as an emblem of social decay, e.g.: 'He admired New York. To him it was a metaphor.' – 'He was as tough as the city he loved.'

The author we've been listening to is of course Isaac, who's given up his lucrative TV comedy-writing job to write a novel about the collapse of civilisation, the success of which will inevitably be judged by its sales and local *réclame*.

Thereafter the film switches between lyrically staged outdoor scenes and deliberately edgy interiors that use the awkwardly angular positioning of people in apartments, art galleries, restaurants, to keep us aware of their problematic relationships. One of many long-held shots features Isaac and Mary, with Yale and his wife reacting touchingly, and hilariously, to each other's presence as they sit in a row listening to a concert.

I've mentioned *Rhapsody in Blue*, and in fact every sequence is keyed to some familiar Gershwin tune, ironically in the case of 'Lady Be Good' as Miss Keaton goes for a rural ride with her current lover and ex-lover in the latter's Porsche, openly romantic when my favourite Gershwin song, 'Someone to Watch Over Me', accompanies a night walk culminating with Allen and Keaton watching dawn break over the East River.

This film establishes Allen beyond doubt as one of the most gifted moviemakers and one of the finest film actors at work today. It was a fitting choice to open this year's Edinburgh Film Festival.

Man of Marble (Andrzej Wajda)

The Observer, 30 June 1979

Twenty years ago, with Hollywood dormant, Italian neo-realism dead, the so-called British renaissance yet to take place, the French New Wave a cross-Channel rumour, Antonioni not even a name to drop and Bergman just emerging on to the world scene, two directors above all others commanded the admiration of young British cinéastes: Akira Kurosawa and Andrzej Wajda.

For cultural reasons Kurosawa was a rather remote figure, but Wajda, then in his early thirties, seemed closer than any British filmmaker of the time. And his World War II trilogy (*A Generation*; *Kanal*; *Ashes and Diamonds*) was what we thought the cinema ought to be: wryly romantic, popular, committed, concerned about the changing nature of post-war life, delicately weighing present despair against hopes for the future. Although there has always been in his films a level of local political and historical nuance accessible only to fellow Poles, he was able to invest his generation's experience with a striking universality.

Then his gifted protégés, Skolimowski and Polanski, emigrated; his star actor, the charismatic Zbigniew Cybulski, was killed; and Wajda lost his way, with only his autobiographical requiem for Cybulski,

Everything for Sale (1968), to remind us of what his career had once meant. So the belated arrival of his three-year-old *Man of Marble* is a major event. For this Eastern European *Citizen Kane*, one of the few serious analyses of Stalinism the cinema has given us, represents an astonishing return to form, though not, I'm afraid, to any bright confident morning.

The film's heroine is a twenty-four-year-old movie student, Agnieszka (Krystyna Janda), a willowy blonde dressed in the international uniform of flared jeans and denim jacket and armed with an aggressive viewfinder and an arrogant sneer. Much of the film is shot with the wide-angle lens and hand-held camera that she believes are the keys to the truth.

She wants to make her diploma film, to be backed by a reluctant TV producer, about one Mateusz Birkut, a Stakhanovite bricklayer of the early 1950s, who was briefly a national hero before falling foul of the party bureaucrats and disappearing into the local Gulag and subsequent obscurity. Her first expedition takes her into an art gallery, where embarrassing social realist works of the post-war period are hidden in the vaults, among them a massive marble statue of Mateusz, now as fit an object for satire as Ozymandias's fallen image. Our heroine symbolically rapes it with her camera.

Next she goes through old newsreels and documentaries, both officially approved and suppressed footage, and she looks up a celebrated director, now middle-aged, who established his reputation with a slick propaganda film built around Mateusz, a chillingly risible piece called *Architects of Our Happiness*. She also tracks down former comrades and an ex-wife, and through their testimony Wajda builds up a picture of a shadowy forgotten era and the shakily affluent present-day Poland.

On the way a simple cardboard paragon is transformed for us into a truly complex hero. What Wajda is talking about is a society that has passed from Stalinism to opportunism, and has lost along the way that idealism the Stalinists exploited. Whether as a clean-limbed labourer achieving 323% productivity, as an uncompromised victim of rigged trials who can help others thrive in the thaw, or as a peg for an ambitious girl's provocative documentary, Mateusz is always a victim.

One of the great delights of this film is the sophistication with which it handles the idea of cinema itself. At various times film is a metaphor for history, for memory, for life, as well as for the hubristic belief that we can ever fully reconstruct and understand experience. In what is possibly a sentimental touch at the end of what is possibly an overlong movie, Agnieszka curls up in a helpless foetal position on her bed because the TV company has taken away her camera, film and technical crew, and it is only the solid working-class common sense of her railwayman father that drives her on to complete the task unarmed. Finally, it should be stressed that for a work said to have weighed on its author's mind for fourteen years, *Man of Marble* is gratifyingly unponderous.

Apocalypse Now (Francis Ford Coppola)

The Observer, 16 December 1979

Unreasonable demands are being made on films about the Vietnam War, both by their directors and their critics, just as they were on the fiction that followed an equally divisive conflict, the American Civil War, when John De Forest coined the term that has loomed over American authors ever since – 'The Great American Novel'.

Francis Ford Coppola's *Apocalypse Now* and Michael Cimino's *The Deer Hunter* aspire to be 'The Great American Film', and both turn to classic literature to underpin their epic intentions. Cimino, in a generalised way, draws on Fenimore Cooper, Hemingway and Tolstoy for his proletarian *War and Peace*; Coppola and his co-screenwriter, John Milius, have transposed Joseph Conrad's *Heart of Darkness* from late nineteenth-century Congo to Indo-China in 1969 for their operatic, metaphysical thriller.

In their version, that commonsensical seadog Marlow becomes a half-crazed special services officer, Captain Willard (Martin Sheen) who is also dispatched up-river by 'the Company', in his case the CIA, not Leopold's exploitative colonial cartel. Willard's task is to 'terminate with extreme prejudice' (i.e. assassinate) one Colonel Walter Kurtz (Marlon Brando), a brilliant career officer now leading a private army of Montagnards over the Cambodian border. Like his Belgian namesake, Kurtz has gone insane, turning his civilising mission into a campaign of atrocities. Though I had major doubts about the closing minutes, this bold, finely acted picture greatly impressed me at Cannes. It still does.

Willard travels on a naval patrol boat called *The Erebus* (in Greek legend, according to a handy dictionary, 'the personification of darkness, and a dark cavern through which the dead passed on their way to Hades') manned by some sixties types. With them he accompanies a helicopter attack on a Vietcong-held village led by a posturing cavalry colonel (Robert Duvall), who is by Joseph Heller out of John Ford. Then they attend a grotesque, erotic variety show mounted in a jungle clearing by *Playboy* bunnies for sex-starved GIs, participate in a mini-My Lai massacre on board a sampan and pass through a crazy night battle at a border bridge that is like a great Crystal Palace firework display, in which the stoned spectators get blown up on the fiery tableaux.

None of this will be unfamiliar to those who have read Nick Tomalin's *The General Goes Zapping Charlie Cong,* Mary McCarthy's report on the Calley trial, Michael Herr's *Dispatches*, and seen newsreels of Bob Hope's visits to the front with Miss World. What Coppola and his brilliant Italian cameraman, Vittorio Storaro, along with his superb film and sound editors, have done is to draw all these scenes together into a nightmare journey. They make us experience at first hand the crazy conditions of this mendacious, drug-fuelled, technological, rock 'n' roll war in a funny, frightening, edgy fashion.

The fundamental difference between Conrad's story and Coppola's film is that we never see the semblance of a stable world or a moderately well-adjusted personality. Willard is cut off from his society when we first meet him, and he is given a voice-over narration (written by Michael Herr) in the hardboiled American idiom that makes him sound more like Chandler's Philip Marlowe than Conrad's Charlie Marlow. He makes sardonic cracks such as, 'charging a man with murder in this country is like handing out speeding tickets at the Indianapolis 500' and utters compassionate asides like 'Charlie doesn't get USO shows, and he has only two ways to go home, death or victory'.

The film sticks surprisingly closely to the original story, often in curiously small details, and the transformation of the renegade Russian sailor who worships Kurtz into a spaced-out cameraman (Dennis Hopper) is brilliantly successful. But what at first seems to fit Vietnam like a glove eventually comes to constrict Coppola like a straitjacket.

The knowledge that Brando is Kurtz sustains our interest in the outcome of the journey, and when we encounter this shaven-headed figure lurking in the shadows of a crumbling jungle temple, looking like a cross between the Buddha and Welles's Kane, we are not disappointed. Unfortunately, at this point Coppola becomes twitchily self-conscious as he proceeds to draw on other key modernist texts that *Heart of Darkness* has led him to, Eliot's *The Waste Land* and *The Hollow Men*, Jessie L. Weston's *From Ritual to Romance* and Fraser's *The Golden Bough*. From these he produces a heady mystic brew about the ritual slaying of kings, the redemption of the land and the gods know what else. There's even the implication that Kurtz, in arranging for Willard to kill him, is consciously fulfilling the twentieth-century destiny as he has read it in these books. I was captivated by the sheer bizarrerie, while remaining unconvinced by the psychological, political and mythical thrust.

The Shining (Stanley Kubrick)

The Observer, 6 October 1980

It is an important week that brings us new work by three of the major directors of our time, the bold, primitive Samuel Fuller, the sophisticated traditionalist Stanley Kubrick, and the wayward innovator Jean-Luc Godard.

All three emerged in the 1950s as popular filmmakers obsessed with warfare, then underwent a decisive change in the 1960s, each becoming, in his different way, a victim of the decade.

After 1963, Fuller could no longer find backers for his low-budget genre movies, and for the past seventeen years has been seen largely as an actor in the films of his young admirers – as a pontificating party guest in Godard's *Pierrot le fou*, a director of westerns in Dennis Hopper's *The Last Movie*, a gangster in Wenders's *The American Friend*, a World War II general in Spielberg's *1941*.

Kubrick withdrew after *Dr Strangelove* into a private world to make expensive, grandiose films behind closed studio doors, to be released at four-yearly intervals in a solemn hush appropriate to the delivery of Mosaic tablets.

Following his deep involvement in *les événements* of 1968, Godard renounced anything remotely resembling the commercial cinema, and has since devoted himself in his Alpine retreat to a technical and political interrogation of the cinematic process and to the production of gnomic anti-cinema films for no known audience.

Kubrick's quadrennial offering is *The Shining*, a horror movie adapted by himself and Diane Johnson from a fat Stephen King novel about an alcoholic failed novelist (Jack Nicholson doing his crazy laughing-man act), his dim wife (Shelley Duvall providing a slim variation on her banal nurse of *Three Women*) and their six-year-old son (Danny Lloyd, cast for his eyes) occupying a labyrinthine luxury hotel in the American Rockies as winter caretakers. Back in 1970, another caretaker, stricken by so-called cabin fever, butchered his wife and twin daughters, and it is merely a matter of how and when history will repeat itself.

Even before the family take up residence, the boy, who possesses the extra-sensory gift known as 'the shining', is in touch with the bloody past and later proves capable of communicating his unease to a fellow sensitive, the hotel's black cook two thousand miles away in sunny Florida. Ghostly presences soon make themselves felt to the frantic father (a room full of revelling, Gatsbyesque revenants, a demonic bartender, a sinister waiter played by a Kubrick regular, Philip Stone). When knives and axes are out, these manifestations of evil banality even impinge on the bland consciousness of the distraught wife.

The result is a polished, low-key horror picture of a rather conventional kind, with those fluid tracking shots we associate with Kubrick, and some remarkable sets for them to play in. But we never become involved either intellectually or viscerally with the characters. They are played too much on single notes, we know nothing about them and care little for their fates. Our pants flutter occasionally, but the film comes nowhere near scaring them off us.

Clearly Kubrick didn't spend so much time, energy and money to compete with Roger Corman, and perhaps in paring down his picture from the 146-minutes American running time to its current two hours, he's left something vital out. What starts in obliquity finishes in obscurity. One can only guess at his intentions, and I'd say the picture was a further, deeply misanthropic exploration of man's position in an absurd scheme of things, another story about imperfect creatures destroyed by their pursuit of perfection.

Kubrick began in *The Killing* with crooks planning the perfect robbery, moved on to campaigning soldiers and conniving politicians, then to explorers of the cosmos and adventurers in history. Here, in this deceptively domestic setting, a clue to his enormous ambitions is the image of a maze, both an actual maze in the gardens and a model of it in the hotel lounge. At one key moment the two are elided so that we have a God-like view of the wife and son appearing to negotiate the table model. This Borgesian labyrinth is opposed to the corrupted gothic world of the hotel and is some emblem of life itself. In the film's climax, the son escapes the sacrificial intentions of the Minotaur father by learning how to use the maze. Anyway, I have heard less plausible, and less generous accounts of Kubrick's intentions.

Caligula (Bob Guccione) & Diabolo Menthe (Diane Kurys)

The Observer, 2 November 1980

I returned to the critical fray last Monday after three weeks in the United States spent largely listening to radio, watching TV and visiting plays and exhibitions.

I saw only two movies, Woody Allen's *Stardust Memories* (about which I will wax, or wane, unenthusiastic come December) and the much-vaunted patriotic nonsense *The Great Santini* (which I only took in because it was showing at Chicago's tastefully restored Biograph, the cinema where John Dillinger saw his last picture show on 22 July, 1934).

It looked like a bad-news week that lay ahead. In fact it turned out rather well.

The first piece of good news was hearing that the dedicated classical scholar Bob Guccione had rescinded his PR advisers' invitation to the critics to attend a preview of *Caligula*. This 'powerful film that faithfully recalls some of the most realistic images of pagan Rome ever seen' might not have been understood by the Press, thus preventing the impressionable public from having 'the opportunity to fully experience this landmark motion picture for themselves'. Perhaps there are some prejudiced, prurient critics who would approach this 'controversial' work convinced that a Guccione life of Caligula might more closely resemble the results of five randy gibbons let loose with a movie camera than one sober Gibbon working with a quill pen. Anyway, I shall not lay down *The Observer*'s good money at the box office to see this chaste offering of Mr Guccione and his associates (or dissociates) until five readers have assured me that it will enrich my life.

The second piece of good news was the discovery that the unattractively titled *Diabolo Menthe,* which I thought might be a horror flick about a cancer-inducing mentholated cigarette, but actually translates as *Peppermint Soda,* is a directorial debut of great distinction by Diane Kurys. The French have a remarkable tradition of movies about education, from *Zéro de conduite* through *Les Quatre cents coups* to *Une Semaine de vacances,* and they are now joined by this wholly unsentimental account of the school year 1963–64 as experienced by the teenage Weber sisters.

Philip Larkin assures us that this was the 'Annus Mirabilis': 'Sexual intercourse began in 1963 – between the end of the Chatterley ban and the Beatles' first LP.' But life was not so simple or schematic for the thirteen-year-old *jolie laide,* Anne (Eleonore Klarwein), who stands in awe of her conventionally attractive fifteen-year-old sister Frédérique (Odile Michel), and their autobiographical director hasn't got the budget that can put Beatles' songs on the sound track.

The girls' teachers are cranky, insensitive, weak; their friends puzzling, passionate, inconstant; their divorced parents demanding, unpredictable, exploitable. The small excitements, the big shames, the lack of that sense of time and proportion that age and maturity are supposed to bring, these aspects of being a teenager, of being a member of that extraordinary thing – a school community, of growing up in a fluid society, all this is caught in a succession of brief, precisely delineated sequences. There's none of the seductive pop nostalgia that undermines so many American pictures on this theme.

In *Diabolo Menthe* we see the *graffiti français* on the wall for 1968 in a sharply related succession of short scenes linking teachers, pupils and parents, wherein the elder of these Jewish sisters (whose mother has almost forgotten that she is Jewish) comes to recognise an undercurrent of fascism and anti-Semitism beneath the complacent surface of Gaullist France. But it isn't insisted on.

We first meet the Weber girls as they leave their father at a Normandy beach in September. We feel we know them very well, far better than he knows them, when they return to him the following summer. The film's final image is a freeze-frame of Anne looking over her shoulder as she trots towards the sea. By the time Diane Kurys makes this explicit reference to *Les Quatre cents coups*, she has repaid her debt to Truffaut.

Kagemusha (Akira Kurosawa)

The Observer, 16 November 1980

With his superb *Kagemusha*, Akira Kurosawa is at the age of seventy back where he belongs, in the highest critical esteem and readily available to popular audiences.

This is a film of Shakespearean design, a profound, beautiful and exciting historical movie on which I first reported from Cannes last May. Since then Kurosawa has trimmed it to a leisurely 158 minutes and clarified certain aspects of the narrative. It might be instructive, however, before looking at the film again, to recall the vicissitudes of the director's career and reputation, because a lot of people seem to have forgotten.

Kurosawa's arrival in the West with the screening of his *Rashomon* at the 1951 Venice Festival was as confident a cultural breakthrough as Commodore Matthew Perry's entry into Tokyo Bay ninety-eight years before. Less than a year later, in 1952, I saw the film on Liverpool's Lime Street hold an audience spellbound at a cinema that didn't exactly specialise in prestige programming. It was a political event of the first order, for in this and the pictures that followed Kurosawa was helping to heal recent wounds and open new cultural vistas. After *Seven Samurai*, who could ever say again that he couldn't distinguish one Japanese from another?

When *Throne of Blood* opened the first London Film Festival in 1957 (a modest fourteen-movie affair), everyone raved over the greatest adaptation of Shakespeare the screen had yet seen. Kurosawa's reputation was at its zenith, and until now it has been going downhill almost ever since. Ray, Visconti, Bergman, the post-neo-realist Fellini, Antonioni, the French New Wave, were about to emerge on the international scene.

Critics were soon to discover Mizoguchi and Ozu and promote them as more 'authentically Japanese' than the allegedly Westernised Kurosawa.

The London Festival remained loyal to him, but from 1961, when his powerful radical melodrama *The Bad Sleep Well*, was sneered at, his films mostly failed to find distributors here. The wry anti-epic *Yojimbo* (1961) is little known in this country, though everyone has heard of its plagiarised spaghetti western version, *A Fistful of Dollars*.

Soon his local finance dried up, and he had to go to Russia to make his humanist masterpiece *Dersu Uzala* (1975). Three years passed before it found a British distributor, most critics patronised it, and the film finished up being shown on BBC 2 opposite *The Sound of Music* on a Christmas afternoon. *Kagemusha* is only his second Japanese picture in fifteen years and was made possible through the support of his American admirers, George Lucas and Francis Ford Coppola.

Kagemusha, meaning 'a shadow warrior' or *doppelgänger*, is set in the late sixteenth century when several clans were competing for control of Japan. Cavalry, firearms and Christian missionaries had recently arrived from the West, but traditional martial codes and forms of honour and morality had survived intact, as they were to do for centuries.

Just as he is approaching his moment of triumph, the fifty-two-year-old clan boss Shingen begins to falter in body and spirit. His younger brother, who can get away with a little Hollywood-style distant doubling, discovers a genuine double, a craven thief, whom he rescues from the gallows and brings secretly to court. The lord and the thief immediately recognise their common humanity, as well as the very scale of theft and murder that distinguishes the warlord from the criminal.

What follows is a fascinating alternation between kinetic and contemplative, personal and public, epic and anti-heroic, Zen and Zenda, as Shingen dies and the thief is compelled by external and internal pressures to take his place. Meditative scenes are succeeded by sequences of violent action, pawky humour modulates into painful sadness. Sometimes Kurosawa carefully prepares scenes so that we may appreciate the ironic undertones. Just as often he springs a surprise on us, then unravels its implications.

He finishes up with a film that combines the dramatically unexpected with the tragically inexorable. The thief does not succeed effortlessly à la Rudolf Rassendyll, and the spiritual grandeur he attains is betrayed by simple physical ineptitude that might equally be hubris or fate. Kurosawa uses the idea of the double as a way of discussing the relationship of men to their private selves, their public roles, their political and patriotic allegiances. A key line inquires about the existence of a shadow after the body has gone, and later the camera poignantly takes up the image.

There are wonderful set-pieces in this film: a battle by night, the burial of Shingen in a vast lacquered urn in a mist-shrouded lake, the double meeting his late master's grandson, bodyguards and concubines. There are also some elaborate nightmares and post-battle scenes that I find less attractively memorable. All in all it is a masterly achievement, not my very favourite Kurosawa but nonetheless a definition of maturity.

Atlantic City (Louis Malle)

The Observer, 25 January 1981

Ever since he co-directed *The World of Silence* with Jacques Cousteau twenty-five years ago, Louis Malle has been inviting us to view life from a variety of disturbing perspectives, and rarely with more ambiguity than in his second American movie, *Atlantic City*.

Atlantic City is a richly suggestive metaphor for America and the American Dream, a fashionable turn-of-the-century holiday resort gone to seed; a favourite inter-war playground of underworld figures and adulterers; the home of the Miss America pageant; the setting of the original Monopoly board, a game conceived at the very depth of the Depression that harnessed the local geography to a rigid hierarchy of capitalist values; a town now making a controversial comeback as the Las Vegas of the East, with anonymous casinos going up just as soon as the wrecker's ball can demolish the baroque hotels that line the celebrated Boardwalk.

A screenplay by the American playwright John Guare, which is as elegant in construction as it is quietly eloquent in its dialogue, brings together in this changing city a trio of desperate losers. They're a shifty Canadian hippie (Robert Joy) who has snatched a consignment of cocaine from the Philadelphia branch of the Mafia and arrives in Atlantic City with his inane, pregnant, flower-child mistress; the hippie's estranged wife, Sally (Susan Sarandon), who's working at a casino fish-food counter and studying at a school for croupiers; and an elderly crook, Lou (Burt Lancaster), whose shabby livelihood as a numbers-runner is threatened by legal gambling.

Lou is a failed crook kept by a hypochondriac widow who came to Atlantic City during the war to take part in a Betty Grable look-alike competition. He boasts of once sharing a cell with the notorious hoodlum Bugsy Siegel, a claim based on his having been in a local slammer on a drunk and disorderly charge when Siegel stopped there overnight on his way to a Federal penitentiary.

The stolen cocaine that brings the hippie to an early grave (by way of the Frank Sinatra wing of the Atlantic City Medical Center) enables Lou to live out his fantasies. He cheats, steals, lies, betrays and kills, and in the process both sends Sally on the road to freedom (a Sunrise Semester radio lecture on French champagne ringing out from the radio of her stolen car) and attains a self-respect and social standing that has hitherto eluded him.

This is a very funny, precise, ironic, deeply sad movie that escapes being aridly cynical or sentimentally patronising because of the wry affection with which Malle and Guare observe the central characters. The film scarcely puts a foot wrong, and Lancaster gives one of the major performances of his career. His Lou combines two different sorts of role he has played, that sad *film noir* loser sitting in his singlet on a flop-house bed waiting for the hitmen to get him in *The Killers* (in which he made his debut in 1946) and the dignified, slightly prissy American professor in Visconti's *Conversation Piece*.

Excalibur (John Boorman)

The Observer, 5 July 1981

A few years ago, the late Sean Kenny retrieved *Gulliver's Travels* from both nursery and study by putting all four voyages, not just the sojourns in Lilliput and Brobdingnag, on the stage of the Mermaid in a striking piece of total theatre.

In a comparably bold and rather more refined way John Boorman's *Excalibur* encompasses the whole of Malory's *Le Morte Darthur* from the acquisition of the numinous sword by Arthur's father Uther to the dying king's departure for Avalon. In so doing he repossesses the Arthurian legend on behalf of a truly popular cinema from the Monty Python team, who punctured it with self-protecting ironies; from Bresson and Rohmer, who desiccated it with Gallic severities; from MGM, who stretched it to fill the wide screen for the first CinemaScope movie shot in Britain; and from Walt Disney, who turned T.H. White's *Sword in the Stone* into a candied cartoon and prevented the Twain from meeting anywhere by dropping a Connecticut Yankee astronaut into King Arthur's court.

There are themes and scenes from every Boorman movie here, for in *Excalibur* he faces head-on a body of potent mythology that has under-lain his work since his debut with *Catch Us If You Can* sixteen years ago. Quests, encounters by rivers, dreams merging into reality, symbolic temptations, the concept of honour, man's divorce from nature, the conflict between free will and destiny, they are all powerfully brought together in a magnificent film that rounds out the first phase of one of the most important careers in the history of British cinema.

His film presents these legendary incidents with the magic that has always captured the romantic imagination of children, and it manages to be both precise and timeless. There are battles and jousts (the one between Arthur and Lancelot beneath a thousand-foot waterfall is a beautiful ethical parable), breath-taking moments as Excalibur is delivered from the lake and taken back, the excitements of a boy being snatched from the crowd to be trained as a king.

At the same time the picture comprehends those metaphysical patterns and darker, mystical aspects that in the past century have largely become the property of high culture. The conception-by-deception of Arthur, and the parallel events some thirty years later by which his nemesis, Mordred, is unwittingly sired by Arthur himself, are complex transactions, subtly presented and charged with an erotic power that involves us at a deep emotional level.

Matching his style to his story's varied sources, Boorman is eclectic in his choice of music and visual references. One notes the influence of Kurosawa on the smoky battle scenes, of glowing pre-Raphaelite paint-ings on the idyllic sequence where Lancelot accompanies Guinevere to her marriage, of Klimt and the glittering corruption of Viennese art nouveau when the court of Camelot enters its decadent phase. In a most interesting score by Trevor Jones, Wagnerian themes are deployed as key motifs: Siegfried's funeral march, for instance, is identified with Arthur to suggest that his dreams contain the seeds of their own destruction.

But the film is held together by Boorman's singular eye. He and his cameraman Alex Thomson are sensitive to the mood of the season, to the endless ways light can fall in the forest. The remarkably varied Irish locations they use are moral arenas, never there simply to beguile. This eye is part of a controlling vision, which a strong cast, made up largely of character actors rather than stars, is there to serve. Cherie Lunghi is a gentle Irish Guinevere; Nigel Terry is an Arthur who matures persuasively.

The only stars are Helen Mirren as the evil Morgana and Nicol Williamson as Merlin. (They were once memorably teamed in *Macbeth*.) This Merlin mediates between present and future, between reality and legend. Bearded, dressed in a black cloak and silver skull cap, he is the conscious embodiment of the film's sense of the tragicomic nature of human aspiration. He has the most important dialogue – and generally the script steers a plain line between Hollywood fustian and fancy Fry – but Williamson speaks it in a curious mixture of Celtic accents and sometimes sounds as if the dragon's breath has got into his sinuses. Like others considering this extraordinary picture, I took to Williamson's performance more the second time around, which was perhaps due to seeing it with a more sympathetic audience.

Heaven's Gate (Michael Cimino)

The Observer, 13 September 1981

The hostility that greeted *Heaven's Gate* last November has perhaps more to do with the psychopathology of American life than the quality of Michael Cimino's picture. Just as there seemed to be some shared national intention to will success upon *Raiders of the Lost Ark* this summer, so there appears to have been some concerted desire that *Heaven's Gate* should not merely fail but be the occasion of a positive debacle.

In the wake of Reagan's victory, conservative critics must have been shocked by a national epic that presents a band of well-heeled xenophobic Wasps conspiring to murder hapless immigrants while the US cavalry stands idly by. Timid liberal critics were waiting to make amends to Jane Fonda for their extravagant admiration of *The Deer Hunter*, a film she denounced as racist and fascist. Right and left now united in dismissing *Heaven's Gate* as incoherent, overlong, tedious.

Their reaction reinforced, and was reinforced by, a feeling that the arrogant new directors needed disciplining, as Stroheim had been tamed in the 1920s, Welles in the 1940s and Dennis Hopper in the 1960s. And who better to choose as a scapegoat than someone who had been allowed to run wildly over budget?

Cimino was still reeling when he brought his re-cut version (reduced by an hour to 148 minutes) to Cannes, where jackals slow-handclapped the overture and then put a series of insulting questions at the subsequent press conference, before the French critic Michel Ciment rose to suggest that we might talk about *Heaven's Gate* as a western.

As a western, *Heaven's Gate* is a handsome, intelligent, carefully considered contribution to a series of Hollywood films reappraising the frontier myth in the light of recent radical thinking and under the influence of the violent, quasi-Marxist spaghetti westerns of Sergio Leone. It resembles several of these fairly closely, because the same cameraman, Vilmos Zsigmond, photographed Altman's *McCabe and Mrs Miller*, the same star, Kris Kristofferson, appeared in Peckinpah's *Pat Garrett and Billy the Kid*, and the same designer, Tambi Larsen, was responsible for the appearance of Clint Eastwood's *The Outlaw Josey Wales*.

More insistently, however, than any of these, it connects the western experience with the social crises in the burgeoning cities of the industrial Northeast. Cimino presents the infamous Johnson County War of 1891, when Wyoming cattle bosses dispatched a mercenary army to punish the newly arrived homesteaders, as a microcosm of the conflict between entrenched interests and the unwelcomed huddled masses that threatened national stability and racial homogeneity.

Early in the film, a death list of 125 Johnson County 'rustlers, anarchists and criminals' is drawn up in the elegant headquarters of the

Cattle Growers Association at Casper, Wyoming (incidentally, one of the most dynamic and convincing re-creations of a bustling western town I've seen). As the neatly dressed fat cats assent to this declaration of bloody class war, we hear a roll call of traditional Wasp names. This scene is echoed later on (the movie is composed of echoes and parallels), when a horrified audience meets at the Johnson County community centre – the *Heaven's Gate* roller-skating rink offering a moral and exhilarating experience – to hear the list of condemned men and women read out, virtually all of them Eastern European. Only very reluctantly do they decide to fight, and in the process they discover some of the central contradictions of American life.

At the film's centre are two men, mirror images of each other as one of them explicitly asserts to his own mirror image, both dubbed class traitors. One is the federal marshal of Johnson County, John Averill (Kris Kristofferson), whom we have encountered in a prologue set in 1870 when graduating from Harvard with a sense of high social duty and a belief in America as the last best hope of the world. The other is Nate Champion (Christopher Walken), a whey-faced dandy gunslinger hired by the cattlemen to execute rustlers, a man of innate decency drawn by pride and ambition to take this job. Both men share the favours of Ella Watson, the local brothel-keeper who accepts cash or cattle from whoever comes to the door. Played with great warmth by Isabelle Huppert, Ella is a passionate, generous woman, at one with the land as the men are not, and representing the spirit of compromise.

Like Visconti and Coppola, Cimino eschews carefully graded narrative in favour of powerfully animated, operatic set-pieces that are often extended beyond what puritanical northern temperaments would think reasonable limits. On the other hand, the epic, emblematic conception of character is tempered by scenes of a touching intimacy. And like *The Deer Hunter*, it concludes with an ambiguous epilogue that relates personal tragedy to national experience.

This rich, bold film is not without its flaws, but they are not the yawning fissures you may have gathered from other reports.

Once Upon a Time in the West (Sergio Leone)

The Observer, 13 June 1982

Sergio Leone's *Once Upon a Time in the West* is being shown in this country for the first time in its original 167-minute version. It is a beautiful, moving and poetic film, one of the best westerns ever made, though I have not always thought it so. Back in 1969 I was so in thrall to the notion that serious westerns represented an essential transaction between Hollywood directors, the American landscape and US history that I was incapable of taking spaghetti westerns seriously.

The first person I heard speak up for Leone was Graham Greene, who in the course of a 1971 National Film Theatre lecture cited *Once Upon a Time in the West* among the two or three recent films he most admired. I assumed then that he had been attracted by the combination of Catholicism and Marxism so evident in Italian westerns. But during the past seven years, I've often thought of a quotation from Chekhov about his fellow Russian novelists that recurs in Greene's movie criticism of the 1930s:

> 'The best of them are realistic and paint life as it is, but because every line is permeated, as with a juice, by an awareness of a purpose, you feel, besides life as it is, also life as it ought to be, and this captivates you.'

This ideal that Greene proposed for the popular cinema about 'life as it is', accompanied by the implication of 'life as it ought to be', is to be found in Leone's movie.

Leone made his rich, affirmative film in 1968, immediately after the immensely successful 'dollar trilogy' of cynical, highly stylised westerns starring Clint Eastwood. Co-scripted by the young Bernardo Bertolucci, this long, expansive epic drew together the main themes of the genre without having recourse to the sort of synoptic *Reader's Digest* plot that made *How the West Was Won* so thin on the prairie.

The time is vague, the period detail very specific, the locations combining John Ford's recognisable Monument Valley with anonymous dusty corners of Wild and Woolly Spain. Interwoven are the stories of Jill (Claudia Cardinale), a prostitute who inherits some land coveted by a railway company, the crippled railway tycoon Morton (Gabriele

Ferzetti), Morton's hired gun, Frank (Henry Fonda), an honest anarchic outlaw called Cheyenne (Jason Robards) and a mysterious avenger known simply, because of the instrument he plays, as Harmonica (Charles Bronson).

They are familiar types, powerfully embodied, both mythical figures and representatives of the historical process. In every major scene they are joined by a familiar character actor from Hollywood or Rome's Cinecittà (Jack Elam, Lionel Stander, Keenan Wynn among them), and they are underpinned by Ennio Morricone's elaborate score, the theme for Cardinale beginning in an elegiac vein and modulating into an anthem of hope for the future.

The dominant motif for this film is water. The opening theme, where three killers wait at a railroad station for the arrival of Harmonica, is punctuated by the creaking of a wind-wheel and the dripping of water onto a gunman's Stetson. The ambitious homesteader defying the railroad is killed beside his well at the arid ranch he has named *Sweetwater*. At a sleazy saloon, his bride (soon to be revealed as his widow) asks for water, only to be told by a leering bartender (providing a biblical echo) that 'the word is poison around these parts, ever since the days of the Great Flood'.

The railroad tycoon is obsessed with reaching the Pacific before he dies and has a seascape on the wall of his elegantly appointed railway coach. He dies grovelling in a muddy pool, the sound of waves splashing in his mind. At the end, Cardinale goes out to the railway workers with jars of refreshing water, an emblematic task recommended to her by the dying outlaw Cheyenne.

There is plenty of sporadic violence in *Once Upon a Time in the West*, but Leone's American backers were clearly disappointed with the slow, sombre, mysterious picture he delivered to them. That has so often been the way in the movies: directors from Stroheim to Cimino have failed to deliver a carbon copy of their previous successes.

Attempting to make the film more commercial, the English language distributors added incoherence to its other apparent vices by dropping the crucial sequence in which Jill, Harmonica and Cheyenne first meet as fellow outsiders; trimming the odd couple of minutes here and there, and reducing the running time to 144 minutes. No one complained back in 1969. After all, who cared about pasta pastiches? Fortunately the film hasn't suffered the fate of *Napoleon*. We haven't had to wait half a century for a dedicated cinéaste like Kevin Brownlow to restore it to us. Largely unprompted, the distributors have brought back Leone's picture, as last year they did *New York, New York*.

The Chosen (Jeremy Paul Kagan) & Georgia's Friends (Arthur Penn)

The Observer, 20 June 1982

A film with an original screenplay by one of America's brightest younger writers, Steve Tesich, and directed by one of the country's outstanding senior moviemakers, Arthur Penn, arouses immense expectations. A screen version by Jeremy Paul Kagan of a Chaim Potok novel is something few film critics would climb out of a sickbed to catch. In the event, the manner in which Kagan's modest *The Chosen* succeeds illuminates the way in which Penn's grandiose *Georgia's Friends* fails.

Both pictures are set without excessive nostalgia in the recent past and deal with the perennial topic of immigrants' children coming to terms with America. Both are about intense friendships over several years between urban males shaped by the circumstances of their parents and the times. In each case a vindictive outburst of violence leaves the focal character blind in one eye, and in the course of his recovery he moves towards a clearer perception of the world. As reputable examples of what has been called the New Optimism, they conclude with what their makers intend to be seen as a hard-won affirmation.

Let us now look at the instructive differences. Kagan's film never sets foot outside the Brooklyn Jewish community and takes place very precisely between the late spring of 1944 on the eve of D-Day and the creation of the state of Israel five years later. Penn's film sprawls rather vaguely from 1960 to the end of the decade and shifts from the back streets of a Midwestern steel town to a palatial mansion on Long Island Sound.

Kagan and his screenwriter Edwin Gordon (admittedly with a masterly novel to fall back on when in doubt) have a clear idea of how public events relate to private lives. Penn and Tesich, on the other hand, contrive to drag in every issue of the era without deciding which are relevant to their characters' development.

Even if we didn't much care for the people in *The Chosen*, we would still find them of compelling interest because of the important philosophical ideas, moral principles and political currents they embody and articulate. Penn relies to a dangerous extent upon us being affectionately engaged by the naïve charm and provincial vulnerability of his essentially mindless young people.

Georgia's Friends is superior to *The Chosen* in only one respect. Both are schematic, but whereas Kagan manages to produce a neat artefact with scarcely a loose end, Penn's anarchic sense and his surrealistic eye inject into *Georgia's Friends* some of the messiness of everyday life. His film has the kind of puzzling and disturbing images *The Chosen* lacks.

The principal characters of *The Chosen* are a pair of intellectually gifted, physically unprepossessing adolescents, Reuven Malter (Barry Miller), the only son of a liberal Jewish professor (Maximilian Schell), and Danny Saunders (Robby Benson), the eldest child of a stern, Hasidic rabbi (Rod Steiger). Although they live within a few blocks of each other, the pair inhabit totally different worlds. Reuven dresses like any other American kid and enjoys swing, movies and radio comedy; Danny wears the anachronistic garb of his ultra-orthodox sect and has been carefully protected from the twentieth century.

They meet as opponents at a softball game that takes place only because Brooklyn Jews feel that they should draw together during the war, and their friendship is initially founded on their similar, restlessly inquiring intellects. After the war, at college, they're driven apart again for a while on a theological matter that links personal principle to international politics – Zionism. Reuven's father destroys his health through his selfless activities on behalf of the Jewish homeland; Danny's father vehemently denounces 'Ben Gurion and his gang' as heretics for attempting to return to the Promised Land before the coming of the Messiah.

In the course of their emotional and intellectual education, the boys come under the influence of each other's father, and in a sense they switch roles, so that Reuven elects to be a rabbi, and Danny breaks with the family's rabbinical tradition to study psychology across the East River at distant Columbia. This is schematic, as I have said, but not contrived. The two fathers, for example, never meet, and there's nothing pious or sentimental about this sensitive, intelligently acted movie.

Georgia's Friends is the spiritual odyssey of the Yugoslav-born Danilo (Craig Wasson) in search of the American Dream, and if you can imagine a combination of the first episode of Frederic Raphael's *Glittering Prizes* (the one about the Jewish undergraduate drawn into the world of a doomed aristocratic room-mate) and *The Deer Hunter* with odd snatches of *Taxi Driver* and *American Graffiti* thrown in, you'll have some idea of the direction he takes.

After a touching prologue, in which the twelve-year-old Dan arrives to join his steelworker father in East Chicago, we cut to him as a high-school senior in 1961, his Balkan flute having been exchanged for a clarinet. With his bosom friends Tom (a handsome Wasp) and David (plump son of a Jewish undertaker), he's courting Georgia, a local beauty bent on emulating Isadora Duncan as a way of escaping from her drab surroundings. As played by Jodi Thelen, however, she is a sadly inadequate receptacle for their passion. When the shy Danilo refuses to take her virginity, she offers herself to Tom, becomes pregnant and marries poor David.

There are a lot of 'meanwhiles' in this plot. Tom goes off to Vietnam. Danilo, in defiance of glum, defeated Dad ('I'm tired and I have to work – that's America'), goes to smart Northwestern University (no classes, no term or vacation jobs), and falls in love with the beautiful sister of his terminally sick, eternally optimistic room-mate, scion of a wealthy East Coast family. Instant idylls are followed by equally perfunctory explosions of violence, one of them on Danilo's wedding day, that seeks to suggest both the 1963 assassination in Dallas and the killing of social-climbing Gatsby.

After a sequence of cross-cutting in which Dan's search for his ethnic roots among the Serbian community of Pennsylvania is contrasted with Georgia's desperate passage through the decadent late stages of 1960s hippiedom, the couple meet up again in East Chicago. There they join David (with a cosy Jewish wife) and Tom (back from service in Indo-China with a beautiful Vietnamese bride) on the shores of Lake Michigan for a symbolic burning of the trunk that Danilo has been carting around with him ever since he arrived in America.

There are scenes that remind one that Tesich scripted *Breaking Away* and *The Janitor*, and that Penn directed the three finest movies to emerge from the American experience in the 1960s, *Bonnie and Clyde, Alice's Restaurant* and *Little Big Man*. The movie always looks good and sometimes comes up with an unforgettable image (the burning of the Stars and Stripes in slow motion in front of the windscreen of the hero's car, for instance). We are looking at America here through a great pair of eyes, those of the late Belgian lighting cameraman, Ghislain Cloquet.

Angel (Neil Jordan)

The Observer, 7 November 1982

Carol Reed's *Odd Man Out* is our only indigenous *film noir* thriller of the 1940s that compares favourably with the best Hollywood examples of the genre, and it was shot on location in Belfast, with James Mason as an IRA fugitive and his gun as a symbol of contagion. Interestingly, the idiom and iconography of the *film noir* and the hard-boiled thriller are attracting another generation of Irish artists attempting to deal with the current troubles.

First, the Belfast playwright Bill Morrison followed his radio adaptations of the complete Raymond Chandler canon with *Maguire*, a brilliant radio play in the wise-cracking 'Black Mask' style, where a petty crook from the Falls Road is hounded by the police and terrorists after witnessing a sectarian killing. Then the Ulster poet Paul Muldoon composed a modern version of the ninth-century Celtic epic, *Immram Maele Dúin*, in Chandleresque vein. Now the Dublin novelist Neil Jordan has made one of the most auspicious directorial debuts of recent years with *Angel*, a poetic thriller that presses the anxieties and tensions of Northern Ireland into the mould of the classic *film noir*.

Jordan's central character is Danny (Stephen Rea), a saxophonist dubbed 'the Stan Getz of South Armagh' by the other members of the seedy showband he tours with around Ulster's second-rate halls and discos. He is a withdrawn, laconic young man, using his music to spin a protective cocoon around himself. But one night, outside a garish dance hall in a suburban wasteland, he is an unseen witness when three masked terrorists murder his manager and machine-gun a deaf-mute girl

(Veronica Quilligan) who has strayed on to the scene. At dawn the shattered Danny staggers from his shelter behind some drainpipes, carrying the girl's body and saying, 'I will teach you to sing', an echo of Lear's last words to Cordelia, and the first of several Shakespearian references.

This gesture dispels any lingering doubts we might have about the film's mode. The setting is a bleak, tangibly real Ulster, but the vision is heightened to a mythic, surrealistic pitch. Nearly every line of dialogue is charged with wit or poetic resonance, virtually every frame is studiously composed (and superbly lit by the British cinematographer Chris Menges). This produces a certain sense of strain, but the error is in the right direction.

Jordan is a protégé of John Boorman, who produced this film, and Danny makes a circular journey similar to the one taken by the avenger-hero of Boorman's seminal thriller *Point Blank*. He returns at the end of the nightmare for a final confrontation in the gutted shell of the dance hall, appropriately called *Dreamland*. A series of random clues leads to the killers – a built-up shoe in a shop window, a police photograph of a beach hut, a chance meeting in a café. His victims seem to be waiting for him almost fatalistically, and he clutches one of them in a *pietà* position as the man dies.

Danny's music and mission merge. Finding a machine gun, he assembles it with the deft fascination hitherto reserved for his saxophone, and he carries it in a spare instrument case. 'You haven't played your soprano,' someone says. 'I'm waiting for the right tune,' he replies. This avenging angel becomes mystically aware of having a charmed life, and, in his heightened state, discovers new depths of musicianship.

His girlfriend, the band vocalist Dee (a remarkable performance by a newcomer, Honor Heffernan), recognises the transformation, thinking it at first some benign spiritual release, before sensing that Danny is touched by evil. He has the power to enchant and to destroy: the film's most haunting scene involves Danny playing to an audience of elderly patients in a mental hospital, and its most harrowing one sees him unwittingly drive a farmer's widow (Sorcha Cusack) over the brink of despair.

The only evidence of communal violence is a car seen burning in the street at night, the only sign of the military presence a patrolling soldier Danny fleetingly views from a tenement window. But the film is full of hidden terror and suggests a national malaise that either saps people's energy or misdirects their will. The most active figure is the god-like Inspector Bloom (Ray McAnally), the cop who monitors Danny's progress. The most passive is Danny's ageing aunt (Maire Kean), who has abandoned fortune-telling because death rears its head too monotonously. All in all, *Angel* is one of the most exciting pictures of the year.

The Atomic Café (Kevin Rafferty) & Dead Men Don't Wear Plaid (Carl Reiner)

The Observer, 28 November 1982

The single pastime of the Ik tribe is creating unpleasant situations for their fellows and then laughing like drains. So short on laughter has the cinema been this year that I was on the point of imitating the Ik and planting banana skins in the aisles to trip fellow critics, when suddenly two hilarious American pictures arrived on the same day, *Dead Men Don't Wear Plaid* and *The Atomic Café*.

Both are masterpieces of editing, drawing much of their laughter from a classical manipulation of film footage shot for quite different purposes in the forties and fifties. The makers of *Dead Men* are snappers up of well-considered trifles from the vaults of the major Hollywood studios. Like many young American documentarists, the compilers of *Atomic Café*, Kevin Rafferty, Jayne Loader and Pierce Rafferty, are raiders of the locked archives who have spent years sifting the film libraries (in some cases only recently prised open) of the armed forces and government agencies. Both teams clearly revel in the sheer excitement of re-ordering film. But *Dead Men* is innocent of any purpose other than to make us laugh, while *The Atomic Café* has palpable designs on us.

With no formal commentary, *Atomic Café* charts the interplay between the American public's nuclear angst and an officially sponsored domestication of the bomb over the fifteen post-war years. The picture is made up entirely of contemporary material drawn from cinema newsreels, radio, television, pop music, army indoctrination films and civil defence documentaries.

Some awesome colour film of the Alamogordo test explosion is followed by an interview with Colonel Paul Tibbetts, commander of the plane that dropped the bomb on Hiroshima, recalling that he showed that Alamogordo footage to his crew as 'preliminary indoctrination' before take-off. Later that day he knew how horrendous was the act that he had committed.

We don't laugh at Tibbetts, but we begin to crack up a little when Harry Truman smiles at the newsreel cameraman before composing his face for a grave speech thanking God who 'gave the bomb to us and not to our enemies, and we pray that He will guide us to use it for His ways and His purposes.' The conspiratorial smile and the solemn speech symbolise the compact between the American political establishment and the media that continued until the 1960s.

After Truman's speech comes a newsreel clip of the long forgotten leader of the Nagasaki raid, a less reflective figure than Tibbetts. 'That was the greatest thrill,' he says of the moment he released the bomb. We are freed at this point to laugh aloud, and we do so at endless bland politicians, civil defence experts, the cartoon character of Bert the Turtle teaching school kids to 'duck and cover' when the bomb falls, the PR men coaxing the natives off Bikini Atoll, a chaplain putting soldiers at ease before they walk into a radioactive battlefield, and priests reassuring the owners of nuclear shelters of their God-given right to shoot intruders.

The film is accompanied by a string of Country songs from patriotic Nashville, like 'My Atomic Love' and 'The Iron Curtain's Falling on My Cold War With You', that were no doubt played on the juke-box of the eponymous Atomic Café, a roadside diner in Utah with a flashing neon mushroom on top. In a final montage the producers weave their material into a ghastly vision of a nuclear holocaust that recalls the epilogue to *Dr Strangelove*.

Before that, however, there are passages of total sobriety. One of these predictably concerns the execution of the Rosenbergs. Another, rather surprisingly in this satirical context, is a paternalistic speech by Eisenhower about current anxieties over the bomb that is accompanied by some film sympathetically re-creating the complacent, affluent America he ruled over.

By restricting themselves to contemporary American film, the makers of *Atomic Café* have accepted limitations and disciplines. The view of the Cold War, for example, is lopsided in a fashionably revisionist manner.

But their picture has the ruthless qualities of John Heartfield's photo-montages, and it's provocative in a number of useful ways.

The previous collaboration between the comedian Steve Martin and the writer-director Carl Reiner, *The Jerk*, scarcely made me smile. A couple of minutes into *Dead Men Don't Wear Plaid*, their black-and-white spoof on a 1940s private-eye thriller, and I was gasping for breath. Keaton's *The General* and Chaplin's *Gold Rush* are no doubt more formally perfect, but I can hardly imagine laughing more in a period of eighty-nine minutes than I did watching this movie.

Martin plays a Los Angeles gumshoe hired by a beautiful socialite (Rachel Ward) to investigate her father's disappearance. Just another send-up, we think. But going down the mean streets of the 1940s, he encounters Alan Ladd, Ray Milland, Burt Lancaster, Cary Grant, Ingrid Bergman, Bette Davis, Lana Turner, Kirk Douglas, Jimmy Cagney, Fred MacMurray, Humphrey Bogart, Joan Crawford, Charles Laughton and Vincent Price in scenes culled from eighteen movies, mostly *film noir* thrillers made between 1941 and 1950.

The screenwriters work these borrowed sequences into their script with great ingenuity, and the cinematographer Michael Chapman (who shot the monochrome *Raging Bull*), the dress designer Edith Head (whose last film this was), the composer Miklós Rózsa (who provided the music for several of the 1940s classics drawn on here), the production designer John DeCuir and the editor Bud Molin have combined to give the picture a seamless look and feel.

What we have here is a technical exercise of extraordinary virtuosity and a rare case of a film that is as much fun to watch as it must have been to make. Not all the humour derives from the use of the old films – Steve Martin contrives some clever comic business, and there is much delightfully adolescent word play, like the marvellous misunderstanding over the initials FOC. In fact, anyone who likes old movies and dirty jokes will love *Dead Men Don't Wear Plaid* (the gnomic hard-boiled title is an apocryphal *obiter dictum* of Philip Marlowe), and I will not spoil their pleasure by revealing more.

Gandhi (Richard Attenborough)

The Observer, 5 December 1982

At the centre of this week's major movie is a small, bald, bespectacled figure who has walked with crowds and kept his virtue and talked with kings without losing the common touch, an astute politician with a steely sense of destiny, yet renowned for his modesty and revered by his followers as an almost saintly person. He is, of course, Sir Richard Attenborough, and his book, *In Search of Gandhi*, is both an autobiography and an account of a twenty-year struggle to realise a dream.

Just as a book about how Thomas Keneally researched *Schindler's Ark* would be more interesting than the non-fiction novel Keneally wrote, so a movie about Attenborough's two decades trying to set up his cinebiography of the Mahatma would perhaps be more stimulating than the honourable, honestly affecting, carefully crafted film, *Gandhi*, that opened on three continents last week.

Attenborough came to the film well prepared. Since becoming obsessed with Gandhi, he had directed *Oh! What a Lovely War*, *Young Winston* and *A Bridge Too Far*, three ambivalent epics with all-star casts that brought the British establishment sharply into question. Moreover, among his varied acting assignments, Attenborough ventured into the Indian cinema to give, in Satyajit Ray's *The Chess Players*, an impressive impersonation of General Outram, the self-confident imperialist who set the final seal on the British Raj that it became Gandhi's destiny to shatter.

In the course of these movies, Attenborough was able to explore various ways of treating his subject, and I would have liked to see him choose the flexible, investigative technique adopted by Welles in *Citizen Kane* (and flirted with in Carl Foreman's screenplay for *Young Winston*). But with a budget in excess of twenty million dollars, he and his American screenwriter, John Briley, have played fairly safe with a film that is by Bertolt Brecht out of Warner Brothers.

By this I mean that the texture recalls those solid, inspirational Hollywood biographies of the 1930s, associated with Paul Muni, while the structure, as in Brecht's *Galileo*, is a succession of exemplary sequences, each built around a single proposition.

Ben Kingsley's performance as Gandhi, ageing fifty years in three hours from dapper, status-conscious lawyer to emaciated ascetic in a loincloth, is certainly as fine as anything Muni ever did and likely to take its place among the cinema's great historic portraits. Around him some famous Western actors and some little-known Eastern ones lend presence, if not depth, to a variety of real and composite personages.

We first see Gandhi in 1948 at that fateful prayer meeting when he was shot down by a Hindu fanatic, and as millions gather for his funeral in Delhi and the world's leaders make their lapidary tributes, the film flashes back to a chronological account of his life, beginning with his arrival in South Africa in the 1890s at the age of twenty-three. Firmly in possession of a first class ticket, he is thrown off a train in the middle of the night by an irate railway guard at the behest of an indignant white passenger.

This is the first personal lesson learnt by an ambitious conformist. Thereafter each scene of this didactic movie involves learning and teaching as Gandhi develops his ethical system, beginning by encouraging a handful of Indian immigrants to defy the police in a dusty South African township and ending up trying to unite the teeming millions of the subcontinent in passive resistance against the British Empire.

For instance, when Gandhi comes home to India in 1915, he is advised by his mentor, Professor Gokhale, to spend a year seeing the country, and he does so, travelling third class (to the eloquent accompaniment of Ravi Shankar's music). On his return he urges the middle-class intellectuals at a Congress Party rally to go to the villages and begin a grass roots mass movement.

Later, in introducing his fellow Congress leaders to the idea of non-violence, he demonstrates, through his treatment of Jinnah's house servant, that they themselves act towards the lower orders the way the British treat India. 'Forgive my stupid illustration,' he says, 'but I want to change their minds – not kill them for weaknesses we all possess.'

Back in 1939, John Gunther called Gandhi 'an incredible combination of Jesus Christ, Tammany Hall and your father', and all three aspects are brought out by Ben Kingsley. This isn't a pious portrait. There is much sly humour and human warmth in this man, and his relationships with his illiterate wife, Ba (Rohini Hattangadi), and his friend, the Anglican priest Charlie Andrews (Ian Charleson), truly glow.

But the film deliberately leaves out his eccentricities, presumably to prevent the viewer attempting any glib psychoanalytic reading of his character, and has little to say about his religious or political ideas. Much of what made Gandhi controversial in his life and death is hardly touched on.

With the help of his cinematographers, Billy Williams and Ronnie Taylor, Attenborough has produced a beautiful-looking movie that is maybe a little too seductive for its own good. Almost the only touch of real poverty is a ragged mother breast-feeding her child, whom Gandhi sees from the carriage bringing him through the streets of Bombay on his return from South Africa.

But Attenborough shows once again his skill in managing the big set-piece, and whereas in his Arnhem picture he excited us with well-staged battle scenes, here he involves us in the very idea of non-violence during the march on the Dharasana Salt Works, and he denies us any pleasure in his three major action sequences – the massacre at Amritsar, the assault on the police station at Chauri Chaura by Gandhi followers who lose their heads, and a clash between two columns of refugees moving in different directions during the partition. In each case we watch with mounting horror as a peaceful scene turns ugly, then violent, and finally explodes in senseless slaughter.

First Blood (Ted Kotcheff)

The Observer, 19 December 1982

At the height of the Vietnam conflict, Hollywood carefully gauged World War II movies like *Patton* and *Tora! Tora! Tora!* to appeal both to hawks and doves. Now, ten years later, Ted Kotcheff's thriller *First Blood* is designed to appeal to former hawks *and* former doves.

Sylvester Stallone plays Rambo, a longhaired drifter in a combat jacket decorated with the Stars and Stripes, passing through the ironically named small town of Hope in the mountains of Oregon. Hope's redneck sheriff (the excellent Brian Dennehy), taking Rambo for a hippie, books him on a vagrancy charge. Rambo is in fact the familiar figure of the current American cinema, the disturbed Vietnam veteran, a Green Beret with a Congressional Medal of Honour, visiting the Pacific Northwest to look up a black comrade, the only other survivor of their elite jungle squad.

The brutal arrest follows immediately on Rambo's discovery that his old buddy recently died of cancer contracted through exposure to the defoliant Agent Orange in Nam, and the effect is to unhinge him. Some rapid flashbacks to an Indo-China prison camp identify his current treatment by the cops with his torture at the hands of the Gong, putting us on Rambo's side as he devastates the Hope police station and takes to the winter forest.

Armed only with a special combat knife and clad in a home-made hessian outfit that makes him resemble Hereward the Wake or Elmo Lincoln, the silent Tarzan, Rambo defies the local cops, the state police and the National Guard, fending off helicopters, garrotting Doberman pinchers and surviving anti-tank rockets. The events are ferociously violent, though only one man is killed and his death is accidental.

This fascinatingly ambivalent picture is a cross between two influential liberal melodramas, *Bad Day at Black Rock* (1955), where Spencer Tracy, just back from World War II, exposed the nasty little secrets of a shabby desert town, and *Lonely Are the Brave* (1962), where ex-Korean War GI Kirk Douglas, the last cowboy in New Mexico, was hounded through the hills by vindictive cops. It's also the final working out of a cycle of allegorical westerns, *Tell Them Willie Boy Is Here*, *Ulzana's Raid* and *Chato's Land* among them, that reflected the anxieties of the Vietnam war through tales about posses of assorted American types (one of whom invariably comes to dissociate himself from his dishonourable companions) pursuing an increasingly sympathetic quarry.

The troubled pursuer in *First Blood* is initially a naïve young cop, and then, more powerfully, Rambo's Special Forces colonel (Richard Crenna), who is dispatched from a Washington DC desk to mediate, philosophise, and bring his boy home. The film's key line, linking soldier and anarchic dissenter as opponents of a complacent society, is Stallone's surly riposte to his former commander's call for him to surrender to the sympathetic authorities: 'There *are* no friendly civilians.'

There are strong echoes of Walter Hill's *Southern Comfort* in *First Blood*, and indeed the screenwriter David Giler and the cameraman Andres Laszlo worked on both. Compared with Hill's masterly movie, Kotcheff's picture is pretty crude stuff, though gripping enough as a gutsy action thriller, well acted and tightly edited. But whereas *Southern Comfort* failed at the box office, *First Blood* has taken over from *ET* as America's number one attraction. Stallone's blend of machismo and masochism is part of the American dream too.

Fanny and Alexander (Ingmar Bergman)

The Observer, 24 April 1983

Twenty years ago Ingmar Bergman reached the peak of his career and plumbed the depths of his spiritual despair with *Through a Glass Darkly*, *Winter Light* and *The Silence*, his unremittingly bleak chamber trilogy on the solitariness of man. He immediately followed this with his first colour movie, *About All These Women*, a brightly lit comedy about the ménage of a much misunderstood womanising musical genius in the 1920s, that sourly reflected on his own relations with obtuse critics and a prying press.

Bergman then reverted to his customary pessimism, and two years ago concluded his German exile with the starkly monochrome, nihilistic *From the Life of the Marionettes*. Now, returning to Sweden, he has made in *Fanny and Alexander* another glowing movie also set earlier in this century and again consciously autobiographical.

This magnificent three-hour film (which also exists in a five-hour television version) is proposed as his farewell to the cinema and is certainly testamentary in character. Peter Cowie's illuminating, admirably researched critical biography of Bergman, published to coincide with the picture, shows just how much *Fanny and Alexander* draws on the director's own early life, recapitulates characters, themes and motifs from his work, and seeks to reconcile conflicting aspects of his thinking.

Set in a Swedish provincial town, the film begins on Christmas Eve 1907, at the opulent apartment of Helena Ekdahl, a wealthy widow and ex-actress with three middle-aged sons: Oscar (Allan Edwall), an actor-manager of much good will and little talent, who runs the family's prosperous theatre; Gustaf (Jarl Kulle), a successful, Pan-like restaurateur; and Carl (Börje Ahlstedt), a drunken, embittered academic.

Gradually we work out the relationships between the family, their friends and servants, as the Christmas festivities proceed, and the film comes to centre on Oscar's young wife Emilie (the strong, handsome Ewa Fröling) and their children, the ten-year-old Alexander and eight-year-old Fanny.

The town is clearly Bergman's birthplace, Uppsala, the elegantly cluttered apartment we recognise as his grandmother's home, and the enchanting opening shot of Alexander raising the curtain of a toy theatre to look through the stage at the world is the first of numerous references to the theatre.

Oscar and Emilie are first glimpsed as Joseph and the annunciatory angel in their theatre's nativity play, and soon after Christmas Oscar has a fatal heart attack playing the Ghost in a rehearsal of *Hamlet*. As part of the film's supernatural dimension, Oscar returns to haunt the family with characteristic ineffectuality when Emilie marries a sadistic, puritanical bishop (Jan Malmsjö), who takes her away from the theatre to live a life of 'austerity and purity'.

In the bishop's spartan palace Fanny and Alexander are subjected to a regimen reminiscent of testing Dickensian childhoods or Kipling's *Baa Baa, Black Sheep*. The implied notion of the theatre as true father and the church as stepfather reverses the course of Bergman's own life, for the bishop has much in common with the stern Lutheran cleric who was the director's own father.

He is called Vergerus, a recurrent name in Bergman movies from *The Face* (1959) onwards, always attached to those opposed to the mystical, intuitive, sensuous. There ensues a contest of power, magic and will for the possession of Emilie and the children between the bishop's household and the Ekdahls, involving the family's devoted Jewish friend, Isak Jacobi (Erland Josephson).

This exuberant, richly textured film, packed with life and incident, is punctuated by a series of ritual family gatherings for parties, funerals, weddings and christenings. Ghosts are as corporeal as living people; seasons come and go; tumultuous, traumatic events occur; yet, as in a dream of childhood (the film's perspective is that of Alexander), time is oddly still.

The enormous cast, mostly members of the repertory company Bergman has created during forty years in the theatre and cinema, is uniformly excellent. The photography of Sven Nykvist is as fine as ever, conveying with great subtlety the difference of moral tone between the bishop's icy palace, the Ekdahls' warm household, and the mystical Aladdin's cave where the antique-dealer Jacobi provides a refuge for the fugitive children.

The Ekdahl sequences have a depth of focus rare in Bergman's colour movies and are framed and lit to evoke the geometric composition and shadow-less, all-over light of Carl Larsson, Sweden's most perennially popular artist, who celebrated the attractions of middle-class family life at the turn of the century. It is part of the magnanimity and maturity of Bergman's vision that this film can pay tribute simultaneously to Larsson and to Strindberg.

The Ploughman's Lunch (Richard Eyre)

The Observer, 29 May 1983

Three years ago, the novelist Ian McEwan and the director Richard Eyre collaborated on *The Imitation Game*, a first-rate television play about an idealistic young woman destroyed by uncomprehending officialdom during World War II.

The same month, Eyre directed Jonathan Pryce at the Royal Court in one of the most memorable *Hamlets* of the past decade. Now McEwan, Eyre and Pryce have joined forces to produce, in *The Ploughman's Lunch*, a major film with an urgency, seriousness, wit and intelligence rare in our native cinema.

Set in the Falklands year of 1982 – its first shot is a BBC teleprinter tapping out news about the South Georgia landings, its climax was actually filmed during the Tory conference in Brighton – *The Ploughman's Lunch* has the same topicality *The Entertainer* had back in 1957. Osborne's state-of-the-nation play was on the stage while the ashes of the Suez invasion were still glowing; McEwan and Eyre have struck while the ironies of the Falklands conflict are still hot.

Their central character, Jimmy Penfield (superbly played by Pryce), has echoes of the 1950s too. He's the Jimmy Porter and Joe Lampton of the 1980s, a hungry young man of thirty-six, looking back with revisionist anguish as he edges his way to the top. Only to his suburban lower-class Mum and Dad, though, is he Jimmy.

In the company of his smart media friends (who have been told his parents are dead) he's James, a news editor with BBC radio and part-time popular historian. He has contributed the chapter on the Berlin Airlift to *The Cold War*, a symposium just brought out by Tom Gold (a wickedly accurate amalgam of four leading London publishers by David De Keyser), and is currently engaged on a new interpretation of the Suez affair. This book will dismiss the sentimental talk about national humiliation and base conspiracy and justify British policy in terms of political pragmatism and imperial honour.

Ambitious, insecure, eager to please, James is weak rather than wicked. He has professional standards instead of ethics, opinions in place of beliefs, and an edgy diffident charm that passes for sincere concern. He is more vulnerable than his cynical, Oxford-educated Fleet Street chum Jeremy (Tim Curry). He has retained more feeling than the brittle, upper-middle-class TV researcher Susan (Charlie Dore) he pursues, and with whose socialist historian mother (Rosemary Harris) he becomes painfully involved.

But moral chameleon that he is, James's restless thoughts are always elsewhere. At a BBC meeting he reads a letter from his publisher; apparently listening with sympathy to activists at a women's peace camp by a Norfolk air-base, he's only really interested in borrowing a jack to get his stranded Daimler back on the road; as Mrs Thatcher rants on about 'the spirit of the South Atlantic' at the Tory conference, James can only think of his own emotional betrayal; at his mother's funeral, he looks anxiously at his watch as the coffin is lowered into the grave.

The Ploughman's Lunch engages with major themes and issues: the relationship of private actions to public events, the connection between personal and political morality, the consequences of successive cycles of optimism and disillusion since the Labour victory of 1945, the individual's responsibility as historical witness, the continuing pressures of class in Britain, the way reality is perceived and mediated in our society.

But they are handled without wind or rhetoric through characters with authentically observed jobs. Their conversation is concrete and convincing, their professional problems real. At a London university the students are hooked on video games. A poet at a public reading has verse of distinction put in his mouth. The characters visit the Barbican Gallery, read the *TLS* and *Private Eye*, reveal themselves through their responses to Wajda's *Man of Iron*, drink at the Zanzibar and lunch at Langan's.

Where there is some slight exaggeration it is for legitimate satirical purposes, and the acting all around is excellent. There are splendid contributions from Frank Finlay as a burnt-out director of TV commercials and Bob Cartland as a blandly contained BBC news chief.

George Orwell would have liked the harsh symbolism of the homely title. A 'ploughman's lunch' is the simple fare provided in saloon bars throughout Britain, a traditional repast with roots in our rural heritage, but in fact the enduring centre of a successful advertising campaign launched in the 1960s to get people to eat in pubs. It is a metaphor for the film's vision of present-day Britain.

Return Engagement (Alan Rudolph)

The Observer, 11 September 1983

In Shakespeare's only venture into the Americas, the first reaction of the jester Trinculo to Caliban is to contemplate the fortune this bizarre inhabitant of the New World would bring him in a freak show. In this he anticipated the great nineteenth-century showman Phineas T. Barnum, who believed that anything slightly out of the ordinary could be installed for profit in what he called his 'American Museum', in the process creating a metaphor for that function in American life that transforms everything into a branch of show business.

The latest addition to that great American Museum is the double act of Timothy Leary, the former Harvard psychology professor, naïve utopian guru and advocate of freedom through drugs, and G. Gordon Liddy, mastermind of the Watergate break-in, samurai of the suburbs and staunch upholder of victory through willpower.

This past year they have been touring America, lecturing and debating together, and Robert Altman's former assistant Alan Rudolph has made an engrossing, very funny documentary about a week this odd couple spent in Los Angeles, *Return Engagement*.

This title refers to revisiting the sixties and seventies through these emblematic figures, and to the fact that, back in 1966, Liddy, as an eager young district attorney in an ultra-conservative New York county, arrested Leary's whole commune several times on drugs charges. This harassment led, so Leary argues, to Liddy being hired as a narcotics expert by the White House and thus on to Watergate, justifying Leary's claim that the pair helped bring down Nixon.

For commercial reasons the two need each other. Until Liddy came along, Leary was a drug on the market as a lecture-circuit performer, while Liddy needed a way-out stooge to make him sound more humane and reasonable. Together they can attract a mixed house of doves and hawks. But though, as Liddy remarks, 'we disagree about everything it is possible to disagree about', the pair have taken to each other. Whatever each may actually profess, they are representatives of a cranky American individualism at its most extreme that took both to jail for long sentences.

Appropriately the movie begins with Liddy's hoarse baritone rendition of 'America, America' to what he terms Leary's 'psychedelic' piano accompaniment, and their good-humoured public dialogues take place before a giant *Stars and Stripes* backdrop that recalls the pre-credit sequence of *Patton*.

Rudolph's film (with Altman operating one of the cameras) is as deceptively loose-textured and as artfully contrived as his directorial debut, *Welcome to LA*, with exposition as carefully planted as in a well-made play. We have the pair doing their act on stage and separately interviewed by the Los Angeles journalist who moderates the public sessions. A roof-top hotel breakfast with their wives presses on family issues and allows us to observe the acquiescent femininity of Leary's young wife and the toughness of Mrs Liddy; when Liddy refuses to talk about his sex life, saying 'I plead not guilty on all counts', she retorts, 'You always do, that's why they gave you twenty years.'

Rudolph crosscuts between Liddy working out in the gym to the point of extreme pain and Leary playing with his mind-expanding word processor. When Leary goes off to talk a load of mystical guff to a largely nude audience of 'Me Generation' zealots at the Esalen Institute, Liddy is out on the road with a local motorcycle gang, whose leader did time with him in a Federal penitentiary.

When Liddy visits an indoor shooting range, keeping up his skills with shotgun and pistol, Leary drops in on a computer games arcade, preaching his message that with computers 'you can double your intelligence in a week'. Both have a session with a class of high-school seniors, Liddy lecturing them on ethics and social responsibility, Leary flattering them with his ideas on the imminent and necessary take-over by post-war youth.

What they have to say is usually eloquent, and in Liddy's case often shrewd. But sooner or later (usually sooner) their particular brands of authoritarianism and anarchism are pushed so far that each disappears into the wide blue yonder on the back of the great American eagle with a maniac gleam in his eyes. But they're a genial couple, deep in the American grain. There are few dull moments in their company, and *Return Engagement* is as much a testimony to the resilience of American democracy as it is evidence of a national addiction to show business.

Little Ida (Laila Mikkelsen)

The Observer, 30 October 1983

In the summer of 1960, with a couple of hours to kill one wet Monday night in Oslo, I slipped into a cinema showing *Conspiracy of Hearts*, a British movie about Italian nuns saving Jewish children from the Nazis.

In one climactic scene a hostage was tied to a chair in the village square before a Nazi firing squad. Just as the soldiers were about to shoot, there came from the back of a packed, totally silent cinema a piercing scream, the like of which I had never heard before.

What was for me a contrived, sentimental war movie was, I suddenly realised, stirring painful memories and tapping powerful emotions in an audience most of whom had experienced a particularly brutal German occupation which had lasted from before Dunkirk in 1940 until VE Day in 1945.

The feeling I had in Oslo that evening came back most vividly while seeing *Little Ida*, a modest, low-key Norwegian film that deals with children in World War II in an honest, elliptical manner far removed from the vulgar *Conspiracy of Hearts*. It is adapted by Marit Paulsen from her semi-autobiographical novel in collaboration with the director, Laila

Mikkelsen, and looks at the last year of the Occupation through the eyes of the seven-year-old daughter of a woman who cooks in a German prison camp kitchen and has an affair with an SS officer.

Ida must have been three when the Germans arrived, and the world around her is an impenetrably confusing place. At Sunday school in the small northern port where she lives, the other children shun her as a 'Kraut kid' while singing hymns about returning good for evil and forgiving the transgressor. Her elder brother sits apart from Ida and their mother in the communal air-raid shelter and soon manages to vanish across the fjord.

A kindly German sentry gives her a toffee at the camp gate and then later in the day is seen clubbing a starving prisoner with his rifle butt. Her mother, a sad, fading beauty, more stupid than wicked, beats little Ida for making her feel guilty, and the child in turn beats her rag doll. In an excruciatingly painful sequence, Ida makes a shrine in her bedroom, beseeching God 'to forgive us for being different from other people'.

Two happy interludes – one with an older girl whose father has been deported, the other lodging with a stern farming family in the countryside – end in shameful perplexity. Dispatched home by a secretly vindictive farmer after joining the family in a victory toast, Ida arrives to observe her mother's hair being cut off by Resistance stalwarts, just as the Germans shaved the heads of their Norwegian prisoners.

Not realising that her mother's sins are going to be visited on her, Ida decks herself out in patriotic bunting to join a liberation parade. In the street, her Sunday school teacher angrily slaps her and strips off the necklace of flags.

This is by implication a memory film. For more than a year the landscape remains a bleak late winter that refuses to break out into spring. The context in which *Little Ida* must be seen is that of a country where (though Vidkun Quisling, leader of Norway's fanatically Nordic minority of Nazi sympathisers, gave his ignominious name to the language) the level of collaboration was incredibly low.

United from the start behind the government-in-exile in London, the Norwegian people conducted themselves with a dignity and courage unequalled by any other European country. The guilt and moral ambivalence attendant upon any French work about their Occupation are inapplicable in Norway.

So what happened to Ida was part of a necessary ethical cruelty.

Sunniva Lindekleiv gives a heart-rending performance as a tragic innocent, a victim of historic circumstance. But we would be reacting sentimentally, refusing to learn from history, if we did not, at the same time as we extend our easy liberal compassion to Ida, sympathise with the anger her mother's actions excited and understand why parents encouraged their children to boycott the families of collaborators.

Rear Window (Alfred Hitchcock) & A Star Is Born (George Cukor)

The Observer, 4 December 1983

The Year 1954 was not a particularly happy time anywhere. Though America was enjoying a period of exceptional economic prosperity, the Rosenbergs had recently been executed, the manufacture of tranquillisers was becoming big business, McCarthyism was rampant and blacklisting in the media was at its height. In Hollywood, this sense of malaise was further increased by the inroads of television, which was being nervously combated by 3-D and the wide screen.

There was scarcely a film that year directly touching on domestic politics, but a good many reflected the tensions of the early Eisenhower era. *On the Waterfront*, a movie defending the role of the informer, made by a group of ex-Communists who appeared before the House UnAmerican Activities Committee, is an obvious example.

So too are a pair of exceptional movies from 1954 that have just been re-released, Alfred Hitchcock's *Rear Window*, now available for the first time in twenty years in a beautiful new print, and George Cukor's *A Star Is Born*, painstakingly restored to its original three-hour version.

Rear Window, though a comedy thriller, is about suspicion, paranoia, surveillance, the breakdown of community. *A Star Is Born*, though a show-biz musical, is a bleak, ambivalent look at Hollywood with a self-destructive hero who eventually commits suicide.

In addition to reflecting their own times, these films have taken on new meanings with the passing of thirty years. What we now know about Hitchcock's life leads us to think of the film's central character, an inhibited, class-conscious voyeur spinning sinister fantasies around his distanced neighbours, as being a portrait of the director himself. Equally, *A Star Is Born* now has a peculiar edge through our knowledge that the actual careers of Judy Garland and James Mason were exactly the reverse of the film's dependable, sober, understanding heroine and her damned, drunken, wilful husband.

The meaning of *Rear Window* is located in its narrative method, and it is a film carefully planned and immaculately executed by its director, his screenwriter, John Michael Hayes, and his cameraman, Robert Burks. As in *Rope, Lifeboat* and *Dial M For Murder*, Hitchcock set himself an elaborate technical problem – to present a story almost entirely from the point of view of a disabled man living vicariously by observing his neighbours.

As even those too young to have had the opportunity of seeing this film know, he's the New York photojournalist J.E. Jeffries (James Stewart), confined to a wheelchair with a broken leg one hot summer, whose cinema-screen-sized window affords him a constant view of his neighbours around a Greenwich Village courtyard.

Initially alienated from each other, all are in some way troubled, and from the start Jeff appears to partake of their disturbance. At one crucial point he raises his wine-glass to the fantasising neighbour he calls 'Miss Lonelyhearts' instead of to his own, too perfect fiancée, a rich, socialite model played with charm and an easy erotic power by Grace Kelly,

The first moment of terror, connecting fear and desire, love and death, comes when a sinister shadow falls on the face of Jeff asleep in his wheelchair. A subjective shot from the waking Jeff's point-of-view reveals that the shadow is cast by the beautiful Kelly, seen for the first time in the film bending down to kiss him.

Kelly's normal, healthy Park Avenue girl and Thelma Ritter's sharp-tongued, sensible middle-aged nurse make scornful fun of Jeff's voyeurism. Consequently, when he believes he has seen evidence of a travelling salesman across the way murdering his wife, he is doubly determined to draw them into his prying world. Soon the two women have joined him in the obsessive quest, the nurse asking if she too can look through his 'portable keyhole', i.e. his long-lensed camera.

When Jeff's detective chum apparently proves them wrong, he remarks on the trio's obvious disappointment at not having identified a brutal murderer in their midst. Later, when Jeff's surmise proves correct, the killer turns out to be a sad fellow, and we are free to infer that the climactic assault upon the crippled photographer is a response to extreme provocation.

Rear Window is a masterpiece. As a comedy thriller it is not as funny or as exciting as *The Lady Vanishes* or *North by Northwest*. But it has a formal perfection Hitchcock had never attained before and a many-layered moral and psychological complexity that looks forward to another, not dissimilar collaboration with Stewart, *Vertigo*, which many consider the Master's finest achievement.

Though a reasonably close remake of the 1937 Janet Gaynor-Fredric March film, Cukor's version of *A Star Is Born* feels more like the dark reverse side of *Singin' in the Rain*, to which there are a number of specific visual and verbal allusions. Indeed, the twenty-minute 'Born in a Trunk' number, which Garland and her husband forced upon a reluctant Cukor (who refused to direct it), is virtually a reworking of Gene Kelly's 'Broadway Melody' ballet.

It was one of the three CinemaScope films from the bunch released in Britain during 1955, that opened our eyes to the creative possibilities of the wide screen, the other two being *Bad Day at Black Rock* and Anthony Mann's *The Last Frontier*. Cukor never tried to fill the giant space with meaningless action. Often he leaves two thirds of the screen dark and just highlights a face, or holds one character in close-up at the right with another in profile on the far left.

Where the meaning of *Rear Window* is in the point-of-view, in *A Star Is Born* it's in the décor. The rising star, Ethel (Garland), has bright red lips and is always surrounded by red lights or wearing red clothes, the colour suggesting danger, adventure, optimism, while the falling star, her alcoholic husband Norman Maine (Mason), wears sombre browns, blacks and greys.

The version of the film released in America and Britain was half-an-hour shorter than the one premiered in September 1954. The producers, Warner Brothers, thought it simply too long. Now, with remarkable assiduity, Ronald Haver, curator of the film department at the Los Angeles County Museum, has reassembled the whole picture, using a complete soundtrack and filling in with a montage of stills where blank passages remain. The technique not only works well, it gives additional pathos to the film.

In the shortened version, the film moved glibly from Norman offering the dazed Esther a screen test to her appearance in the studio make-up department the following morning. We now have nine scenes between these two events, as Esther drifts from job to job and a distraught Norman searches for her.

Then there's a deliberately embarrassing proposal scene at a studio recording session (a very theatrical, Cukoresque occasion), a long musical number in a film-within-the-film, and an affecting short sequence where the nervous Esther, on the way to a sneak preview, alights from a car to vomit beside an oil derrick.

It would have been far better to drop 'Born in a Trunk' than these episodes. But I wouldn't have wanted this wonderful picture any shorter, and, though it remains an imperfect work, we are all in Mr Haver's debt. Perhaps he'll now set about restoring Orson Welles's *The Magnificent Ambersons*.

Scarface (Brian De Palma)

The Observer, 5 February 1984

In American crime movies of the 1930s a monochrome portrait of Franklin D. Roosevelt on the wall of an earnest lawman's office was a reassuring sign of hope, compassion and justice promised by the New Deal. In Brian De Palma's masterly updating of *Scarface*, a colour photograph of Jimmy Carter, grinning with lunatic innocence, has precisely the opposite effect.

Seen over the shoulders of exasperated immigration officials interrogating the rodent-like Cuban crook Tony Montana (Al Pacino), the Carter picture is a savage comment on the liberal naivety that enabled Fidel Castro to empty his jails of criminal psychopaths by slipping them among the 125,000 refugees allowed to sail from Mariel in 1979 to join relatives in the States.

This little touch is characteristic of the careful detail that marks every sequence of a long, self-aware, lovingly crafted movie that is so obviously a collaborative exercise between its star, who is rarely off the screen for 170 minutes, the producer Martin Bregman (whose idea it was to remake the 1932 Howard Hughes/Howard Hawks/Ben Hecht classic), the director Brian De Palma, the scriptwriter Oliver Stone, the visual consultant Ferdinando Scarfiotti and the composer Giorgio Moroder.

It is perhaps misleading, though, if this scene suggests that the picture exploits a current American xenophobia – a fear that is encouraged at the outset by the presence of Oliver Stone, author of the racially insensitive *Midnight Express*. *Scarface* is no more an attack on a vulnerable ethnic minority than were the classic gangster pictures of the 1930s. To this model it returns, firmly putting aside the sentimental domestication of professional crime in *The Godfather* and the socially scientific pieties of the New Deal era that insisted on seeing criminals as victims of society and elevating FBI agents as heroes.

Like *Little Caesar*, *Public Enemy* and the original *Scarface*, De Palma's movie is a cynical morality tale about the rapid rise and vertical fall of a ruthless immigrant seizing his share of the American Dream. The scene is switched from the gloomy northern cities to the sun-belt south of Florida. Prohibition liquor as the central illegal commodity becomes cocaine imported from Latin America.

The Italian-American bootlegger Tony Camonte, played by the Jewish actor Paul Muni, is transformed into the equally dynamic Cuban hoodlum Tony Montana, played by the Italian-American Al Pacino. The language is fouler, the violence more explicit, but essentially the career is the same brutal parody of the Horatio Alger success stories. We are not invited to admire or pity Montana, but we are expected to be stirred by the energy with which he reaches his goal.

In a famous essay, *The Gangster as Tragic Hero*, Robert Warshow compared the protagonists of the early 1930s crime films to Shakespeare's alluring villains. De Palma has certainly read it. When the doomed Montana is at bay, awaiting his fate, he sits agonising in his high-backed, black-and-gold monogrammed chair, photographed from below, looking like Macbeth or Richard III on a tainted throne.

Like most people seeking power and success, Montana doesn't know what to do when he has them. Absolute power bores absolutely; as kingpins in the drugs business probably learn, it is better to traffic hopefully than to rise. Our hero and his consort break the rule, 'Don't get high on your own supply,' and finish up sticking their noses into piles of cocaine as big as ant hills.

Montana's tragic flaw turns out to be a dangerous thread of warped

1984

human decency – the incestuous love that makes him so solicitous for his sister's purity (a precise carry-over from Ben Hecht's script here) and a refusal to kill the children of a Bolivian journalist, whose crusading activities threaten his Latin American connection. The sequence involving these kids, in which Montana follows a booby-trapped automobile around News York, is De Palma's obligatory homage to Hitchcock, a variation on the boy carrying the anarchist's bomb across London in *Sabotage*.

As in the 1932 movie, a neon sign beckons and mocks Tony with the slogan 'The World is Yours', and he dies beneath it. But this evil man in a hopelessly corrupt world believes he has been true to his own sense of macho probity: 'All I have in this life is my balls and my word, and I don't break them for anyone.'

Under Fire (Roger Spottiswoode)

The Observer, 12 February 1984

America's love affair with the Press began when newspapermen helped fuel the War of Independence and were rewarded with special protection under the Constitution. Hollywood continued this national romance, and with the coming of sound its stars were shouting 'hold the front page' not many minutes after Al Jolson had told astonished audiences that, 'you ain't heard nothin' yet'.

So *Under Fire*, Roger Spottiswoode's exhilarating movie about journalists covering the fall of the Somoza dictatorship in Nicaragua, is fresh, bold and timely, while at the same time being deep in the American grain and operating within a grand Hollywood tradition.

In the 1930s its central trio – two tough guys in love with the same independent lady – would have been played by Spencer Tracy, Clark Gable and Myrna Loy, or Cary Grant, Gary Cooper and Jean Arthur. But they wouldn't have been better than Gene Hackman, corrugating his brow with integrity as the grizzled *Time Inc* correspondent Alex Grazier, Nick Nolte as the cool, quizzical freelance photographer Russell Price, and Joanna Cassidy as the lithe radio reporter Claire, viewing the world through sharp green eyes. Together they visit small Third World wars the way other pros circle the globe on the golf and tennis circuits. 'I don't take sides. I take pictures,' Nolte tells a rebel priest he's thrown in jail with. 'We validate the readers' ignorance,' quips Hackman of the journalistic style that helps them keep tragic events at a safe distance.

But Nicaragua proves to be more than 'a neat little war with a good hotel'. For the first time they're pushed into taking sides. Where do their loyalties lie? With the underdogs (here the Sandinista rebels) whom Americans are traditionally supposed to help? With the fascistic Somoza regime the US Government is supporting as a bulwark against Communism? Or with some kind of detached professional integrity that believes in the possibility of locating and reporting an objective truth that will, as St Paul assured us, make us free?

Variously pressing the reporters to commit themselves are an apologetic American PR man putting the case for the cruel, child-like Somoza in the latest Madison Avenue jargon; a suave French businessman, Jazy (Jean-Louis Trintignant), go-between for the CIA and the regime, arguing for defending the bad against the worse, for stability, for *Realpolitik*; and the Sandinista themselves, fighting for their lives and land, and though thankfully they are not given any eloquent, thick-accented spokesman out of *Viva Zapata!*, their politics are never directly examined. The picture favours them in a variety of romantic ways, not least through the music, a bamboo flute theme entering Jerry Goldsmith's complex score whenever they appear, giving the scene a heady sense of regional mystery,

Nolte as the cameraman Price is put on the spot when the guerrillas take him to meet the man he most wants to photograph, their charismatic leader Rafael. In a shot lit by the distinguished British director of photography, Jon Alcott, to resemble an academic painting of Lazarus or the entombed Christ, Price is shown Rafael's dead body and asked to fake a photograph of the man alive – in the cause of the revolution.

Photography is central to the morality and dramatic structure of this elegantly shaped movie. In the opening scene we are aware of Price's presence as camera eye picking out the expressive frames during a battle between government forces and insurgents in Chad, though we do not see him until the fight is over. A surreal picture he takes during the African fracas (a guerrilla mounted on an elephant firing at a helicopter gunship) appears on the cover of *Time* the week Price arrives in Nicaragua.

1984

Pictures provide clues to the shifting relationships between Hackman, Nolte and Cassidy. There are direct references to the debate over various key war photographs. For instance, Capa's legendary (possibly faked) picture of the Spanish Civil War soldier struck by a bullet, and the initially distrusted photos of the dead Che Guevara, lie behind Price's dilemma about helping the Sandinistas. When some young guerrillas demand that Price photograph them killing Trintignant, we recall that picture of the Viet Cong officer executed during the Tet Offensive.

Invariably, and sometimes with an appalling irony, the photographs are used in ways Price has not anticipated. They are indeed moral acts, not neutral records. Price realises that he is becoming emotionally involved when Claire points out that he has helped carry a wounded man to cover rather than take a picture of him.

But I don't want to give the impression that Spottiswoode, his screen-writers Ron Shelton and Clayton Frohman, and his other collaborators have made a film that seems calculated and schematic. There is no alienation effect at work here (though the device of a universal, unstoppable mercenary called Oates forever popping up in Price's tracks is a Brechtian concept).

Under Fire is an immensely physical experience; the feeling of a society on the brink of disintegration, then falling apart in the chaos of civil war, is more palpably caught than in any picture I know. It is superior to such comparable recent movies as *Missing, Circle of Deceit* and *The Year of Living Dangerously*. In my view, one of the best American films of the 1980s and the most provocative about the Press since Haskell Wexler's *Medium Cool*.

The Right Stuff (Philip Kaufman)

The Observer, 4 March 1984

In 1972, the writer-director Philip Kaufman made a cult reputation with *The Great Northfield Minnesota Raid*, a remarkable western examining the way the Jesse James gang turned themselves into legendary heroes at a time when respectable bourgeois life was stifling the old frontier spirit.

NOTES FROM THE DREAM HOUSE

Twelve years later Kaufman has returned to the same themes of heroism, the creation of national myths and social change in *The Right Stuff*, an engrossing movie based fairly closely on Tom Wolfe's breezy, eye-opening book about the American manned space programme from the breaking of the sound barrier in 1947 to the 1963 flight that took Gordon Cooper, the last of seven original astronauts to go into space, circling the world for thirty-six hours. The sky is now the frontier and the widow-maker, and *The Right Stuff* begins with the post-World War II funeral of a test pilot at a remote hillside cemetery, filmed in the elegiac manner of John Ford.

The movie's true hero, Captain Chuck Yeager, rides his horse across the desert to inspect the plane that will make him the first man to break the sound barrier in a little publicised flight over California, risking his life for a regular officer's pay of $285 a month.

This laconic loner, beautifully embodied by the playwright Sam Shepard, has that combination of courage, recklessness and insouciance known in the test pilot's world of macho postures and Mach speeds as 'the right stuff'. When we last see Yeager, in what is perhaps the finest sequence in the picture, he's walking across the desert from a terrible plane crash like a cowboy whose horse has been shot beneath him, while across the continent at Houston the astronauts are the guests of honour at a grotesque Texas barbecue hosted by Vice-President Johnson in the Astrodome.

Yeager, the ironic, self-contained individualist, was not what the ASA recruiting officers were looking for when President Eisenhower decided that 'the first American in space is not going to be a chimpanzee'. The Government needed clean-cut, crew-cut, well-adjusted organisation men with obedient, well-groomed military wives, to be moulded into heroes by *Life* magazine and help restore national morale after the humiliation brought on by the Russian Sputnik in 1957.

The seven men chosen from the Navy, Air Force and Marine Corps are pawns in the Cold War, 'Spam in the can' for the projected space lobs, a way of humanising and raising funds for a scientific programme that really has no need of them. They go along with the publicity process out of a mixture of duty and ambition, but are guiltily aware that they are being turned into cardboard heroes before actually having done anything.

They become true heroes, in Kaufman's and Wolfe's view, at the moment they rebel against the system, a magnificent seven facing the establishment, refusing to be treated as guinea pigs, insisting on being given individual responsibility and demanding the restoration of their personal dignity.

A very American amalgam of the romantic and the cynical, the movie gives a proper account of the excitement of space travel, while holding up the backstage manipulations to ridicule. It celebrates real heroism while lampooning the social machinery that exploits the heroes. This effect is attained by giving individual identities to Yeager, the astronauts and their wives (though only Sheppard, Grissom, Cooper and Glenn are properly developed characters), and treating the Press, the politicians, the bureaucrats and the scientists in a deliberately stylised way. This often verges on strip-cartoon treatment, and the film's Lyndon Johnson is a ripe caricature. But some figures have a sober, symbolic function, most notably the black-suited clergyman played by the old western actor Royal Dano, who's a sort of *memento mori*.

The Right Stuff is a bold, confident picture that makes its point with visual flair and tells us a great deal about the American character and the forces that have been working on it in the post-war era. There are longueurs and odd sticky moments, but at the end Kaufman has fully justified a running time of over three hours.

Uncommon Valor (Ted Kotcheff)

The Observer, 24 March 1984

Ted Kotcheff's last film, *First Blood*, brought the Vietnam War back home to complacent rural America in the shape of an angry veteran drive beyond endurance by provocative cops. Now, in a companion piece, *Uncommon Valor*, another splendidly vigorous action movie, Kotcheff makes a spiral movement, from the battlefields of 1972 Vietnam, around America and Southeast Asia, and back to a prison camp in Laos eleven years later.

The movie begins with a stunning slow-motion sequence of a desperate army in flight. It is a US Marine platoon splashing through the paddy fields to two helicopters. A lieutenant stops to carry an injured man, and their distraught comrades are borne away, leaving them to be captured by the advancing Viet Cong. The lieutenant is the son of the emblematically named Colonel Jason Rhodes (Gene Hackman); the marine he helps is the son of a Texas business tycoon.

In the face of an indifferent, and at times hostile, officialdom, Rhodes sets off on a ten-year odyssey, searching for news of his son, one of the forgotten 2,500 Americans recorded as POWs or missing in action, who were not repatriated in 1973. Eventually finding evidence that suggests his son is in a remote Laotian labour camp, he is subsidised by the Texas tycoon and recruits for a hazardous rescue mission five of his son's Vietnam buddies and a zealous young ex-officer without combat experience.

The film begins like a right-wing *Missing*, modulates into a modern *Magnificent Seven*, has a training sequence reminiscent of *The Dirty Dozen*, and ends up with a jungle assault that recalls *Bridge on the River Kwai*. But the movie that *Uncommon Valor* invites comparison with is John Ford's *The Searchers*, to which it pays explicit homage when one of the assault team says, 'Okay Buddy, we're going home,' to an emaciated POW cowering in the corner of a wretched cell, his English almost forgotten.

There is no attempt here to justify the American involvement in Vietnam, any more than there was in the three other movies touching on the Indo-China war that its producer, John Milius, was associated with as writer (*Apocalypse Now*) and director (*The Wind and the Lion*, *Big Wednesday*). There is no breast-beating or liberal baiting. The film does attack a government and a nation, dishonest and infirm of purpose, who let down the men who served them, treating them, Rhodes says, in the way a capitalist society treats bankrupts.

There are seeds of fascism here, yet the film is too good-humoured for them to sprout. And it is at heart celebrating some old-fashioned virtues – comradeship, heroism, self-sacrifice, personal honour – with the knowledge that they are as unfashionable on the right as on the left.

The film is well enough acted, has an attractive score by James Horner (composer of *The Dresser*), is bleakly photographed, and has been assembled for full emotional impact. But what gives it a special distinction is the presence of Gene Hackman.

Led by a gung-ho right-winger like Wayne or Eastwood, or an

anguished liberal like Fonda or Redford, this team would have been on a different errand. Hackman's contained, inward Jason Rhodes transcends ideology, suggesting a man of probity from a long line of soldiers who have always done their duty. When, before his group splits up for battle, he quotes the Shakespearian exchange between Brutus and Cassius on the eve of Philippi, the reference is appropriate. *Uncommon Valor* is, at its best, a Roman movie.

Sunday in the Country (Bertrand Tavernier)

The Observer, 1 July 1984

'The hero is back,' the posters for *Indiana Jones and the Temple of Doom* scream at us. But Spielberg's wise-cracking, cliff-hanging adventurer represents a very limited, *Boy's Own Paper* notion of heroism. As a young critic for *Cahiers du Cinéma*, Bertrand Tavernier celebrated Hollywood's action directors and their gun-toting protagonists. Yet when he came to make his own movies in the mid-1970s, he focused on the every-day heroism of ordinary people, who re-examine their lives, confront the reality around them, and learn to live with the flaws and talents they have and the mistakes they have made.

In his first film, *The Watchmaker of St. Paul*, a petit-bourgeois craftsman comes to terms with his son's involvement in political crime. In my favourite movie of his, *Une Semaine de vacances*, a schoolmistress on the brink of a nervous breakdown gains a new perspective on her vocation. Now in his new film, *Sunday in the Country*, a seventy-six-year-old widowed painter, Monsieur Ladmiral, reviews his achievements and limitations as artist and father one hot summer's day in 1912 at his country house outside Paris where he's visited by his son and daughter, and by memories of a loving marriage.

Adapted by Tavernier and his wife from a novella by Pierre Bost, this beautifully paced and exquisitely textured movie has at its centre a performance of quiet authority by the seventy-three-year-old stage actor Louis Ducreux that brings to mind that of Victor Sjöström in Bergman's *Wild Strawberries*. From the moment we see him rise and prepare himself to receive his devoted son Gonzague and family, we sense a confidence that continues to the final frame.

Ladmiral's small, decent reputation is based on continually painting corners of his studio and the garden of the house where he has spent his whole life. He has been true to his gifts, but he has never taken risks. He grew up beside Impressionism, was thrilled by Cézanne, his exact contemporary, but reflects that had he tried to imitate these innovators he'd have been less original than he has been by remaining true to his traditional academic self. The staid, middle-aged Gonzague (Michel Aumont) and his pious, complacent wife (Geneviève Mnich, excellent in an unsympathetic role) are viewed by the bohemian side of Ladmiral with a patronising affection tinged with derision. His real love is reserved for his daughter, Irène (Sabine Azéma), the attractive, independent owner of a Paris shop and embodiment of the New Woman.

Gonzague and his wife and children come down by train and after a stately walk from the station (filmed in the long, elegant tracking shots Tavernier favours) they settle into post-prandial somnolence. Intercut with their slumbers is Irène, barrelling along dusty country roads in her gleaming motor car rather like Mr Toad. She's on her way to disrupt their composure with one of her rare, brief visits, and to galvanize them with her neurotic energy. In one of the movie's finest sequences, she drives Ladmiral to an open-air restaurant beside a river, the setting for the kind of vital Renoir paintings he has so assiduously eschewed. They dance together, this handsome woman towering over the withered old man, and he is indescribably happy, yet at the same time aware of the world he will soon be leaving and of excitements he has never had.

Sunday in the Country is elegiac and affirmative without being nostalgic or sentimental. At the end we have not only seen a day in Ladmiral's life, but experienced his life in this day. The picture is verbally and pictorially witty, and genuinely wise about age, death, ambition and family love. We are unlikely to see anything more perfectly achieved this year.

1984

Red Dawn (John Milius)

The Observer, 11 November 1984

John Milius, one of the most talented writer-directors to emerge in the United States this past decade, is a right-wing maverick whose patriotism and old-fashioned concern for honour and heroism have put him at odds with the prevailing leftish stance of Hollywood's more fashionable filmmakers. And never more so than in the case of his latest picture, the widely execrated *Red Dawn*, wherein he thinks impermissible thoughts about the unthinkable.

The title *Red Dawn* suggests something put on in the 1930s at London's Unity Theatre or an uplifting drama staged in China during the Cultural Revolution. It refers in fact to the morning in some future September when a division of Russian and Latin American paratroopers takes over a small Colorado town and a band of teenagers takes to the hills to form a guerrilla force that harasses the invaders over the next six months.

The opening twenty minutes are breathtaking, both for the dynamic brilliance of the filmmaking and the shock that the notion of a non-nuclear World War III administers to the nervous system of a *bien-pensant* liberal like myself. After all, the liberal idea of a good Cold War movie is *The Russians Are Coming, The Russians Are Coming*, where the loveably eccentric crew of a Russian submarine grounded on Cape Cod is taken to the warm bosom of the middle-class summer community and protected from the uncomprehending military. The acceptable liberal idea of a film about World War III is *Threads*, in which a community of innocent, beer-swilling proles is nuked back into the Stone Age as a result of their leaders' incompetence.

The antecedents of Milius's movie are political science fictions like *Nineteen Eighty-Four*, Constantine Fitzgibbon's *When the Kissing Had to Stop* and Kingsley Amis's *Russian Hide-and-Seek* or Michael Frayn's *Liberty Hall*, which turns on the idea that the Bolshevik Revolution took place in Britain rather than Russia.

Red Dawn is a compelling 'what if?' fantasy which asks how America would react if it were occupied like Czechoslovakia, Afghanistan, or World War II Europe. It evokes old movies of guerrilla warfare, including wartime Hollywood propaganda pictures set in Russia, as well as

Lawrence of Arabia. In particular it takes scenes from the most celebrated Marxist anti-colonial picture, Pontecorvo's *The Battle of Algiers*, and turns the role of the hard-line French para colonel into a Russian, a borrowing boldly announced by the way he marches into town with his men and then gives a lecture on the technique for eliminating guerrillas.

As in all big-budget war movies, *Red Dawn* accompanies its rousing combat sequences with reflections on the brutalising effects of war, though Milius argues that war can both degrade and ennoble. That it is an anti-Communist picture is undeniable, and no worse for that; but in tone and treatment it's far removed from the Hollywood Red Scare pictures of the early 1950s.

The Communists are not presented as inhuman fanatics, their arguments are clearly put in subtitles, and one of the most sympathetic characters in the film is the Cuban, Colonel Bella. His natural instinct is to side with the rebels, and he becomes increasingly disgusted with his role as policeman. Bella goes some way towards taking the edge off the distasteful exploitation of the current American paranoia over the increasing illegal immigration from the South.

Of course all films of this kind, whether left or right, feed on deep-seated anxieties. The other mischievous aspect is the explicit support the picture gives to America's gun lobby. But then, the mystique of guns, hunting and associated male camaraderie is part of Milius's ethos (Theodore Roosevelt is one of his idols) and belongs to an American tradition that we would be better advised to study rather than sneer at.

Anyway, *Red Dawn* is not to be dismissed with glib discussion-stoppers like 'adolescent macho fantasy', 'fascism' or 'Reaganite posturing'. Indeed there seems to me to be a proper freedom of expression in a film industry that can in the same year produce *Red Dawn* and Roger Spottiswoode's film about American journalists espousing the cause of the Sandinistas, *Under Fire*.

1984

A Private Function (Malcolm Mowbray)

The Observer, 2 December 1984

Older moviegoers will recall Jack Warner and Kathleen Harrison as the British cinema's favourite cockney couple in *Here Come the Huggetts*, bedding down in the street for the night to catch a glimpse of the Royal Couple on their way to be married at Westminster Abbey on 20 November 1947, and Fred Astaire and Jane Powell finding romance with British aristocrats in London that very week in the MGM musical, *Royal Wedding*.

Now, nearly forty years on, *A Private Function* looks at the response of some equally enthusiastic royalists to that same event and presents a rather different view of the time. It's directed as his first feature by Malcolm Mowbray, a recent National Film School graduate (born 1949), and scripted as his first screenplay by Alan Bennett, one of our most gifted playwrights (born 1934). They have come up with a sharply anti-nostalgic comedy that is not only the funniest film I've seen this year, but as authentic a picture of the darker side of post-war Britain as our cinema has given us.

The loyal celebrants of the film are four prominent citizens of a small Yorkshire town: a doctor (Denholm Elliott), a solicitor (John Normington), an accountant (Richard Griffiths) and a police inspector (Jim Carter), who are planning a civic dinner on the night of the Royal Wedding, with a black market pig as the main course.

This quartet are not rebellious, Ealingesque eccentrics à la *Passport to Pimlico*. They're a collection of snobbish, vicious, anti-Semitic North Country grotesques. Elliott's snarling Dr Swaby is the kind of backwoods Tory GP who thought Nye Bevan the devil incarnate, and he finds his opposite number in the local inspector for the Ministry of Food, Mr Wormold (Bill Paterson), a puritanical Scottish socialist lacking a sense of taste and smell. This Robespierrean incorruptible paints all confiscated meat sea-green after his nocturnal raids on black-marketeering butchers and suspects that some large conspiracy is afoot.

Standing between these ideological extremes are the kindly chiropodist, Gilbert Chilvers (Michael Palin), who merely wants to set up practice in the high street, and his pathetic but ruthlessly ambitious wife

(Maggie Smith), who's willing to undergo any humiliation to be accepted socially. A series of accidents leads Gilbert to hi-jack the royal porker from a rural hideaway and hold it for ransom. As his wife says, 'It's not just pork, Gilbert, it's power.'

This movie sees Bennett at the height of his form, working in his chosen area of Yorkshire lower-middle-class life, halfway between Hoggart and Hogarth, with an acute ear for the weird turn of phrase and a beady eye for the surreal in the everyday. The vision of the period is mercilessly unromantic and unglamorous.

The excellent cast catch to perfection that uncomfortable look of the 1940s, the men in lumpy utility suits or shabby pre-war outfits, their badly cut hair greased down, their raw, over-shaven faces ignorant of after-shave and talc, the women with rigid perms, too much makeup and coarsely fashioned dresses. When Maggie Smith decides she will reward her husband with a little sex, she gets out a rubber-bulb-and-tube device that looks like a deep-sea diver's equipment.

Bennett and Mowbray know how to use bad taste to make moral points comically. Most obviously there is the loose-bowelled pig being chased around a semi-detached house by an amateur butcher. More courageously they present a hero who spends his time cutting away at corns and toenails all day, then talking about spectacular encounters with verrucas when he gets home at night.

Unquestionably Gilbert the chiropodist is the star of the film, for he embodies those qualities of gentleness, civility, decency and reticence we know Bennett admires. And in the interstices of a Darwinian world, Gilbert survives. The movie is indeed a commentary upon post-war Britain and what undermined our great socialist experiment that recalls a celebrated essay on the period by Michael Frayn.

Frayn saw the Festival of Britain as the last flourishing of the liberal idealists he called the Herbivores, and contrasted them with the Carnivores who were to shape the callous Affluent Society that followed Attlee's Age of Austerity. Gilbert is a Herbivore; those who set about the roast pig with such relish at Bennett's and Mowbray's *Private Function* are Carnivores.

Blood Simple (Joel Coen)

The Observer, 3 February 1985)

Some directors start their careers with a triumphant explosion they never quite manage to repeat. Orson Welles is an example. Others, more wisely, choose to announce their revival with a small, confident, solidly crafted film, more like a neatly engraved office doorplate than a dazzling display of pyrotechnics.

This is how Steven Spielberg and Walter Hill arrived in the 1970s, how Neil Jordan emerged two years ago, and how the twenty-nine-year-old Joel Coen and his younger brother Ethan Coen have presented themselves with *Blood Simple*, a taut thriller in the *film noir* mode, directed by Joel, produced by Ethan and scripted by the pair of them.

They establish the bleak setting of West Texas with a montage of unpeopled shots – a two-lane highway stretching into infinity; a distant cityscape on a flat plain; the screen of an abandoned drive-in cinema in the scrubby countryside; untended oil pumps dipping away like mechanical birds on a hostile planet. Then comes an anxious dialogue between a man and a woman, a long take viewed from the back seat of a car as they drive through blinding night rain, the headlamps of oncoming cars cutting across them like searchlights from a prison tower. This is the iconic shot from the *film noir*: two people in a storm heading guiltily in the wrong direction.

They are, it transpires, Ray (John Getz), bartender at a garish small-town dive called the Neon Boot, and Abby (Frances McDormand), the young, sluttish wife of his employer, Marty (Dan Hedaya). The trio look more like people on the cover of a hard-boiled novel of the 1930s than the stars of a movie of that decade. On the other hand, they are beauties compared with the obese, ill-shaven private detective (M. Emmet Walsh) whom Marty first hires to shadow his wife and her lover, and then to kill them.

Things don't turn out as planned or as expected, either by the characters or by us, the audience. Without too much cheating, the Coens have pulled off the trick of making a thriller that is as unpredictable as Clouzot's *Les Diaboliques* and as inexorable as Wilder's *Double Indemnity*, while playing out the tension and the grim humour to the last line.

As the title (a quote from Hammett's *Red Harvest*) suggests, *Blood*

Simple is about people stirred by primitive emotions – lust, greed, anger, fear. If we care for them, it isn't because they are attractive, but because an excellent cast draws us into recognising the basic and base humanity we share with them. There is also quite simply a lot of blood, giving an ironic edge to the notice on the Neon Boot's lavatory door: 'All employees must wash hands before resuming work.'

This is a very physical picture; people sweat with terror, Marty vomits when his wife kicks him in the groin, killers can't sleep. The Coens deliberately borrow from the famous but clumsy scene in Hitchcock's *Torn Curtain*, where Paul Newman has difficulty killing an East German policeman, and extend it to near breaking point. Another homage to Hitchcock is the cigarette lighter left as incriminating evidence under some rotting fish.

There are some misjudgements in this splendid little film, but they're excusable ones. Above all I'll remember *Blood Simple* for its palpable low-life atmosphere and for some astonishing, almost surreal images. A ceramic money box in the form of a fish is used as a murder weapon, then smashed on the floor, scattering silver coins among the debris of broken glass. A garbage incinerator blazing in the night like the jaws of hell mocks and beckons Marty from a vacant lot opposite his saloon.

My Beautiful Laundrette (Stephen Frears) & King Solomon's Mines (J. Lee Thompson)

The Observer, 17 November 1985

A happier outcome [than in Istvan Szabo's *Colonel Redl*] to a homosexual relationship is to be found in *My Beautiful Laundrette*, about which I am still as enthusiastic as when I acclaimed it at the Edinburgh Film Festival. The film's moments of true gaiety come in a gay love affair between a young Pakistani and a white Londoner, that transcends race, class, upbringing and social chaos. It is as if the director, Stephen Frears, and his screenwriter, Hanif Kureishi, had decided that E.M. Forster would like to have ended *A Passage to India* by getting Fielding and Aziz into bed together rather than having them ride off in different directions.

The Pakistani is Omar (Gordon Warnecke), neatly turned-out son of an alcoholic Bombay-born journalist; the Londoner is Johnny (Daniel Day-Lewis), butchly handsome Lambeth tearaway with a bleached white strip down his black hair that makes him look as if he's balancing a well-groomed skunk on his head. So unlikely is their affair that it takes us quite by surprise. But it is made wholly convincing and provides a positive centre to an acute comedy that for the rest of the time swings a satirical wrecker's ball at the shaky moral edifice of Thatcher's Britain.

The symbolically named 'Churchill's Laundrette' is in a run-down corner of the South London empire ruled by Omar's Uncle Nasser (Saeed Jaffrey's richest performance to date), an immigrant entrepreneur whose toasts to free enterprise always include the name of Mrs Thatcher. Nasser gives Omar the Churchill to run. Financing himself by hijacking a consignment of heroin from Karachi, the quick young learner transforms a moribund establishment into a kitschy gathering place with flashy décor and muzak, called Powder's Laundrette, the pun on its laundered finance echoing the sexual/detergent joke in the nickname of its proprietors, Omo.

Omar is assisted in the emblematic transformation by his old school-mate Johnny, who becomes his servant, partner and lover. As a quirky metaphor at the film's centre, the laundrette separates Omar from his idealistic father just as decisively as it draws Johnny away from the racist thugs he has been squatting with.

As in *Bloody Kids*, Stephen Frears confidently modulates between a casual naturalism and a highly charged expressionism. The ultimate triumph of the movie is to deal with the problems of unhappy, uprooted people without for one moment becoming glum or patronising.

In his brilliant new book *Holy Smoke*, the Cuban cinéphile, polymath and punster G. Cabrera Infante warns us that 'those who forget the movies of the past are condemned to see re-makes'. But what have we done to deserve this fourth version of H. Rider Haggard's grand imperial adventure yarn *King Solomon's Mines*, a novel published exactly one hundred years ago and never out of print?

The first sound adaptation in 1937 was counted by Graham Greene 'a disappointment to anyone who like myself values Haggard's book a good deal higher than *Treasure Island*', though he liked Cedric Hardwicke's Allan Quatermain. What he would make of this I can predict, for the only truly Haggard part of it is the way the spectator feels at the end, and if the author isn't turning in his grave he must at least be a most uneasy Rider.

Indeed this attempt to cash in on the Indiana Jones vogue is more Raider than Rider, with director J. Lee Thompson (who twenty-five years ago was capable of turning out passable adventure movies like *North-West Frontier* and *Guns of Navarone*) trying to replenish his lost art with a rejuvenating injection of Lost Ark. Quatermain is now an American (played by Richard Chamberlain as if only too aware of being sold as a second-hand Ford), and the period being updated to German East Africa just before, or possibly during, the Great War. His task is to escort the pert American archaeology student Jessie Juston (Sharon Stone) into what he calls 'beautiful downtown Tongola' to help find her kidnapped father, who has a map revealing the whereabouts of King Solomon's Mines.

Jessie's Dad has fallen into the hands of the evil Turkish merchant Dogati (John Rhys-Davies) and the shaven-headed Hun, Colonel Bockner (Herbert Lom), who wants the diamond hoard to swell the Kaiser's war chest. Between the seekers and the treasure lie many dangerous miles of native territory and endless pages of comic strip dialogue. Quatermain's devoted African helper Umbopa (his name changed here to Umbopo) is turned into a Stepin-Fetchit character who puts his hands over his eyes for fear whenever travelling by car or train, and stops just short of saying 'Feet be mah friend'. All the other natives, save one quaint tribe that lives upside-down as a gesture against world disorder, are bent on eating Allan and Jessie ('apparently they prefer white meat') or sacrificing them to their gods.

In one extended cannibal joke (a sequence not borrowed from Spielberg), the pair are put into a giant pot to cook – 'Look on the bright side, at least we're the main course,' quips Allan. When the explorers get into Solomon's cave, Bockner swallows a fistful of diamonds, boasting that 'German laxatives are the best in the world'.

What the filmmakers are doing here isn't sending up adventure yarns. They're jumping on a bandwagon and their tongues are not so much in their cheeks as obsequiously busy elsewhere. However, the washed-out images and shoddy back projection are authentically bad rather than homages to old B-movies, and the picture lacks style and purpose. There is no hint of that excitement engendered by the myths of the Dark

Continent we get in the aptly named 'Lost Magic Kindoms' exhibition that Eduardo Paolozzi has just arranged at the Museum of Mankind.

Over all hangs a sweaty pall of desperation, typified by the scene in which Chamberlain's Quatermain stumbles into a railway carriage full of armed German soldiers and resorts to an impersonation of Eddie Murphy to talk his way out.

King Solomon's Mines was filmed in Zimbabwe with the full cooperation of the country's air force and Ministry of Defence. A definitive answer to the question of whether Robert Mugabe has a well-developed sense of humour would be given should Thompson and the heads of Cannon Films, Menahem Golan and Yoram Globus, attend the movie's premiere in Harare.

Silverado (Lawrence Kasdan)

The Observer, 29 December 1985

Nothing could please me more than winding up the year enthusing over *Silverado*, directed and co-scripted (with his brother Mark) by Lawrence Kasdan.

Kasdan showed his intelligent admiration for Hollywood traditions through his scripts for the second and third *Star Wars* films and *Raiders of the Lost Ark*, and his directorial debut, the *film noir* thriller *Body Heat*. Now he addresses the greatest, and currently least fashionable, Hollywood genre, the western, and the result is two-and-a-quarter hours of pleasure that attracts, appropriately enough given its title, a term-of-art of the assay office and cliché of the critical profession, the adjective 'unalloyed'.

Kasdan has returned to the genre's golden age to recapture both its vitality and its essential optimism, and his title, *Silverado*, suggests, perhaps fortuitously, a conflation of two cult movies by old masters, Allan Dwan's low-budget, covertly anti-McCarthy western, *Silver Lode* of 1954 and Howard Hawks's expensive right-wing *El Dorado* of 1967.

The film's principal theme, a perennial one in the western, is about the tug between the settled, domesticated existence and the free, roving life, and it is spelt out in an early exchange between two former, *One-Eyed Jacks*-style partners-in-crime.

'I think I've found my place in the world,' says the grinning heavy, Cobb (Brian Dennehy), who, it transpires, is the crooked sheriff appointed by a corrupt cattle baron to run Silverado. 'I think I'll still go on looking for mine,' replies Paden (Kevin Kline), though he accepts a job in a saloon that Cobb owns.

The film tells the story of four men who temporarily make common cause, first for mutual protection, subsequently to achieve justice, and three women who variously attend to them. The men are Paden, a charming former outlaw determined to go straight but not become rigidly respectable; the quiet, resourceful gunslinger Emmett (Scott Glenn), a decent man heading for California with his mercurial, near psychopathic brother Jake (Kevin Costner); and Mal (Danny Glover), a black cowboy on his way from the Chicago stockyards to his father's New Mexico ranch.

The women are the proud, philosophical saloon-keeper (the diminutive Linda Hunt) who needs a ramp to get her head and shoulders over the bar; Mal's sister Rae (Lynn Whitfield), who has left the family ranch to become a whore and mistress of a slimy gambler (Jeff Goldblum); and Hannah (Rosanna Arquette), a young homesteader who attracts both Emmett and Paden when they come to the aid of the wagon train she's with.

Hannah's role is the least satisfactorily developed, but she does have one of the film's most affecting speeches: 'I want to build something and make things grow,' she says. 'That takes hard work, a lifetime of it, and that's not why a man comes to a pretty woman, and after a few years of living like this a woman's not so pretty anymore.'

The film has a lot of plot, a little too much in fact, and the chief fault is that as it rushes from one action sequence to the other, there is insufficient time for repose. But the set-pieces are superbly staged, opening with a stunning assault on an isolated cabin (this is the first western I can think of since *The Searchers* to start indoors) and ending with a showdown in a cattle-town, a finale preceded by this neat dialogue:

Old timer: 'What's going on, sheriff?'
Sheriff: 'Hide and watch.'

There is much carefully judged humour in *Silverado*, none of it, I'm glad to say, self-mocking, and the casting of John Cleese as a bearded English sheriff, sternly upholding the law in a town the quartet pass through, is inspired.

There are echoes in this film of Ford, Peckinpah, Hawks, Mann and Leone, but no specific or self-conscious homages, and so far as I can tell only two of the actors in a uniformly splendid cast have been in a western before, the septuagenarian Sheb Wooley, one of the four killers in *High Noon*, who turns up briefly as a grizzled cavalry sergeant, and Scott Glenn, who back in 1980 rode with Burt Lancaster in *Cattle Annie and Little Britches*.

The cinematographer, John Bailey, and the editor, Carol Littleton, are both new to the genre and each has done an excellent job. Shooting in autumn and winter, Bailey has produced a study in various shades of black, brown and beige, with pale blue skies complementing the sand, bleached grass and snow.

Defence of the Realm (David Drury)

The Observer, 5 January 1986

The paranoid thriller, of which David Drury's *Defence of the Realm* is a superior British example, has its roots in Kafka, who in turn drew on Dickens's image of the minatory metropolis. It is appropriate therefore that one of the state's victims in this disturbing movie, the decent alcoholic left-wing journalist Vernon (inevitably played by Denholm Elliott), should occupy apartment K in an ordinary block of London flats lit by the skilled cameraman Roger Deakins to look as sinister as anything in *The Trial*.

Vernon's suspicious death, following immediately upon the ransacking of his flat by some intelligence agency, is one of the pieces in a jigsaw puzzle that must be assembled by his fellow *Daily Dispatch* reporter, the handsome slob Nick Mullen (Gabriel Byrne). The completed picture will explain the connection between the mysterious death of a borstal escapee in the vicinity of a US Air Force base in East Anglia and the framing of a Labour MP (Ian Bannen), who's forced to resign his seat after Mullen's paper has revealed that he shares the services of a call girl with an East German diplomat suspected of being a KGB agent.

Nick is an investigative reporter a few rungs above Paul Slickey but a couple of storeys below Woodward and Bernstein, and the movie is about his education in the ways of the State, just as the denser, though in many respects similar, TV serial *Edge of Darkness* is about the education of Inspector Ronald Craven. Both Mullen and Craven discover to their fatal detriment the covert interconnectedness between the Special Branch, the intelligence establishment, the Ministry of Defence, NATO, the media, the civil service and big business, in an essentially malevolent system operated by people of individual goodwill.

The film's depiction of Fleet Street life and practice seems wholly convincing, and while, when considered in retrospect, there are loose ends in Martin Stellman's screenplay, we're seized by the lapels from the teasing opening shots and dragged with the hero to the edge of an abyss. Like Nick Mullen, we're bombarded with aural and visual information, and to sustain an almost vertiginous pace Drury crosscuts and interlocks sequences, so that just before a scene ends we're shown a fragment of the one that follows. But above all, as in *Edge of Darkness*, the film feeds our current fears and anxieties into its nightmarish narrative, and the genre to which it belongs throws some light on the course of our collective thinking over the thirty-nine years since Orwell wrote *Nineteen Eighty-Four*.

The cinematic paranoid thriller began in the late 1940s with right-wing Hollywood movies about externally controlled left-wing conspiracies. It ended up (via the 1962 watershed of *The Manchurian Candidate* where deft sleight-of-hand established a fantastic link between the Maoists in Peking and witch-hunting McCarthyites in Washington) with liberal movies about internal right-wing conspiracies.

The latter films, exemplified by *The Parallax View*, *All the President's Men* and *Three Days of the Condor*, are the stylistic and ideological source of *Defence of the Realm*. However, the movie that I think made possible both *Defence of the Realm* and *Edge of Darkness* was a dangerous little SF thriller produced back in 1962, Joseph Losey's *The Damned*. This was the first British film to suggest that the Cold War had created in our country a lethal State-within-a-State that was the enemy of its own citizens and believed itself to have the right to take lives in the public interest.

Revolution (Hugh Hudson)

The Observer, 2 February 1986

Only someone who has spent the past six weeks as the subject of a sensory-deprivation experiment will be unaware that Hugh Hudson's *Revolution* is an 'Epic Adventure' made in England and set in North America between 1776 and 1783, which went wildly over budget and has been given the same treatment by New York critics as a party of their colonial ancestors accorded to a cargo of imported tea in Boston harbour.

This ambitious film, which treats a period that Hollywood has largely shrunk from, does not deserve to be treated with such contempt. The re-creation of eighteenth-century New York by the designers Assheton Gorton and John Mollo is impressive; the battles between the English redcoats and the makeshift rebel army are rendered in all their ugly confusion (Hudson has learned valuable lessons from Welles's staging of the Battle of Shrewsbury in *Chimes at Midnight* and from *Barry Lyndon*.)

There are scenes that lodge in the mind: the heroine lending her patriotic red-and-white sash to be used as a tourniquet by a doctor sawing off a soldier's leg at the battle of Brooklyn Heights, or the hero forced to drag an effigy of George Washington across the countryside for fox-hunting British officers and their hounds to pursue. As these incidents suggest, Hudson and his American screenwriter, Robert Dillon, cannot be said to court easy popularity with their emphasis on pain, sacrifice, muddle, humiliation and, at the end, hopes deferred.

Yet the movie is a failure, and about two-thirds of the way through, at the point where the middle-class revolutionary heroine embarrassingly joins the working-class hero at Washington's Valley Forge winter quarters in 1778, I was reminded of a great surreal scene from Hollywood fiction. The hero of Nathaniel West's *Day of the Locust* wanders onto the set of an expensive epic called *Waterloo*. As rival armies storm around the mock battlefield under the guidance of an anxious production team, each soldier authentically dressed, the historical circumstances carefully researched, there occurs what at first appears to be an earthquake, but it is in fact a canvas hillside collapsing, because the carpenters hadn't completed the scaffolding. The impending defeat of the French is transformed into a rout of both sides, economic catastrophe faces the producer and,

NOTES FROM THE DREAM HOUSE

as West quietly predicts, there'll be 'big losses sustained by an insurance company'.

The fault in the infrastructure that leads to the collapse of *Revolution* lies in a script that ultimately fails at every level, including that of simple, coherent narrative. The three main characters whose paths cross and re-cross over the years – the fur-trapper Dobb (Al Pacino with an all-purpose Celtic accent) unwillingly forced into the army to protect his one remaining son, the martinet English sergeant-major Peasy (Donald Sutherland adopting a perennial Hardy Mummerset), and the middle-class idealist Daisy (Nastassja Kinski speaking in showbiz American) – remain cyphers. They don't engage our sympathy as individuals or command our interest as emblematic figures.

Hudson's 'epic adventure' ends up neither as Brechtian epic (though it echoes *Mother Courage*) nor as run-of-De-Mille adventure. Partaking of the confusion it observes, the movie falls between the stools of a romantic entertainment set against the background of the American Revolution like Ford's *Drums Along the Mohawk* and a serious study of political change like Visconti's *The Leopard*, where the foreground fictional characters embody the issues involved in the *Risorgimento* far more cogently than do real-life political figures in the background.

Out of Order (Carl Schenkel)

The Observer, 2 March 1986

The British locomotive pioneer George Stephenson and the American inventor of the fast, safe elevator, Elisha Graves Otis, made possible the horizontal and vertical growth of our cities. In doing so they prepared their Victorian passengers for the new visual experiences that the cinema would bring at the end of the century through the smooth camera movements known as tracking and crane shots,

But while the railway, from Lumière's 1895 *Train Pulling into a Station* and Porter's 1903 *Great Train Robbery* onwards, has been endlessly celebrated by the movies (and much written about), the screen's approach to the lift has been more equivocal (and largely ignored).

The mechanics and the enforced intimacy have of course been a great source of comedy, starting with Chaplin two-reelers and continuing through the early sound era when chatting girls up in, or while waiting for, lifts became a Hollywood convention. But it is the claustrophobia, our hopeless dependence upon their proper function, and the sense of the lift shaft as an abyss at the centre of our buildings, and thus our lives, that 'cable hangers' or 'shaft operas' exploit.

To name but a few examples: Olivia de Havilland as the trapped invalid in *Lady in a Cage*; Angie Dickinson reflected in the convex lift mirror of *Dressed to Kill*; the reporter searching for the documents concealed beneath the lift in *Defence of the Realm*; the machine that assumes a malevolent life of its own in the Dutch horror movie *The Lift*; the painfully slow elevator taking fugitive thieves down a skyscraper in *Kiss of Death*; and endless group jeopardy and disaster movies.

The latest of these films is Carl Schenkel's thriller *Out of Order*, the melodramatic side of the coin whose comic face was the classic 1961 TV programme *The Lift* where Tony Hancock was the ninth man on an eight-passenger BBC lift, causing it to stick in the shaft all night.

One Friday evening in a West German city, four people find themselves trapped halfway up a deserted forty-storey office block. They're a familiar enough bunch from *Stagecoach* or *Towering Inferno* – an elderly clerk decamping with a suitcase full of deutschmarks; a young dropout with a ring in his ear and a contemptuous smirk on his handsome, unshaven face; a coolly attractive, self-confident woman; her ex-lover and advertising agency superior, a good-looking man whose aggressive confidence hides a deep insecurity.

But they are given substance by the performances of Wolfgang Kieling (best-known as Gromek, the sinister East German policeman whom Paul Newman has trouble killing in *Torn Curtain*); Hannes Jaenicke; the Dutch actress Renée Soutendijk (one of the most strikingly and erotically provocative stars in European cinema today); and Götz George who played Commandant Hoss of Auschwitz in *From a German Life*.

Once they've registered the fact that Mr Otis regrets he's unable to winch today, tempers fray and snap along with the elevator cables (the convincing sets are designed by Toni Lüdi), and the writer-director effectively keeps up the pressure and the suspense. When you emerge from *Out of Order*, you'll feel as much like taking the lift as you feel like taking a drink at the end of *The Lost Weekend*.

Ran (Akira Kurosawa)

The Observer, 9 March 1986

In 1955, John Gielgud toured Europe as a Japanese Lear in an austere Stratford production designed by Isamu Noguchi, and two years later Akira Kurosawa stunned the world with *Throne of Blood*, his magnificent transposition of *Macbeth* to mediaeval Japan.

We have thus been long prepared to receive Kurosawa's version of *King Lear* and rarely can the highest of hopes have been so completely fulfilled as by the seventy-five-year-old maestro's *Ran*, a towering achievement that sets the capstone on one of the greatest bodies of work in the history of world cinema.

Ran means chaos, and it begins and ends with variations on the same image – man at the edge of an abyss. In the opening sequence, groups of horsemen stand at high noon on a precipitous verdant mountainside, poised, confident, completely still as the camera moves closer towards them. At the end a blind man taps his way to the edge of a bleak precipice only to stop just in time, while the camera draws back to leave him a distant, lonely figure against a darkening sky. In between we have seen the breakdown of order and reason, the destruction of a family and a state, a world shattered, yet the dignity of man is ultimately affirmed through a movie of great visual power, moral authority and psychological perception.

Kurosawa's Lear is Lord Hidetora (played by Tatsuya Nakadai), a sixteenth-century warrior-chief who at seventy decides to divide his kingdom between his three sons, with the eldest *primus inter pares*. When the youngest son, Saburo, questions the wisdom of attempting to impose so rational a system on a kingdom created by violence, he is banished, Cordelia-like, along with the film's Kent figure, the outspoken courtier Tango. For most of the way, indeed, the movie adheres to Shakespeare's dramatic line, and includes a Fool played with graceful vivacity by a transvestite artist called Peter.

The chief difference is the cropping of the Gloucester-Edgar-Edmund subplot. But this loss of symmetry is made up for by the introduction of a blind Prince whose eyes have been gouged out by Hidetora himself after slaughtering his father. This blind youth's sister has been forcibly married to the Lord's second son but has found tranquillity through

Buddhism. By contrast, another princess, made the captive bride of the Lord's eldest son, has become an implacable avenger.

Gloucester's line about 'flies to wanton boys' has been incorporated into a speech delivered by the Fool, who now survives Lear to rail against the gods. 'Why must you crush us like ants?' he demands, to be rebuked by Tango the humanist, who speaks passionately of the gods and Buddha weeping to see the folly of men who, given their free will, constantly choose evil over good.

As the subtitle I've just quoted suggests, there is little verbal poetry in the translations we're offered. But there is abundant visual poetry – delicately composed interiors and swirling battle scenes with five armies bearing banners and plumes in red, yellow, blue, black and white; stylised costumes and make-up from the Noh theatre.

Most of Kurosawa's artistic collaborators have worked with him for years and here excel themselves. Every department – design, editing, photography, sound – contributes to such unforgettable sequences as the bloody battle at a castle planted in the black ash on the side of a volcano where the Lord goes mad. It concludes with the deranged Hidetora dressed in white, his face a ghostly mask, descending a flight of steps and passing through the ranks of his sons' red and yellow armies to depart into the wilderness of the blasted heath.

The Mission (Roland Joffe)

The Observer, 26 October 1986

In the mid-eighteenth century a complex series of political manoeuvres in Europe and South America culminated in the Pope closing the Jesuit mission in Paraguay. The principal though not the sole objective was to propitiate the Spanish and Portuguese governments and their colonists, who saw the self-sufficient communities of Indian converts the priests ruled over as providing unfair competition.

The blood was still wet on the ground when that celebrated bad-taste comic Voltaire, no friend of the Jesuits, thrust Candide into the Paraguayan fray and had him escape disguised as a priest. More recently and more soberly, Fritz Hochwälder tackled the subject in his play *Das heilige Experiment*, staged with unforgettable power in London thirty years ago as *The Strong Are the Lonely*, with Donald Wolfit as the Jesuit father provincial.

Now five distinctive talents – screenwriter Robert Bolt, producer David Puttnam, director Ronald Joffe, cinematographer Chris Menges and composer Ennio Morricone – have collaborated on a further, earnest rehearsal of the events in *The Mission*, the movie awarded the *Palme d'Or* at the 1986 Cannes Festival. And it stars three of the English-speaking cinema's most accomplished actors, Jeremy Irons as the Jesuits' edgy leader, Robert De Niro as an explosive slave-trading mercenary, and Ray McAnally as the cardinal sent from Rome to adjudicate between missionaries and colonists.

As is usual with Bolt, a principled hero defies a devious establishment (as Bolt himself did twenty-five years ago, when he went to jail as a member of the Committee of 100). Like most Puttnam productions, there is an almost mystical bond between two men. As in Joffe's first film, *The Killing Fields*, we are subjected to an intensely physical experience.

Their film is constructed as a series of journeys on a river in the Paraguayan jungle, each commenting on the preceding one. First a crucified priest is dispatched downstream and over a mighty waterfall by the Indians he's failed to convert. In the second journey, another missionary (Jeremy Irons) scales a cliff beside the falls to continue the dead man's work and found the San Carlos mission. In the third, the mercenary De Niro drags, Sisyphus-like, a huge net containing the equipment of his trade over the same terrain as a redemptive task for killing his brother in a duel, and subsequently joins the Society of Jesus. The cardinal makes the same journey by canoe in joyful mood, but shortly after arriving delivers his fateful verdict that the missions must be closed. Next the Spanish troops come upstream to destroy the San Carlos missions, and finally, in a scene reminiscent of *The Emerald Forest*, some Indian children, survivors of the massacre, paddle further upstream to put down roots far away from the colonists.

This handsome, moving, intimate epic has two perfect elements: Menges's photography and Morricone's elaborate score, which brings together sacred and Indian music to reinforce the images. A central theme is introduced when the cross is raised over the San Carlos mission;

native pipes seductively join the score when the visiting Cardinal is enchanted by the Edenic innocence of the most recent native converts.

The film's weaknesses lie in a refusal to confront head-on the historical, theological and intellectual issues in all their complexity. Like *A Man for All Seasons*, this is a Protestant treatment of a Catholic subject, and its politics are glibly liberal. It lacks the theological sophistication of Hochwälder's *Holy Experiment* and presents nothing comparable with the lucidly articulated Marxist analysis of imperialism in Latin America that Pontecorvo provided in *Queimada!*, which also had a fine Morricone score.

In *The Mission,* the Jesuits and their idyllic Indian converts are simply hapless victims of political trimmers and imperial greed. The only choice left to the audience is whether to identify with the priests who resist passively, or with those who take to arms in a manner reminiscent of retired western gunfighters retrieving their discarded gun belts.

The production team have not immersed themselves in the period the way Brian Moore did in *Black Robe*, his novel about Jesuits in seventeenth-century Canada. Their real interest clearly resides in Latin America today, the relations between the Capitalist West and the Third World, the function of a politicised church and the fate of disappearing aboriginal populations. This is emphasised by the device of returning after the lengthy final credits to the cardinal completing his report to the Pope and then turning a beady accusatory eye on the viewer in a huge close-up. But the tale is too simple to leave us with any thought more complicated than the crude one that Western civilisation is an irresistible juggernaut that crushes anything standing in its way.

Heartburn (Mike Nichols)

The Observer, 4 January 1987

Nora Ephron is the daughter of the celebrated Hollywood husband-and-wife writing team Phoebe and Henry Ephron, and in the 1970s she emerged, through her collections of essays (mostly material from *New York Magazine* and *Esquire*), *Crazy Salad* and *Scribble, Scribble*, as one of the wittiest observers of the American social scene. The second of these books was dedicated to her husband, the Washington journalist Carl Bernstein, and it is no secret that her novel *Heartburn* was inspired by the breakup of their marriage following Bernstein's affair with the wife of a foreign diplomat.

Rachel Samstat, the thirty-eight-year-old narrator of *Heartburn*, is a celebrated New York food writer. A female Groucho Marx or Woody Allen, she uses a brittle, wisecracking style to cover the pain she endures after discovering halfway through her second pregnancy that her husband Mark, a Washington columnist, is having a serious affair. She had married him knowing full well that he was not merely single but 'famous for it', 'very single'; what is for both of them a second marriage proves a short-lived triumph of hope over experience.

To accommodate Meryl Streep as Rachel, Ms Ephron and her director Mike Nichols (who both worked with Streep on *Silkwood*) have made the character less Jewish and more shrewish, less funny and more obviously neurotic. Perhaps because it is also lit by Nestor Almendros, the picture comes over like a post-feminist *Kramer vs Kramer*. But because the husband is now the edgy, unpredictable Jack Nicholson and not the sober, reasonable Dustin Hoffman, it has a comic, dangerous tone. (Hoffman's appearance in *All the President's Men* necessarily precluded him from playing the role.) It is an amusing and affecting look at a marriage doomed, after a couple of happy years, to failure because the partners are wilful people who (for reasons we can only guess at) merely play at being adults.

Streep and Nicholson are both good. Richard Masur, Stockard Channing and Jeff Daniels as their friends are excellent, and in the film's single funniest sequence there is a devastating impersonation by John Wood of Alistair Cooke presenting *Masterpiece Theatre* on *Public Service Broadcasting* television.

Artfully edited by Sam O'Steen, the picture contains the kind of surprising dramatic turns and the playful observations we associate with Mike Nichols. In a particularly arresting scene, a drunken Mark, on hearing that Rachel is pregnant with their first child, insists on singing all the songs they know about babies. He concludes with the expectant father's sentimental 'Soliloquy' from *Carousel*, which he delivers *in extenso*, word perfect. Now the movie of *Carousel* was produced by Nora Ephron's father and co-scripted by her mother, and this scene directs us towards what is the major subject of *Heartburn* – turning life into saleable words.

In the novel, the heroine's father is an actor. For the movie he's been turned into a widowed screenwriter, and it is well known that the Ephrons took their daughters' college experiences and turned them into their biggest stage success, the 1961 Broadway comedy *Take Her, She's Mine*.

In the movie, Mark (like Chekhov's Trigorin) always carries a notebook in which to jot down his own (and other people's) ideas for his column. When Rachel rhapsodises about motherhood, her New York editor immediately suggests she write a book on the subject. She rejects the notion, but in the next sequence she's busily talking into a cassette recorder while feeding the baby.

And of course we are constantly aware that *Heartburn*, as film and novel, springs directly from the author's broken marriage. Thus this self-reflexive movie is saying something both funny and serious about the inability of articulate professional people to live life for itself and to resist the temptation to turn it into something else, whether it be money, art or deceptive memories.

The Sacrifice (Andrei Tarkovsky)

The Observer, 11 January 1987

Since *Through a Glass Darkly* was shot there in 1961, Fårö, the small island in the Baltic, along with the bleak northern end of its near neighbour Gotland, has been as closely associated with Ingmar Bergman as Monument Valley is with John Ford.

Andrei Tarkovsky, who died on the last Sunday of 1986, chose Gotland as the setting for *The Sacrifice*, the masterwork that has proved to be his testament. Moreover, he used Bergman's regular cinematographer, Sven Nykvist, and the designer of *Fanny and Alexander*, Anna Asp, and cast in the central role Bergman's close friend and cinematic alter ego, Erland Josephson. The result is a movie with a spiritual power, austere beauty and ethical intensity to match the films made on this same moral terrain by the Swedish master himself.

The Sacrifice takes place during twenty-four hours in the life of Alexander, a star actor who has for complex metaphysical reasons abandoned the stage to write and teach after scoring great successes as those antithetical figures, the megalomaniac Richard III and the holy fool Prince Mishkin. It is mid-June, his birthday, and his friend Victor (Sven Wollter) comes for dinner bringing a handsome volume on Russian icons. Victor is the sometime lover of Alexander's wife, a neurotic English actress (Susan Fleetwood), and recently he performed a throat operation on Alexander's small, unnamed son in an attempt to restore his speech.

Also present are Otto (Allan Edwall), a retired history teacher and part-time local postman, who brings a map of seventeenth-century Europe as his present; Alexander's teenage daughter; and two female servants, one of whom, Maria, an Icelander with psychic gifts, bears a striking resemblance to the Virgin in a reproduction of Leonardo's *Adoration of the Magi* on the wall of Alexander's study. The names of the three men, Victor, Alexander and Otto (i.e. Bismarck) all suggest aggressive militarism. The symmetry of the Christian fable is established by a third birthday present, a miniature replica of the family home, built by Alexander's son but never delivered.

A sense of unease hangs over this quintessential Chekhovian gathering. There is no talk smaller than a discussion of Nietzsche's notion of eternal recurrence. Though the depressive Alexander (quoting Hamlet) despairs of 'words, words, words', the book of icons provokes him to articulate the disappearance of our ability to pray, and the map compels him to reflect on the false charts we produce of our world. Then to make sure there will be no smiles on this summer night, a series of sky-rending noises are followed by a TV address, couched in a bureaucratic language at once threatening and reassuring, announcing that World War III has broken out and the nuclear holocaust is imminent.

The sedative syringe is taken from the doctor's bag, which also contains an automatic pistol; a bottle of brandy is produced from the cupboard. But refusing the consolation of the needle and alcohol, Alexander falls to his knees, recites the Lord's Prayer, and proposes a pact with God. He will give up everything he treasures if the world is restored to precisely the way it was that morning. This bargain involves a sexual transaction with the maid Maria, whom Alexander identifies with his mother; their act of love begins as a *pietà*.

1987

Sacrifice is the simplest, most direct of the seven feature films Tarkovsky made. Much of it is ambiguous – we can, if we wish, see the vision of the apocalypse and/or Alexander's response to it, as a dream. Odd incidents here and there are mysterious. But there is nothing resembling the obscure historical allusions and reference to Tarkovsky's family life that made his autobiographical *Mirror* opaque, arcane and virtually impenetrable.

Tarkovsky wrote in his eloquent book *Sculpting in Time* that the aim of his movies was nothing less than to spark 'a spiritual awakening' in his audience. And in this film he puts us on the line as relentlessly as Beckett and Bergman do. We can admire the superb acting and the bravura camerawork of Sven Nykvist that takes in elaborate long takes and modulates between colour and various kinds of monochrome, including for the central visionary passage a silvery chiaroscuro that recalls nineteenth-century art photography. But at the end we must confront the glittering eye of this ancient mariner calling us to our spiritual duties.

For some it will prove too much. Tarkovsky has that wicked ability Solzhenitsyn and other confident zealots have of making their audiences feel morally inadequate if they reject or question what they offer. For all my respect for this great poet of the cinema, I found the penultimate sequence – when Alexander sets his house on fire and is chased around the adjacent watery meadow by men in white coats –more risible than genuinely disturbing. The speed at which the latter arrive on the scene leads one to suspect that their ambulance is permanently patrolling this part of Sweden ready to make house calls.

Blue Velvet (David Lynch)

The Observer, 12 April 1987

Since the 1920s, the avant-garde and the commercial cinema have run on parallel courses. Until recently the only major figure to pass from one to the other was Luis Buñuel, and there was a hiatus of twenty years between the surreal masterworks of the late 1920s and his first seemingly orthodox narrative movies in post-war Mexico.

NOTES FROM THE DREAM HOUSE

Currently a number of young directors are attempting to make that transition, but the only significant success so far in the English-speaking cinema has been achieved by David Lynch. His underground cult hit of the mid-1970s, *Eraserhead*, led to the mainstream feature *The Elephant Man*, the big-budget SF flop *Dune*, and now the riveting, highly personal *Blue Velvet*.

The intriguing thing about *Blue Velvet* is not that it resists classification, but rather that this curious hybrid invites us to push it into numerous different pigeonholes. Lynch's point of departure is simple. A university student, Jeffrey Beaumont (Kyle MacLachlan), returns to his Middle American home town of Lumberton, where his father has had a heart attack while watering the lawn of their archetypal white-painted wooden framed house. Crossing a waste lot on his way back from the hospital visit, Jeffrey discovers a severed ear covered with ants and turns it over as evidence to a police officer, father of the attractive teenager Sandy (Laura Dern), a former schoolfriend of his.

The cop is cagey about the ear's provenance, so with Sandy in tow Jeffrey embarks on a search for its owner. Very rapidly he's drawn into a dark side of Lumberton he's never known, becoming involved in the violent and perverse intrigues of the night club singer Dorothy (Isabella Rossellini) and her lover, the sadistic criminal Frank Booth (Dennis Hopper), who may have kidnapped her husband and son.

That description sounds like a classic 1940s *film noir* thriller, and indeed this is what the film often resembles, with the young hero torn between an experienced raven-haired older woman and a blonde, inexperienced younger one. It also belongs in that literary tradition exposing the corruption lying beneath the idyllic surface of American small-town life that runs from Sherwood Anderson's 1919 classic, *Winesburg, Ohio* to Grace Metalious's 1950 bestseller *Peyton Place*.

But *Blue Velvet* is altogether more mysterious than that. The severed ear reminds us of the severed hands the hero of Dali and Buñuel's *Un Chien andalou* discovered in a Parisian gutter and gave up to the police, a scene generally interpreted as expressing a fear of castration and a capitulation to authority. The use of Bobbie Vinton's soulful ballad 'Blue Velvet' over the opening montage and in the night club recalls another and equally shocking underground movie often compared with Buñuel's – Kenneth Anger played the same recording on the soundtrack of the first sequence of his subversive 1964 picture, *Scorpio Rising*.

1987

The characters' names also direct us towards symbolic readings of the action. Dorothy and the conical wizard's hat belonging to her vanished son suggest connections with the Dorothy swept away to Oz. Her residence on Lincoln Street and the presence of a crazy killer called Booth evoke a century of vainglorious American assassins seeking their niche in history by striking the father dead.

The film is a playful and disturbing mixture of the real, the surreal and the fantastic, realised through a rich texture of sound and wide-screen images. The fashion in cars, clothes and music is deliberately confused so that we cannot tell precisely when it is taking place. A roadside hoarding, for instance, reading *Welcome to Lumberton*, bears the face of a woman out of a 1950s advertisement in *Life* magazine, but the middle-class hero has a gold ring in his left ear. We are drawn into the story through that ringed ear of young Jeffrey. But whether we're seeing a distorted dream version of his rites of passage or some collective American nightmare is ultimately left open. Certainly the film is an allegorical journey of a most arresting sort, and arguably a therapeutic one.

Radio Days (Woody Allen)

The Observer, 28 June 1987

For his sourest autobiographical film, that bleak study of the auteur at bay, *Stardust Memories*, Woody Allen chose Fellini's *8½* as his model. Now for the form of his sunniest autobiographical picture, *Radio Days*, Allen has drawn on *Amarcord*, Fellini's collection of random boyhood reminiscences of Rimini in the 1930s, and how public events impinged on private lives there.

Amarcord is a dialect word for 'I remember', and on the soundtrack of *Radio Days* Allen recalls his childhood in a Jewish working-class home in Rockaway, the seaside district of Brooklyn. His screen persona is the pre-teenage schoolboy Joe (the delightful twelve-year-old redhead Seth Green), and this ingenious, deeply satisfying mosaic of memories, anecdotes, legends and epiphanies is an affirmative picture of one corner of

America from the last years of the Depression up to the final year of the Second World War, just before the Bomb and television.

Joe lives in a raucous household of nine – immigrant grandparents; a long-suffering mother and a feckless father with a wake of failed get-rich-quick schemes behind him; an uncle, aunt, and their teenage daughter; and his mother's unmarried sister Bea. The family are happy without knowing it, getting by through a love none of them can articulate, their ruefully protective Jewish humour, and the dreams, hopes and aspirations engendered by radio.

Everything in the film is somehow related to broadcasting – the programmes they love, the pop music that provides each of them with a personal picnic basket of Proustian *madeleines*, the news that flows in from around the world, the stories they hear about the glamorous lives of the unseen stars whose voices emerge on the domestic loudspeaker. There will never again be anything quite like the magic of radio, and Allen seizes on it as a powerful metaphor.

The overall tone is comic, and the movie is consistently funny, though never malicious or patronising. There is a deal of poignancy in the experience of Joe growing up and of the ever-hopeful Bea (Dianne Wiest), the Brooklyn book-keeper with vast hats, poor eyesight, and a succession of promising swains who turn out to be migrant geese. Two of the film's finest set-pieces involve Aunt Bea and her current man taking Joe on excursions to Manhattan, the first to Radio City Music Hall ('like entering heaven'), the second to attend a radio quiz programme on which Bea wins sixty dollars and buys Joe a chemistry set at Macy's.

The penultimate scene strikes a tragic note as Joe's family and the nation huddle over their wireless sets to hear the live coverage of attempts to rescue a child trapped down a well in Pennsylvania; and the final sequence is positively Chekhovian as radio personalities gather at a New Year's Eve party in 1943 and wonder what, if anything, future generations will know of them.

Radio Days is a realistic companion piece to the surreal *Purple Rose of Cairo*. Both are about the consoling fantasies provided by mass culture in the America of fifty years ago, and both feature Mia Farrow. In the earlier film she's a movie-obsessed waitress escaping from her terrible life by visiting the cinema, in the new one a resilient hat-check girl determined to break into radio as a singer, actress or interviewer, and eventually making it as a gossip columnist. In *Purple Rose,* Jeff Daniels plays a movie adventurer called Tom Baxter; in *Radio Days,* he's the cliff-hanging serial hero Bill Baxter. But unlike the waitress in *Purple Rose,* Joe's family are well aware of the way they use and are used by the mass media.

Students of the effects of broadcasting, film and popular music should study the subtle fashion in which Allen presents their response. When Joe, told that he's neglecting his schoolwork for the radio, points out how much everyone else in the house listens, his mother replies, 'You're different, our lives are ruined already.'

No film this year has given me as much pleasure. I loved every minute, and look forward to seeing it for a third time. If I had to single out two performers from an enormous cast, they would be Josh Mostel as portly Uncle Abbe and Dianne Wiest as Aunt Bea.

Full Metal Jacket (Stanley Kubrick)

The Observer, 13 September 1987

For thirty-five years Stanley Kubrick has combined his two great passions, chess and photography, by making war movies. His first feature film, *Fear and Desire,* centred on a lost patrol in an unidentified twentieth-century war. There followed the Great War in *Paths of Glory,* a Roman civil war in *Spartacus,* World War III in *Dr Strangelove,* an anticipation of Reagan's Star Wars in *2001,* the Seven Years War in *Barry Lyndon,* and now Vietnam in *Full Metal Jacket.*

Like *Platoon* and *Hamburger Hill,* Kubrick's movie is, in formal terms, a conventional war film. Its story of a disparate group of civilians being turned into an effective fighting unit and then being tested under fire resembles Carol Reed's official World War II morale booster *The Way Ahead.* And there are scenes where an educated recruit helps a plump, slow-witted comrade that recall the undervalued *Carry On, Sergeant,* in which William Hartnell reprised his definitive drill sergeant from *The Way Ahead.*

Two things, however, give *Full Metal Jacket* (the title describes a standard rifle bullet) its special distinction. The first is the sheer precision and intensity of the execution. The second is the way Kubrick pursues the twin themes that have run through his work – brilliant plans ruined by human error, and the relationship between the imperfectability of man and the possible perfection of machines. I suspect that Kubrick was initially attracted to his source (a rather good novel by a Vietnam veteran, Gustav Hasford, called *The Short-Timers*) by a line in the book now spoken on the soundtrack by the hero. 'The drill instructors are proud to see that we are growing beyond their control,' says Private Joker. 'The Marine Corps does not want robots. The Marine Corps wants killers.'

Kubrick has adapted the novel in collaboration with its author and a more celebrated Vietnam hand, Michael Herr, and the first part is dominated by a stunning performance as the sadistic, foul-mouthed Sergeant Hartman from another Viet veteran, ex-US Marine Corps Gunnery Sergeant Lee Ermey. Hartman is a theatrical warrior preparing a platoon of shaven-headed recruits for a theatre of war. He speaks a familiar military litany of obscenities and profanities, designed to brutalise his charges, whom he renames, further to rob them of their earlier identities. When so inclined, he physically assaults them to test their self-restraint.

Hartman is a monster, unrestrained by superior authority (officers are conspicuous by their absence); there is no twinkle in his frozen eyes. Audiences amused by his scatological banter will have their smiles wiped away when Hartman commends Lee Harvey Oswald and the Texas mass murderer Charles Whitman as assassins whose marksmanship was a credit to their Marine Corps training. After he has turned the recruits into lethal fighting machines, a Frankensteinian revenge is unleashed upon him in a latrine that shines like a laboratory.

The basic training session is introduced by the patriotic country song 'Goodbye Darling, Hello Vietnam'. The second half, set in Vietnam during the 1968 Tet Offensive, begins with Nancy Sinatra's 'These Boots Are Made for Walkin'' played over a shot of a brash Vietnamese whore strutting along the street towards Private Joker. We are left to decide whose boots are being used to tramp all over whom. Joker (Matthew Modine giving a quiet, controlled performance) is now a Marine combat reporter, a laid-back ironist sporting the legend 'Born to Kill' on his helmet and a peace badge on his lapel. It's a demonstration of Jungian duality, he tells an indignant colonel, who's as stupid as the senior officers in *Paths of Glory* and *Strangelove*.

Joker is disgusted by the lies and bromides put out by the publicity unit he works for, and he regains a purchase on life by rejoining an old barrack-room chum, Cowboy, and his platoon in a desperate battle to retake the ancient city of Hué from the North Vietnamese. Conflating two sections of Hasford's book into a single action, Kubrick mounts one of the best, most terrifying portraits of a long day's military dying I've seen. Without the narrative becoming confused, he shows the mess of a war that's run out of control. Communications and discipline have broken down; objectives once dimly perceived have now become wholly lost. Everything has given way to the simple act of revenge, in this case against a lone Viet Cong sniper picking off targets at will.

Isolated and leaderless, the remnants of Cowboy's platoon make their way among smouldering ruins at nightfall, as if passing from the Halls of Montezuma through some annexe of Hell into the palace of Valhalla. Like the war itself, possibly like life too, the action is absurd. But the troops go relentlessly on. Evoking the end of *Paths of Glory*, a young woman briefly intrudes to question a morally numb male world before they march off once more, singing into battle. This is bravura filmmaking that gets the adrenalin pumping. We enjoy ourselves vicariously while receiving our regular liberal anti-war inoculation.

Empire of the Sun (Steven Spielberg)

The Observer, 27 March 1988

On paper, which is where all movies begin (whether as scripts or contracts), Tom Stoppard and Steven Spielberg were precisely the right team to adapt and direct the film version of J.G. Ballard's great autobiographical novel *Empire of the Sun*.

Spielberg has a feel for epic cinema, is a gifted director of children and has a passion for science fiction. Stoppard understands the surreal landscape, and his father died in a prison camp after dispatching his wife and young children from Singapore shortly before it fell to the Japanese invaders. Ballard's book is based on his adolescent experiences in Japanese-occupied China from just before Pearl Harbor in 1941 (when he was eleven) until just after the atom bomb was dropped on Hiroshima nearly four years later. *Empire of the Sun* is not only one of the finest novels of our time about children and war, it also throws retrospective light on Ballard's career as a major author of surreal, apocalyptic science fiction of – in some instances at least – a rather cerebral kind.

The film's admirable first hour is often stunning in its recreation of the confused Shanghai where the young Jim Graham (Ballard's initials stand for James Graham) lives a protected existence in the privileged international settlement, the arrogant independence of which the Japanese army scrupulously observes. Jim sings in the Anglican cathedral choir and on the eve of Pearl Harbor drives through the madding streets, isolated in the family's gleaming Packard, to a pre-Christmas fancy dress party at the 'stockbrokers' Tudor' mansion of a business associate of his father. In the film's most remarkable scene, Jim goes in search of the model airplane he has been flying on an airfield near the party and stumbles across a company of Japanese soldiers concealed in a fold in the ground. In the film as in the book, we see more through his eyes than he sees himself: he has crossed no man's land a few hours before the declaration of war.

Then the fragile bubble he has been living in bursts. He loses contact with his parents and is left to wander the city. In a striking image that comes right out of the book, he walks in front of a giant poster of *Gone With the Wind*, and for a moment the real backdrop of a smoking, battle-torn Shanghai is surreally replaced by MGM's stylised depiction of a burning Atlanta.

As Jim, the thirteen-year-old Christian Bale is superbly expressive, here as later, and a credit to Spielberg as talent-spotter and director. Moreover, what he registers is not simple bewilderment – Jim Graham is intensely involved in complex emotional and imaginative ways with the political scene as he naively perceives it. He is a remarkable interpreter of the world, and he makes his way through four horrendous years with two contrasted, and equally dangerous, models of moral behaviour before him, both parodies of his domestic, middle-class value system.

On the one hand, he admires the Samurai spirit of the Japanese aviators, a form of hero-worship that comes to focus on the kamikaze pilots sent on their one-way missions from the airfield adjoining his civilian prison camp. On the other hand, he learns the arts of survival from the American black-marketeer Basie, a satanic ex-merchant seaman played (with a complexity that matches Ballard's novel) by one of the finest American actors now at work, John Malkovich. The character is a variation on that played by William Holden in *Stalag 17* and George Segal in *King Rat*.

After the first hour, the picture jumps forward (as the novel does) from 1943 to 1945, and thereafter it loses in clarity, dramatic grip and simple coherence, while John Williams's hitherto restrained, suggestive score becomes increasingly soupy and obtrusive. If you don't know the book, you'll be puzzled by curious ellipses, undeveloped relationships and unexplained icons. And even though you might be impressed by the portentous mood, you'll wonder how a film that comes to look like a sanitised fusion of *The Go-Between* and *Tenko* can have been derived from a novel that has been favourably compared with *A High Wind in Jamaica* and *Lord of the Flies*, not to mention the treatment of adolescent heroes in Dickens and Stevenson.

Wings of Desire (Wim Wenders)

The Observer, 26 June 1988

Our semi-tautological phrase 'few and far between' is a corrupted formulation by the nineteenth-century Scottish poet Thomas Campbell of an old saying to the effect that the visits of angels to our world are 'brief and far between'.

In the movies these past fifty years, however, such visitations by guardian, recording or avenging angels have been lengthy, frequent and have involved stars as varied as Cary Grant, Claude Rains, James Mason and Clint Eastwood. A pattern could be established relating angelic Hollywood films to periods of particular social anxiety.

Our theatre and cinema are currently experiencing a cycle of Faustian bargaining, and in northern European cultures agonising, claw-footed, tail-dragging, sulphur-tainted Mephistos are more common than airborne, deodorised, sympathetic seraphim. For this reason, Wim Wenders's *Wings of Desire*, which treats the plight of angels hovering over Berlin with the deadly earnestness that informs all Wenders's movies, is a welcome and enjoyable occasion. His chief angel Damiel is played by Bruno Ganz, the German cinema's countervailing force of gently-smiling liberal seriousness to the parodic, manically laughing, Teutonic madness of Klaus Kinski.

Wings of Desire is almost plotless. The film only starts to break down in the last half-hour or so when Wenders and his long-winded co-scriptwriter Peter Handke blow a deal of metaphysical hot air into the story of Damiel falling in love with a French trapeze artist (Solveig Dommartin). She wants to be an angel, he would like to be human and experience cold, colour, time and taste. Up to this point the movie is more like a lyrical poem, an ethereal version of the classic German documentary of the 1920s, *Berlin, Symphony of a Great City*.

Following the example of *A Matter of Life and Death*, the angels see the world in a bleak monochrome as they drift around town through a giant library (which they appear to use as a dormitory), in and out of apartment buildings, along the carriages of underground trains, always listening with affectionate concern to the anxious, unspoken thoughts of this divided city. When the world is occasionally presented from a human viewpoint, it is in a slightly heightened colour, and when Damiel takes on a human identity to court his acrobat, it is as if he has crossed the rainbow and arrived in Oz. The cinematography by the octogenarian French cameraman Henri Alekan is magnificent

Wenders's angels dress in overcoats, knot their hair at the back and do not have wings. But the performances of Bruno Ganz and Otto Sander (as his companion Cassiel) create an uncanny sense of people living in some other dimension, and the fluid camerawork and subtle orchestration of sound make us experience the world from a different point of view. We are given a fresh vision of what an extraordinary gift life is and understand why Damiel might wish to be human. Crossing over, he joins another fallen angel, Peter Falk, making an endearing appearance as himself.

Au revoir les enfants (Louis Malle)

The Observer, 9 October 1988

To appreciate the immense emotional gulf between the British and the Continental experience of World War II, you only have to compare two recent autobiographical films by directors now in their mid-fifties, John Boorman's *Hope and Glory* and Louis Malle's *Au revoir les enfants*.

Boorman looks back truthfully and with guiltless affection to a time when British communities were united by the Blitz and shared hardship, when no one got up to anything more wicked than a little dabbling in the black market and adultery with glamorous allied servicemen, and when children willed friendly bombs to fall on schools. There is much that is universally human in Boorman's nostalgic film, but there is also a general absence of 'Le Chagrin et la Pitié'. He did not have to ponder exemplary careers ranging from the craven collaboration of Pierre Laval to the courageous resistance of Jean Moulin that Europeans and Scandinavians must confront when reviewing the war years.

Malle's subtly detailed movie takes place in occupied France during January 1944, less than six months before D-Day, at a school for the sons of wealthy Catholics outside Fontainebleau. The crowded dormitories, poor food, freezing classrooms and stern discipline suggest the world of Dickens. The central relationship, however, contains hints of Alain Fournier's *Le Grand Meaulnes*.

When a new boy called Jean Bonnet is introduced into a class of twelve-year-olds, he is made the object of practical jokes and bullying despite a special request from the priests that he be treated with kindness. Initially the brightest boy in the class, Julien Quentin, joins in to ingratiate himself with his fellows and because he recognises in the clever, scholarly Jean an academic rival.

But gradually the two become friends, sharing an interest in music (in a lovely scene the pair play a boogie-woogie piano duet) and literature. And Julien discovers that this anxious outsider, posing as a protestant, is in fact Jean Kippelstein, one of three Jewish boys being hidden by the fathers – though precisely what a Jew is he cannot understand.

For much of the way, Malle appears merely to be creating a vivid portrait of an enclosed community, its essential austerity simply intensified by war conditions. The occupation is resented, certainly, and this is expressed through a superior distaste for the Boches. Yet, schoolboys can unthinkingly echo their parents' prejudices: 'At least Pétain knows how to get along with the Krauts,' one says. 'Better Krauts than Jews or Reds,' says another.

The occupying power apparently represents little threat to the school-boys. A young German soldier asks one of the teachers to hear his confession. Lost in the forest on a boy-scout expedition, Jean and Julien are brought safely home by a German patrol. When a pair of vicious, anti-Semitic French militiamen demand to see the identity cards in a smart restaurant where Julien's visiting parents are treating him and Jean to lunch (one of the most brilliantly orchestrated sequences in the film), a drunken German officer orders them to leave, largely to impress the middle-class French diners.

Eventually, of course, the Gestapo come, tipped off by an informer. But even here the most violent act by their leader is to snatch offensive allied flags from a war-map on the classroom wall, and he gives the assembled boys a lecture on German discipline. The ending is quiet, understated and shattering. Denying us the easy comfort of tears, Malle makes us share a memory that has haunted him for over forty years, a memory that must have become intensified over time, as Julien increas-ingly understands the background from which Jean came, the destination to which he was being sent, and the historical circumstances that made such a tragedy possible. This can never be exorcised.

Au revoir les enfants is not only the best movie on the subject of the Occupation since Malle's own *Lacombe Lucien*; it is also one of the best pictures ever made about childhood, and the finest French film for several years. The performances that Malle has drawn from Gaspard Manesse and Raphaël Fejtö as Julien and Jean are not to be faulted.

Scandal (Michael Caton-Jones)

The Observer, 5 March 1989

As scandals go, the Profumo affair is tame stuff compared with the sexual carryings-on in Second Empire France or the political enormities of Watergate. But along with the Beatles, the newly created *Private Eye*, John Osborne's film version of *Tom Jones*, and *That Was the Week That Was* on television, it helped to make 1963 a joyous year – up to November. It also created in Christine Keeler the Nana of Macmillan's 'Never-had-it-so-good' Britain and helped to topple a government.

Still the best picture about the moral corruption of the times, Joseph Losey's *The Servant* was being privately screened as the affair emerged in the public view. When it opened in the early autumn of 1963, the film uncannily echoed the obsessive themes and occasions of the preceding months. It is itself now echoed in *Scandal*, a sober and responsible movie by a production team mostly too young to have followed the events at the time.

Directed by Michael Caton-Jones from a script by Michael Thomas, the picture centres upon the relationship between two ambitious provincial outsiders making their way on the metropolitan scene: the gifted osteopath, Dr Stephen Ward (John Hurt) and the teenage good-time girl, Christine Keeler (Joanne Whalley-Kilmer), to whom he becomes Svengali and decadent older brother. Both are sad, vulnerable people compared with the brassy, nail-hard Mandy Rice-Davies (Bridget Fonda), whom Christine befriends, and the people Ward cultivates in the sleazy demi-monde inhabited by the high, low and socially unaccommodated, where at the same party Lord Astor (Leslie Phillips) could rub shoulders with the property racketeer Rachman and the Soviet naval attaché Ivanov. And they, rather than Profumo, are seen as the victims of the scandal.

Ward, a manipulator of bones and people, a vain lover of intrigue, but neither pimp nor traitor, is framed by an Establishment closing ranks to protect its own. Keeler, forced by the authorities into betraying Ward, the only man who really cared for her, is then jailed for perjury.

The movie is not moralising or judgmental on matters of sexual morality, but it is angry about hypocrisy, scapegoating and bad faith. And it finds in 1963 a society much like our own: a political party too long in office; a Prime Minister arrogantly out of touch with currents of opinion; the police and the law used for political purposes; the secret service going about its business without having to give a public account of itself; a Press largely cowed, craven and prudishly prurient.

Scandal makes witty use of contemporary pop music: the Shadows' 'Apache' over a montage of Christine and Mandy dressing and making up for a night on the town; the Peter Sellers/Sophia Loren 'Goodness Gracious Me' as Profumo drives away from the Keeler-Ward mews flat and Ivanov arrives; the Beatles' 'Do You Want to Know a Secret?' when Profumo resigns. But it doesn't much go in for analysis and is restrained by fears of libel from too much speculation.

Profumo (Ian McKellen), who was no tragic romantic statesman in the tradition of Parnell, gets off lightly as an infatuated middle-aged chap straying from the strait-and-narrow into the bed of an attractive eighteen-year-old redhead, who happened also to have a couple of reckless Caribbean lovers and to be keeping company with a Russian intelligence man.

Did he really say to Christine, as they looked at a Guardi on the wall at Cliveden: 'You have never made love until you have made love in a gondola'? Did she really yawn over his bare shoulder as he rutted away? Possibly. What is incredible, however, is the wig McKellen wears, with its sharp triangle of hair in the middle that makes Profumo look as if he's playing Ko-Ko in a House of Commons production of *Mikado*.

The Thin Blue Line (Errol Morris)

The Observer, 19 March 1989

I really feel for Mrs Thatcher this week. If I were a doting mother with a rootless son who'd gone down to Dallas in search of a living, I would have had a sleepless night after seeing Errol Morris's *The Thin Blue Line*, the riveting true-life thriller about Randall Adams, a drifter from Ohio wrongly convicted of murdering a Dallas cop at Thanksgiving 1976. His mother describes Dallas County as 'the nearest thing to hell on earth'.

After a month without clues, Adams must have struck the desperate cops as a dream fall guy, a friendless transient blue-collar worker from out-of-state, and at twenty-seven old enough to go to the electric chair. The chief witness against him, a sixteen-year-old habitual criminal, David Harris had boasted of having committed the murder to friends, then withdrawn his confession and fingered Adams. The pair had met on the morning of the crime when Harris gave Adams a lift in a stolen car. For the sleuths, Harris presented two problems. First, he came from the ultra-xenophobic township of Vidor, headquarters of the Texas Ku Klux Klan, who had formed the impression that the dead cop was, if not exactly black, not quite white either. Second, Harris was too young to be executed.

The day the case came to trial the prosecution produced three surprise eyewitnesses, a trio of colourful low-lifers, all notorious liars out for a reward. The Assistant District Attorney in charge of the case, a man with a 100% conviction rate including two 5000-year sentences for kidnapping, happily quoted the maxim, 'Anyone can convict a guilty man; it takes talent to convict an innocent man.'

Errol Morris stumbled across the articulate, quietly spoken Adams while conducting research for one of his offbeat documentaries on the lunatic fringe (or lunatic centre) of American society. His investigations soon pointed towards Adams's innocence, and his masterly movie is an extraordinary combination of *Rough Justice*, *Rashomon*, *In Cold Blood* and *10 Rillington Place*, using interviews, dramatic reconstructions, mug-shots and photographs from family albums, official documents, pages from newspapers, blown-up maps and courtroom drawings, and clips from old feature films. The repetition in slow motion of key images (e.g. a Burger King milkshake thrown from a car window by the murdered cop's inattentive policewoman partner) and of variant versions of re-created events produces a surreal effect, and this disturbing ambience is reinforced by Philip Glass's throbbing score.

Most interviewees have those authentic Texas faces rarely glimpsed in JR Ewing's Dallas and not produced by a healthy life riding the Marlboro range. Their appearances suggest the effect of too much beer and junk food, too many cigarettes and too little exercise. Several characters and incidents might well have sprung from the bad-taste, darkly comic imagination of that son of Dallas, Terry Southern. We hear about a court-appointed shrink dubbed 'Dr Death', whose expert psychiatric evidence always advised that convicted murderers should go to the chair.

We learn that the dead cop's wife had bought her husband a bulletproof vest and planned to give it to him for Christmas.

But though often wildly funny, Morris's movie isn't callous. He combines a zealous quest for justice with a rare compassion, and concludes by looking sympathetically at the disturbed background of the real killer, David Harris, now on Death Row himself after yet another murder.

Field of Dreams (Phil Alden Robinson)

The Observer, 26 November 1989

American football, officially classified as business, was the favourite game of Nixon's White House and provided Ronald Reagan with his most celebrated film role. In recent movies, football invariably reflects the dark side of American life, the game an image of brutal capitalist conflict, its battered players victims of the system.

Baseball, though no less a business than football, has retained its legal status as a sport and its popular image as the expression of national hope. In movies, baseball players are physically graceful in their movements and touched with a spiritual grace that enables them to transcend the mundane world. This sense of the game's essential goodness is at the heart of the current cycle of baseball pictures that reaches its apogee in Phil Alden Robinson's *Field of Dreams*, a wonderful fantasy movie rising from the heartland of America like two classics to which it affectionately nods, *The Wizard of Oz* and *It's a Wonderful Life*.

Its star, Kevin Costner, is in the tradition of those eager, open-faced all-Americans, Gary Cooper and James Stewart, both of whom went on from Capra movies to impersonate real-life baseball heroes tragically struck down in mid-career, Cooper in *Pride of the Yankees*, Stewart in *The Stratton Story*. Costner plays the thirty-six-year-old Ray Kinsella, a product of the 1960s campus revolution now living a quiet post-Woodstock life on an Iowa farm with his wife (the sharp, spunky Amy Madigan) and their little daughter.

One day, as Ray walks through his cornfield, a god-like voice (a sonorous cross between sports radio and Old Testament) intones: 'If you build it, he will come.' Ray interprets this as an instruction to fashion a flood-lit baseball diamond on his deeply-mortgaged farm, a task as daunting in its way as Simon Rodia setting out to build his Watts Towers in Los Angeles, or mediaeval masons erecting a cathedral on Mont St Michel. When the job is finished, the legendary Shoeless Joe Jackson appears, literally and figuratively, out of the higher corn. The star of the disgraced 1919 Chicago White Sox baseball team (the so-called Black-Sox Scandal is the subject of John Sayles's film *Eight Men Out*). Jackson was the great hero of Ray's broken, rejected father, and his ghost has been wandering in search of a welcoming ballpark. 'Is this heaven?' he asks. 'No, it's Iowa,' Ray replies.

Soon Joe is joined by the other White Sox outcasts, and Ray receives his second divine command: 'Ease his pain.' In W.P. Kinsella's 1982 novel, *Shoeless Joe*, on which the film is based, Ray believes that he has been told to track down the reclusive J.D. Salinger and involve him in the quest. In the film, for rather obvious reasons, Salinger has become Terence Mann (James Earl Jones), a charismatic black novelist who influenced the sixties generation and then withdrew from the world in disgust. The change enhances this aspect of the film by making Mann a fan of the Brooklyn Dodgers infielder Jackie Robinson, the first black American to become a baseball star. The 1957 transfer of the Dodgers from Long Island to Los Angeles and the destruction of their ballpark, Ebbets Field, is evoked as a turning point in American social history.

Attending a baseball match in Boston, Ray and Mann jointly receive a further instruction on the scoreboard. They are urged to 'Go the distance' and seek out the elderly small-town physician Doc Graham, who as a young man took the field for a single inning with the New York Giants before the Great War. Doc is played by the great character star and all-purpose loser of post-war American cinema, Burt Lancaster.

This simple, direct movie suggestively intertwines several themes: the reconciliation of father and son, the redemption of fallen heroes, the recovery of lost dreams, a vindication of what was best in the spirit of the currently reviled 1960s. If you stand back from it, *Field of Dreams* might be embarrassingly sentimental. Seen with a sympathetic audience, it can provide a powerfully affirmative experience. And it is often very funny. Ray's wife has a splendid line putting down a neo-conservative contemporary at a PTA meeting: 'I think you had two 1950s and then the seventies.'

Back to the Future III (Robert Zemeckis)

The Observer, 16 July 1990

The *Indiana Jones* series sagged badly in the second episode. It then recovered with the excellent *Indiana Jones and the Last Crusade*, that discovered its roots in the Old West and drew new sustenance from a father-son relationship.

The same has happened with Robert Zemeckis's *Back to the Future*. The second part was confused and incoherent, but *Back to the Future III*, which takes its characters back to the nineteenth-century West and explores the relationship between the hero and his surrogate father, is funny, charming, inventive and affecting.

Only the final sequence is set in 1985, and Hill Valley 1955 is the launching pad for ageing teenager Marty McFly to rocket back in the time-travelling DeLorean. His mission is to rescue the eccentric Doc Brown (Christopher Lloyd) who's stranded in the recently founded Hill Valley of 1885.

His journey begins in a surreal, powerfully resonant setting – a drive-in cinema in Monument Valley that's showing the low-budget 1955 horror flick *Tarantula*, which happens to feature at the bottom of the cast list the unknown Clint Eastwood.

The accelerating DeLorean heads directly towards the drive-in's screen, but at the point of collision it passes through the time barrier, arriving in the Old West just as an Indian war party is being pursued by a company of US cavalry.

In this frontier community Marty encounters the first generation of the McFly family, recently arrived from Ireland, and gives his name as Clint Eastwood. What he has stumbled into is less the real West than the classic western.

Back to the Future III alludes to, and evokes, numerous famous westerns. Sitting in the local saloon are old-time cowboy actors like Harry Carey Jr, who appeared in Hawks's *Red River* and numerous Ford westerns, and whose father was the star of Ford's first silent pictures. As Marty and Doc Brown prepare their return to 1985, they draw on their knowledge of the genre. Doc, who finds a common bond with the new schoolmarm (Mary Steenburgen) in their love for Jules Verne, overcomes his bashfulness and starts to court this exotic outsider by carefully imitating the way Henry Fonda's Wyatt Earp escorts Cathy Downs onto the dance floor in *My Darling Clementine*. Marty survives a gunfight by remembering Eastwood's cunning strategies in *A Fistful of Dollars*.

But for Marty, the 1985 teenager, westerns are as distant a part of the past as the historical West itself. The genre's values seem to him both comic and romantically appealing, and that gives an edge to the proceedings. So does the *Back to the Future* trilogy's central contradiction.

The supporting characters behave according to a traditional European view of society, which believes that your ancestors and your progeny are likely to be much like you. The bullies in 1985, for instance, are the great-grandchildren of pioneer rotters, and in the twenty-first century their children will still be bad apples.

But though young Marty's jeans determined his name when he returned to 1955 (he was dubbed Calvin Klein), his fate is not determined by his genes. He has that American belief in the ability to challenge fate and re-shape one's life by an act of will.

Home Alone (Chris Columbus)

The Observer, 23 December 1990

A really good Christmas film should entertain the whole family, have a yuletide setting and still be enjoyable after the decorations have come down and the tree's been sawn up. Few films have all three qualities. One thinks of *Miracle on 34th Street*, *It's a Wonderful Life* and, more recently, *Gremlins*.

This year's seasonal treat, *Home Alone*, is directed by Chris Columbus, who wrote *Gremlins*, and its leading characters, separated by several thousand miles, watch *Miracle on 34th Street* in an affluent Chicago suburb and *It's a Wonderful Life* dubbed into French in Paris.

The viewer in Chicago is the eight-year-old Kevin, delightfully played by Macaulay Culkin. The viewers in Paris are his parents, brothers and sisters, cousins, aunts and uncles, who discover half-way across the Atlantic en route to a Christmas holiday in France that they have left Kevin home alone. The producer-scriptwriter John Hughes (the man who virtually invented the Brat Pack film) has contrived a concatenation of events that makes the situation entirely plausible.

The rebellious egotist Kevin wakes up believing that his wish has come true and that his family has disappeared into limbo. Crusoe-like, he starts to enjoy his exclusive, untrammelled reign over the family mansion.

As his worried-sick parents try in vain to contact him (the phone is out of order, the neighbours away), Kevin has the time of his life eating junk food and watching garbage cassettes. But two comic crooks (Daniel Stern, Joe Pesci) have cased the neighbourhood and plan to burgle the houses one by one. At this point the movie comes into its own.

Kevin is as seemingly vulnerable as the blind Audrey Hepburn fighting off hoodlums in *Wait Until Dark*, as resolute a defender of his domestic territorial imperatives as Dustin Hoffman in *Straw Dogs*, as formidably armed and as ingenious a setter of booby traps as Rambo, and as gleeful in inflicting pain on his adversaries as the Road Runner, Bugs Bunny or Jerry the Mouse.

Except in *The Cowboys*, when John Wayne's youthful protégés avenge his murder, I do not recall having witnessed such violence being visited on adults by a child. Roald Dahl would have approved, and the children sitting around me in the cinema loved it. Maybe the Neighbourhood Watch movement should consider recruiting younger members.

Home Alone has some of the cheerful sadism Columbus injected into *Gremlins*, though it lacks the earlier picture's magical qualities. But how to account for the film's phenomenal success in America this past month? Just as *Straw Dogs* reflected anxieties bred by Vietnam, Columbus's picture preys on frustrations created by the Gulf confrontation. It feeds off a desire to solve problems rapidly through heroic combat so that the family can return home to Middle America from threatening foreign parts and hug each other around the tree on Christmas morning.

Dances with Wolves (Kevin Costner)

The Observer, 10 February 1991

Kevin Costner, whose impressive directorial debut, *Dances with Wolves,* is the first western in more than fifteen years to prove a major success at the box office, says that he fell in love with the genre at the age of seven, when he saw James Stewart as the mountain man at the beginning of *How the West Was Won* in 1962.

How the West Was Won was perhaps the last western that could be regarded as an unqualified celebration of the making of America, the fulfilment of Manifest Destiny. By then, westerns had become a highly critical forum for reviewing the national past and appraising the present, and by the 1970s the essentially pessimistic character of the best movies had alienated large popular audiences.

Costner's film partakes of the negativity of the counter-cultural westerns of twenty years ago that turned a jaundiced eye on corrupt white civilisation and embraced the superior life of the Indians that it was destroying. But through the force of his performance as the film's hero, Lieutenant Dunbar, and his sympathetic treatment of the Sioux, Costner has turned his film into an entirely positive experience that reminds us of an earlier James Stewart movie, the optimistically liberal *Broken Arrow*, which began the pro-Indian cycle of the 1950s.

In the opening scene, the severely wounded Dunbar performs a suicidal act of heroism that inspires a demoralised company of Union soldiers to take a Confederate position in 1863 Tennessee. His reward is to choose his next posting, and he elects to go West 'to see the frontier before it goes'.

His journey resembles those physically and psychically wounded Hemingway heroes seeking therapy in the wilderness after the Great War. As the fastidious, puritanical Dunbar leaves the last dismal remnant of civilisation, an isolated fort, the commandant commits suicide from self-disgust, and Dunbar is accompanied into Indian country by a noisome, foul-mouthed trader.

His new post is mysteriously deserted, so with Cisco, his wonder horse, and a neighbourhood wolf for company, Dunbar settles into a disciplined Crusoe-like routine before contacting the Native Americans.

They turn out to be as sharply divided as the Brazilian Indians in Boorman's *The Emerald Forest*.

On the one hand, there are the violent, predatory Pawnees, their heads half-shaven, their faces hideously painted, their bodies nearly naked. On the other hand, there are the Sioux – long-haired, dignified, eloquent, peaceful, generous, democratic, in touch with their inner selves, the environment and the universe.

The film traces the moral journey by which the hero sheds his hollow identity as Lieutenant Dunbar and becomes a Sioux Indian named 'Dances with Wolves'. One of the agents of his change is the forceful widow 'Stands With a Fist', a white woman raised by the Sioux after the Pawnees massacred her pioneer family when she was seven. She's played by Mary McDonnell, whose strong jaw, deep voice and large liquid eyes bring to mind Jane Fonda.

Dances with Wolves is long, simplistic and lacking in irony, though not in pawky humour. The action set-pieces (two ambushes, two pitched battles, a grand buffalo hunt) are dynamically handled.

But the picture lacks the visual and dramatic authority of the best westerns of, say, Ford, Mann and Peckinpah. It is certainly much inferior to *Heaven's Gate*. But the sincerity of Costner's performance, Dean Semler's handsome photography, John Barry's lush score and the striking faces of the Indians give the film a rich romantic aura that sweeps us along.

Life Is Sweet (Mike Leigh)

The Observer, 24 March 1991

The plays and films Mike Leigh has created in collaboration with his chosen casts over the past twenty years make him a major, if somewhat idiosyncratic, witness of our times. *Life Is Sweet*, only his third work for the cinema, is among his finest achievements.

The fact that it is continuously funny, often disconcertingly so (I still laugh a little uneasily when recalling the line 'Fancy going to the States and not going to Disneyland'), should not blind us to the maturity of its vision or the depth of its feeling.

To accompany the picture, Leigh has provided a 'note from the director' listing, in alphabetical order, 104 things that *Life Is Sweet* is about, beginning with accordions and ending with zest. Oddly he fails to include the three main topics: coping, dreaming and everyday heroism.

The film is set in the unprepossessing North London suburb of Enfield, the source of famous guns (the Enfield rifle and the Bren) rather than famous sons. Here Wendy (Alison Steadman) and Andy (Jim Broadbent), both in their late forties, live in a privatised council house with their bespectacled twenty-two-year-old twin daughters, Natalie (Claire Skinner) and Nicola (Jane Horrocks).

Wendy, a cheerful, outgoing survivor with a gift for friendship and an ear for innuendo, works part time in Bunnikins, a children's clothing shop. The self-dramatising, big-hearted, procrastinating Andy has a well-paid job in charge of some commercial institution's kitchen (the film's one bravura take, a hand-held tracking shot, shows him as monarch of all he purveys), but he hates it and dreams of better things.

The boyish, sociable Natalie, embodying her mother's common sense without the warmth, has found congenial employment as a plumber. The withdrawn, unemployed, bulimic Nicola stays at home spouting feminist clichés. Her afternoons are spent in bondage games, her nights guzzling chocolate and throwing up in a plastic bag.

The family's chief friends are a pair of posturing losers. The spivvish Patsy (Stephen Rea) sells Andy a run-down, insanitary mobile café, guaranteed to make his fortune (or get his throat cut) selling hamburgers at White Hart Lane. The awkward, pudgy Aubrey (Tim Spall) opens a high street restaurant called Regret Rien, with a menu less attractive than the one on the lower deck of Battleship Potemkin, and Wendy agrees to help out on opening night.

Unlike the improvisational cinema of John Cassavetes, there are no longueurs in Leigh's movies and no sense of the performers reaching into their guts on the screen. By the time he starts shooting, Leigh commands the text. The final result, despite the naturalistic surface, is as dramatically patterned and thematically orchestrated as a play by Ibsen. Indeed, *Life Is Sweet* bears a close resemblance to *The Wild Duck* and has the same ability to be terrifyingly funny and deadly serious. Perhaps the high point of a magnificently performed film comes when Wendy turns on her defeatist daughter and delivers a passionate speech about family life.

Leigh has been called patronising. The charge is false. The Noel Coward-David Lean film *This Happy Breed*, evoked by Leigh in several panning shots across back gardens, is patronising. Coward and Lean pat their characters on the head, giving them little medals in their own honours list. Leigh shakes them, hugs them, sometimes despairs over them, but never thinks they are other than versions of ourselves.

My Own Private Idaho (Gus Van Sant)

The Observer, 29 March 1992

Lately settled and still sparsely populated, the Pacific Northwest of the United States, a vast terrain of towering mountains and flat plains, is culturally shallow yet not insignificant. Vernon Lewis Parrington wrote his monumental *Main Currents in American Thought* while teaching at the University of Washington; a sojourn in Oregon inspired Bernard Malamud's fine novel *A New Life*; Ezra Pound was born in Idaho and Hemingway died there.

A few years ago, one of America's quirkiest independent filmmakers, Gus Van Sant, decided to give up making TV commercials in Manhattan and moved to Portland, Oregon, where he has been quietly putting the area on the map in a way that might not commend him to the local tourist boards.

His first feature, the ultra-low-budget *Mala Noche*, centred on the disastrous love of a gay liquor store manager for an illegal Mexican immigrant. His second, *Drugstore Cowboy*, took a non-judgmental view of a group of itinerant, thieving drug addicts. His expansive new film, *My Own Private Idaho*, rivetingly played by two of America's most versatile young actors, takes us on a colourful journey through all three states of the Pacific Northwest.

Van Sant's young protagonists, Mike Waters (River Phoenix) and Scott Favor (Keanu Reeves), drift around from trailer park to sleazy motel to squat, and even make an excursion to Italy. Scott is the well-heeled son of the mayor of Portland, in flight from responsibility and respectability, and keeping company with the charismatic, middle-aged coke-sniffing hobo Bob Pigeon (William Richert). Mike is a male prostitute, a narcoleptic who is searching for the mother who abandoned him as a child.

Van Sant brings great warmth to the boys' friendship, and he handles their sexual encounters with a variety of middle-aged homosexual clients without prudery or prurience and with a good deal of offhand wit.

This aspect of the story is treated more or less realistically and at one level this is an engaging road movie set in the new West of anarchic cowboys in pick-up trucks familiar from Thomas McGuane's novels and Sam Shepard's plays. The tale of a woman killing her cheating lover while watching a John Wayne movie at a drive-in is right out of Shepard. There are also numerous surreal touches such as the colloquy conducted between Mike, Scott and their friends as they come to life on the covers of gay magazines (with titles such as 'Joy Boy' and 'Male Call') in the racks of a sleazy 'adult' bookshop.

But the film is also a religious allegory, a mythic quest for an unattainable home and a modern reworking of *Henry IV, Parts I and II*. At one point Scott cradles the dormant Mike in a pietà beside the plinth of a historical monument bearing the inscription *The Coming of the White Man*, and the movie concludes by recapitulating the parable of the Good Samaritan.

In his involuntary sleep, Mike dreams of his mother and of a house that crashes down like the one Dorothy flies in to Oz. And the relationship between Scott, his father and the hobo Bob is that between Prince Hal, Henry IV and Falstaff, with slabs of Shakespeare merged into the scabrous modern dialogue.

In the film's version of the robbery at Gadshill, the Canterbury pilgrims become an advance booking team for a rock group, and the reception of Falstaff outside Westminster Abbey is transposed to a restaurant for yuppies in Portland.

With its striking images and imaginative use of music, it consistently holds the attention. At the end viewers are likely to be divided between those for whom the film's three strands remain just elegantly coloured wires, and those who can wrap them around the poles of the mind to provide a sympathetic current and illumination.

NOTES FROM THE DREAM HOUSE

The Long Day Closes (Terence Davies)

The Observer, 24 May 1992

Terence Davies's *The Long Day Closes* affords the viewer a sublime cinematic experience and rounds out a body of deeply personal work by taking us back to its beginning.

Davies spent ten years over his trilogy – *Children* (1974), *Madonna and Child* (1980), *Death and Transfiguration* (1983) – an austere, compressed, monochrome study of the lonely, guilt-burdened Robert Tucker, a Catholic homosexual deeply attached to his mother and oppressed by a drunken father.

Shot on unromanticised Liverpool locations, it combined the bleakness of early Brian Moore with the asperity of late Samuel Beckett to trace Tucker's life from seven to seventy. Davies then went on to the Technicolor diptych *Distant Voices, Still Lives* (1988), a directly autobiographical account of the same family, drawing on his older brother's and sisters' memories of times good and bad in the 1940s and '50s, but altogether more stylised and elliptical and without recognisable location landmarks.

The Long Day Closes overlaps *Still Lives*, picking up after the death of the overbearing father and focusing entirely on the eleven-year-old Bud Davies's view of the world around him in the mid-1950s. Bud (Leigh McCormack, an impressive newcomer) is another version of the young Robert Tucker, a lonely working-class latent homosexual, devoted to his mother (Marjorie Yates giving a luminous performance).

In a remarkable scene, Bud drops a net curtain down on to the head of his mother in the back yard. It transforms her into a bride and Madonna at just the moment Bud catches the eye of a bricklayer stripped to the waist. The labourer winks in acknowledgment of the erotic gaze, and the same actor turns up as the crucified Christ in Bud's fervent imagination as he prays in church.

But Bud is the boy who will grow up to make a healing movie about the life of Robert Tucker rather than stay in Liverpool to experience Tucker's isolation. *The Long Day Closes* is warm and affirmatory; the *Trilogy* cold and stoical.

Davies is a working-class Merseyside Proust whose madeleine is probably a plate of scouse, though his memories are usually triggered by music (mostly of the cheap, potent kind that reunited Coward's Amanda and Elyot), old movies, embarrassment and rain. The film is not total recall. It is a distillation of experience, a series of epiphanies, a celebration of love and community from the perspective of a perennial if reluctant outsider.

Bud views the world from the linoleum-covered staircase of the family's sparsely furnished terrace house, from its back and front windows, from behind the iron bars over the steps to the coal cellar. Romance he experiences through popular songs and in the picture house after standing alone outside in the rain waiting for some 'mister' to take him into an 'A' certificate film. He runs errands for his brothers and sisters, buying perfume, lipstick, silk stockings, cigarettes, film magazines and other erotica, but he is excluded from their courting.

There are references to the Grafton Rooms dance hall, the Cast-Iron Shore, the Forum cinema. But there is none of the bustle of Liverpool life you get in plays by Alun Owen, Willy Russell and Alan Bleasdale. Nor is there any acknowledgment of the arrival of rock 'n' roll, television or consumerism, though a sweet-tempered black person does accidentally stumble into the family home only to be brutally rebuffed.

The movie is poetry, not sociology. There is however, a hilarious scene involving the Davies family's neighbour, Curly (Jimmy Wilde) and his wife Edna (Tina Malone). Curly does impressions of Hollywood stars, Edna is as funny as Tommy Handley, and we realise that Davies could have earned a living writing gags for Jimmy Tarbuck.

The film's greatest sequence is a succession of overhead right-to-left tracking shots linking the crucial aspects of Bud's life: the front of his home, a packed cinema scanned from projection box to screen, a full Catholic church traversed from porch to altar, a classroom in a grim Catholic secondary modern school. On the soundtrack throughout, Debbie Reynolds sings the title song from her 1957 movie *Tammy*, and any suggestion of sentimentality is undercut by a couple of dryly sardonic lines from the chapel scene in *Kind Hearts and Coronets* as the camera reaches the kneeling priest, and Terry-Thomas's *Private's Progress* outburst about his troops being 'an absolute shower' at the point where the schoolboys are let out. The movie ends with Bud contemplating the mysteries of the universe while clouds pass across the moon to the accompaniment of Sullivan's plangent Victorian choral work that provides Davies with his title.

One False Move (Carl Franklin)

The Observer, 11 April 1993

In his brilliant noir thriller, *One False Move*, the forty-three-year-old actor-turned-director, Carl Franklin, performs with the skill of a master angler.

The audience is hooked by an intriguing opening night-scene of a car coming slowly over the brow of a deserted Los Angeles street to the edgy twanging of a blues guitar. The hook bites deep and painful as the three people in the car – an aggressive white psychopath (Billy Bob Thornton, co-author of the script), his black lover (Cynda Williams) and his cool black ex-cellmate (Michael Beach) – disrupt and destroy two black households leaving six bodies behind them.

With the money and drugs they've stolen, the trio embark on a thousand-mile journey to Houston, Texas. Meanwhile, two Los Angeles homicide detectives, one black (Earl Billings), the other white (Jim Metzler), pick up a clue that suggests the fugitives might be heading for the small Arkansas town of Star City. So they fly there and lie in wait with the brash young local sheriff, Dale Dixon (Bill Paxton).

Cutting between these parallel narratives, Franklin tightens and relaxes his line, but doesn't let us off the hook until we're pulled ashore at the end, gasping with some form of catharsis. There are strong echoes of *High Noon* as well as undertones of Greek tragedy. A series of moral lapses, crimes and errors of judgment that began in Star City ends up there six years later, having described a vast circle around the American Southwest. But this point is never laboured in a picture notable for its economic exposition and its exploration of character through action.

One False Move puzzles, surprises and shocks us first time around. At a second viewing, like Hitchcock's *Vertigo* and Jordan's *The Crying Game*, it satisfies in a different way; we become aware of the deeper psychological and social insights that we only subconsciously perceived as the sheer power of the narrative swept us along.

The acting is flawless, and Bill Paxton brings to the pivotal role of the Star City sheriff a Faulknerian complexity. He is a Southern romantic, frustrated by small-town life, full of naïve dreams, troubled by buried guilt, bent on acting decently and honourably. His sensible, dowdy wife (Natalie Canerday), however, gets one of the film's best lines. Knowing that her husband's desire to impress the big-time Los Angeles cops might have fatal results, she says to one of them: 'There's a little girl in there in need of her Daddy. Dale don't know any better – he watches TV, I read non-fiction.'

The Remains of the Day (James Ivory)

The Observer, 14 November 1993

'A family with the wrong members in control – that, perhaps, is as near as one can come to describing England in a phrase.' Thus wrote George Orwell in his pamphlet *The Lion and the Unicorn*, and a few lines later he comments, 'One of the dominant facts of English life during the past three-quarters of a century has been the decay of ability in the ruling class.' One would be surprised if Kazuo Ishiguro had not read Orwell's essay, for it echoes through his novel, *The Remains of the Day*, and the superlative film that director James Ivory, screenwriter Ruth Jhabvala and producer Ismael Merchant have made of it.

The Remains of the Day has two principal dramatic strands. The first is an allegory of early twentieth-century Britain as represented by that old standby, the stately home, in this case the Oxfordshire pile of Lord Darlington (James Fox, once again the weak aristocrat). A benevolent, blinkered survivor of the Great War, Darlington gets into ever murkier political waters as he attempts to assure peace in our time during the thirties.

First he hosts an international conference designed to establish friendly relations with Nazi Germany. Then he entertains a Mosley-like fascist attended by black-shirt thugs. Finally Darlington Hall is the site of a clandestine meeting between Hitler's ambassador, Joachim von Ribbentrop, Lord Halifax, the Foreign Secretary and Neville Chamberlain.

The other strand to the film is the story of Darlington's butler, Stevens (Anthony Hopkins), a man committed to service, order and hierarchy, who equates the notion of a 'great butler' with Great Britain itself. Stevens's opinions and emotions are as repressed as his hair, and he has both compromised himself by his unquestioning devotion to Lord Darlington and lost his one opportunity of romantic fulfilment by not responding to the open, warm-hearted housekeeper Miss Kenton (Emma Thompson).

The Remains of the Day is, in part, a psychological road movie that brings to mind Bergman's *Wild Strawberries*. In both, a man past his prime, making a sentimental journey across country by car, looks back on an apparently successful life that has, in fact, been blighted by his refusal to express emotion and to open his heart to love.

In the film, Stevens's journey has been moved on two years to 1958, so that he is going to the West Country after the Suez debacle rather than before it. And he is to have his first meeting with Miss Kenton in twenty years not in Cornwall but in the Somerset seaside town of Clevedon, suggesting connections between Darlington Hall and Cliveden, the Thames-side country house where von Ribbentrop was a regular guest. A further sharpening (some might say coarsening) comes in turning the Jewish servants his lordship fires during a bout of anti-Semitism from local girls into Jewish refugees.

The allegorical aspect is somewhat pat and more insistent than in the book. But it provides a moral force that takes the film far away from the realm of nostalgia (though as always with Merchant-Ivory productions, the social detail of the recent past is lovingly re-created) and forms an essential context for the portrait of Stevens.

In the novel, Stevens is a classic case of what Wayne Booth calls 'the unreliable narrator' – someone who tells us less than he knows, reveals more than he intends, and doesn't speak for the author. Rejecting the device of voice-over narration, the makers have wisely decided to rely on Anthony Hopkins's ability to convey every kind of reticence, deference, suppressed emotion, unconfronted doubt, irritation and superiority through the tilt of his head, a slight twitch, the shift of a shoulder, a cold flicker of a smile, a minute tightening of the eyes.

This is great screen acting. It is complemented by Emma Thompson's generous, spontaneous Miss Kenton, and there are obvious parallels with the characters Hopkins and Thompson played last year in *Howards End*. A formidable cast of British character actors surrounds them, and altogether this is a remarkable film that brings honour to everyone involved.

1993

The Age of Innocence (Martin Scorsese)

The Observer, 30 January 1994

In 1921 the trustees of Columbia University, overruling the Pulitzer judges' decision to award that year's fiction prize to Sinclair Lewis for *Main Street*, presented it instead to Edith Wharton for *The Age of Innocence*, now immaculately filmed by Martin Scorsese. They regarded Lewis's book as subversively satirical of current American values, in contrast to Wharton's apparent celebration of the high moral tone of a late-Victorian New York. Ironically, Lewis had dedicated his savage novel to Wharton, regarding her as his mentor, and he would have agreed with Edmund Wilsons's comment a couple of years later that 'Mrs Wharton was perhaps the first American to write with indignant passion *against* American values as they had come to present themselves by the end of the century.'

Edmund Wilson, however, saw that a change had come over Wharton in the course of writing *The Age of Innocence*. At the age of sixty, as she looked back from a long period of European exile to the upper-class New York of her young womanhood, her acerbity was tempered by nostalgia; she lovingly recreated a world that had once stifled her. This ambivalence, like much else in the book, is superbly caught by Scorsese. His subtle, supple, sinuous movie takes its place beside two masterpieces that have clearly influenced him, both based on novels by patrician writers covering much the same period as *The Age of Innocence*: the Orson Welles 1942 film of *The Magnificent Ambersons* (which brought Booth Tarkington the 1918 Pulitzer Prize), and the 1963 Luchino Visconti adaptation of di Lampedusa's *The Leopard*.

The Age of Innocence has a large, detailed *dramatis personae*, is full of complex ethical and moral nuance, and takes place in a wonderfully realised world of an old-money New York threatened by the *nouveaux riches*, where people can gain a reputation as authorities on form, fashion and family. There are great set-pieces of balls and dinners, of summer in Newport and winter in Florida, of households where the paintings, china and silver express and possess their owners. This was a time when Central Park was on the edge of the wilderness and Penn Station was across the Hudson in New Jersey. 'Making love' then meant flowery verbal overtures; unbuttoning a lady's glove was an erotic adventure; a passionate kiss was a commitment for life.

But the essential plot is simple, and it turns on the choices confronting the twenty-seven-year-old Newland Archer (Daniel Day-Lewis), a rich, handsome lawyer whose name is a conflation of the central characters of Henry James's novels from the late 1870s – Christopher Newman of *The American* (1877) and Isobel Archer of *The Portrait of a Lady* (1881). Should Newland do the socially proper thing of marrying the virginal, complacent May (Winona Ryder), member of another established family, or should he follow his heart and pursue May's older cousin, the witty, rebellious Ellen Olenska (Michelle Pfeiffer), who has disconcerted the established order by deserting her husband, a dissolute Polish count, and returning to New York? The dilemma is expressed visually when Newland dispatches yellow roses to the Countess and lilies-of-the-valley to his fiancée from a smart florist, and the wide screen is filled first by an explosion of yellow, then by a calming white that dissolves into Newland escorting May through a white aviary filled with colourful birds.

After Newland marries May, he is given a second, last chance of freedom to escape from a sterile relationship and to elope with Ellen. He does not take it, and thirty years later, visiting Paris as a fifty-seven-year-old widower, Newland rejects his son's invitation to see Ellen again.

Looked at it in one way, Newland, Ellen and May are victims of a narrow, snobbish, hypocritical society that has imported the restrictive class values of the Old World to America. On the other hand it is a society that offers certainty, order and stability, and that rewards the decent, the respectful, the dutiful. To leave all this behind for a romantic passion might prove less satisfying than staying home to fulfil honoura-ble obligations and cherish within oneself the regret for desires denied, for an ecstatic freedom unrealised and probably unrealisable. Countess Olenska demonstrates her strength by returning to Europe. Does Newland prove his weakness in remaining with May?

There is an understandable impulse on the part of readers and viewers to will Newland to go up to the Countess's apartment in the epilogue. In a recent *New Yorker* essay, John Updike called Wharton 'merely perverse' and suggested that 'it seemed possible that Hollywood might exercise its prerogative and have Archer do what any red-blooded widower would do, that is, take the *ascenseur*, give his hostess a hug, and spend the rest of his life with Michelle Pfeiffer'.

But one is reminded of a brilliant epigram coined in 1906 by the novelist William Dean Howells to cheer up Edith Wharton after the failure of a Broadway play based on her *House of Mirth*: 'What the American public always wants is a tragedy with a happy ending.' Scorsese's low-life characters face the choice between conformity and rebellion, between accepting and challenging fate. The complex social web of New York's Little Italy in *Mean Streets* has much in common with the upper-class world of *The Age of Innocence*. While extending his social range, Scorsese is digging deep into familiar territory. He has done nothing better than this masterly film. The uniformly distinguished performances are without hindsight or self-pity, and they are enhanced by the vibrant life that frames them.

And Here's One They Made Earlier – Postmodernism

The Observer, 21 August 1994

Dorothy Parker, who subscribed to Communism and succumbed to alcoholism, said that the only 'ism' Hollywood believes in is plagiarism. That was in the days when serious people exalted originality and left the lifting of plots to less scrupulous folk. Now Hollywood has discovered a respectable 'ism' – postmodernism, in two of its senses.

First, American movies have become highly self-conscious and self-referential. Second, they practise that aspect of postmodernism identified by the French critic Julia Kristeva as 'intertextuality'. Intertextuality is the process by which authors incorporate into their own films, plays and books – by parody, pastiche or direct quotation – the work of other artists, and by implication change our perception of those earlier plays, films and books. An obvious example is the incorporation of whole scenes from *Hamlet* in the 1967 play *Rosencrantz and Guildenstern Are Dead*. Tom Stoppard was, however, only following the example set by Joyce's *Ulysses* and Eliot's *The Waste Land*. Where artistic theft was once covered up, the crooks today positively flaunt their swag.

This sort of rampant postmodernism reaches new heights in the Coen Brothers' *The Hudsucker Proxy*, which opens here on 2 September. The movie conflates Frank Capra's *Mr Smith Goes to Washington* (1939),

Meet John Doe (1941) and *It's a Wonderful Life* (1946), throws in a speech from *Citizen Kane* (1941), features numerous references to Preston Sturges, and has its journalist heroine (Jennifer Jason Leigh) impersonate Katharine Hepburn. This has been the Coens' stock-in-trade from the start. Their debut was the low-budget *Blood Simple* (1983), which took its title from Dashiell Hammett's *Red Harvest*. They went on in *Miller's Crossing* (1990) to bring together the plot and characters of Hammett's *The Glass Key* with those of *Red Harvest*. A legal discussion between the Coen Brothers and the Hammett estate heard before a literate judge would be an instructive cultural occasion.

There have, of course, always been self-referential jokes in movies. Alfred Hitchcock began his brief personal appearances in *The Lodger* (1926), before the coming of sound. In *Hellzapoppin'* (1942), the comedians Olsen and Johnson pass a sledge labelled *Rosebud*. Jean Heather, the juvenile lead in *Going My Way* (1944), appeared later that year in *Double Indemnity*, and in seeking a lift from Fred MacMurray asks if he is 'going my way'. Crosby and Hope made comic walk-on appearances in each other's films, and in *Road to Bali* they come across Humphrey Bogart dragging *The African Queen* through an Indonesian swamp. But these were playful and occasional instances.

It was the *Cahiers du Cinéma* critics-turned-moviemakers of the French New Wave who introduced postmodernist self-consciousness and intertextuality into the movies, some years before these terms entered the critical vocabulary. In Claude Chabrol's *Le Beau Serge* (1958), the first real *nouvelle vague* feature, a copy of *Cahiers du Cinéma* is prominently displayed on a kitchen table. The young hero of François Truffaut's *Les Quatre cents coups* (1959) is entranced by a still of Harriet Andersson from Ingmar Bergman's *Summer with Monika*. Jean-Luc Godard's *Breathless* (1960) has an anti-hero modelling himself on Bogart, contains a shot down the barrel of a gun borrowed from Samuel Fuller's *Forty Guns* (1937), and is dedicated to Monogram Pictures, the low-budget Hollywood studio.

Godard introduced what is now a commonplace device, giving roles to his favourite directors – Fritz Lang appears as himself in *Le Mépris* (1963), as does Sam Fuller in *Pierrot le fou* (1965). The American cinema was slow to follow this fashion, though by 1985, when John Landis gave walk-on parts to a dozen directors in *Into the Night*, it was the scale rather than the practice that attracted attention.

1994

The floodgates opened in America in the sixties when Roger Corman's exploitation studio gave the critic Peter Bogdanovich his first opportunity to direct. The result, *Targets*, is now a landmark in professional ingenuity. Corman provided Bogdanovich with forty thousand dollars and two remaining days on a Boris Karloff contract and several hundred feet left over from *The Terror*, a Karloff movie. From this Bogdanovich shaped a picture about a young director (himself) preparing for the premiere of his first film, a horror flick featuring the final appearance of the great star Byron Orlok (Karloff). A parallel story concerns a middle-class boy killing his family and then shooting motorists at random on the Los Angeles freeway. The two strands come together when the boy, from behind the screen of a drive-in cinema, picks off people sitting in their cars watching Orlok's film.

In perhaps the most significant scene in the film, Bogdanovich and Karloff watch a scene from Howard Hawks's *The Criminal Code* (1930), featuring Karloff in his first starring role. In their book *The Director's Event* (1969), Eric Sherman and Martin Rubin argue that 'this moment marks what is probably the first full-fledged cinematic 'quote' in American cinema'.

In his next movie, *The Last Picture Show* (1971), Bogdanovich again used a cinema as a central image, in this case for the decline of a small town in post-war Texas. The film opens with a quotation from Vincente Minnelli's *Father of the Bride* (1950) in order to establish the middle-class values to which American girls aspired in the early fifties. It concludes with a scene from *Red River* (1948), a celebration of the Texas frontier spirit that has died with the cinema's owner.

Nowadays every movie referred to or watched in a film is significant. Television screens in mainstream features almost always show films that reflect on the characters' lives. In *Sleepless in Seattle* (1993), for instance, *An Affair to Remember* (1957) is on the box day and night.

Much of this self-consciousness comes from the growth of film studies and the fact that most young moviemakers are film-school graduates. The term 'cine-literate' is used to describe their sophistication, but it also suggests the limitations of their experience. On the other hand, in a society where references to the Bible and classical mythology are no longer widely understood, the mass media provide a new body of shared lore, a crude cultural database for the populace at large. In alluding to, parodying and reworking other people's films, moviemakers are following a practice established by Picasso with his versions of Delacroix and Manet, or Bacon with his variations on Velazquez's *Pope Innocent X*, on to which a frame from Eisenstein's *Battleship Potemkin* (1925) is superimposed. In *Western Bathers*, the most recent painting in R.B. Kitaj's current retrospective at the Tate, the nudes of Cézanne's *Bathers* are transformed into characters from westerns. The painting contains references to the films of Ford, Peckinpah and Boetticher, and there are stagger-on roles for W.C. Fields and the drunken gunslinger played by Lee Marvin in *Cat Ballou* (1965).

In a seminal 1953 essay, the American critic Robert Warshow rightly called the western 'an art form for connoisseurs'. A sense of connoisseurship, of shared social and cultural experience, is confirmed and consolidated by the referential postmodernist style. Where once spectators were invited to interpret the elaborate iconography of a Renaissance painting, now they can spot references to Billy Wilder's *Double Indemnity* in Lawrence Kasdan's *Body Heat* (1981) and John Dahl's *The Last Seduction* (1994). Or take a special enjoyment in the familiarity of *The Hudsucker Proxy*.

Three Colours: Red (Krzysztof Kieślowski)

The Observer, 13 November 1994

What makes trilogies so attractive? Is it the association with the Holy Trinity, altar triptychs, the Marxist thesis-antithesis-synthesis, the philosophical syllogism and the three-card trick? Or just the satisfactory notion of a beginning, a middle and an end. The Pagnol and Gorky trilogies brought the form to the cinema in the thirties. In the forties came Ford's 'cavalry trilogy', followed by trilogies by Wajda and Ray in the fifties. Antonioni, Bergman and Leone gave us trilogies in the sixties. In the seventies and eighties it was Britain's turn with the Bill Douglas and Terence Davies trilogies. Now for the nineties there is Krzysztof Kieslowski's trilogy, completed by *Three Colours: Red.*

Film trilogies are either biographical or thematic. Firmly in the latter category, Kieslowśki's takes its title from the French *Tricolor*, identifying the colours blue, white and red with liberty, equality and fraternity. The films are in effect meditations on the contemporary meaning of the trio of revolutionary demands made two hundred years ago, locating the first film in France, the second in France and Poland, and the third in Switzerland. As with his treatment of the Ten Commandments in the *Dekalog* sequence, the themes here are buried, rather than paraded in an Aesopian fashion. And like all this films, the trilogy has a strong element of mysticism and an elaborate patterning to suggest parallels between the characters' lives. But since he became a Euro-director with *The Double Life of Véronique* (1991), Kieślowski has moved away from the gritty, dangerous world he portrayed in such early masterpieces as *Camera Buff* (1979) and *No End* (1984), though he returns to it in the Polish part of *Three Colours: White*.

Three Colours: Red is very much an art-house movie and uses an archetypal art-house plot. In this familiar scenario, a crusty old artist-intellectual figure – always played by a former matinée idol like Max von Sydow or Michel Piccoli and invariably protected by a beautiful younger woman – has holed up in a remote château or Alpine village. The man (or in the rare case of *The Aspern Papers*, the woman) has a secret or special gift that a questing stranger comes to obtain. In stage versions this story is most often set on a Greek island to show that the playwright recognises its source in Sophocles's *Philoctetes*. The encounter between crabby recluse and liberating intruder is an occasion for heady debates on the meaning of life, turning on reasons for the great man's decision to withdraw from the world, though the explanations tend to be disappointingly factitious and unconvincing.

The recluse in *Three Colours: Red* is a retired judge (Jean-Louis Trintignant), disgusted alike with mankind and the law, living alone on a hill above Geneva and eavesdropping on his neighbours' telephone calls. Into the misanthrope's life comes a lovely, soulful model (Irène Jacob) who has accidentally run over his pregnant dog. Their redemptive bonding is paralleled by the break-up of the romance between a weather forecaster and her law student lover, and Chance, Fate and Destiny dance attendance upon them. From the very beginning, the portents of earnestness are all around, and underlined by the swirling, often choral, music of Zbigniew Preisner.

The picture is of course superbly crafted. It gleams and purrs like a Rolls-Royce, but like a Rolls-Royce it passes aloofly through the world, oblivious to the real pain and suffering in the surrounding streets. The designer angst builds to a climactic tying together of the trilogy on a channel ferry that is little more than the higher kitsch. This is not to deny the film's pictorial beauty and its occasional power. In one unforgettable shot, young people crowd shoulder to shoulder in a record shop, each listening on headphones to different music. What a remarkable image of people isolated from each other by taste and technology, yet apparently joined in some shared brotherhood.

Heavenly Creatures (Peter Jackson)

The Observer, 12 February 1995

According to one of last week's obituaries of Patricia Highsmith, the late Marghanita Laski threatened to resign from the critics' panel of the Crime Writers' Association if Highsmith was given an award for what Laski regarded as an immoral portrait of a psychopathic killer, *The Talented Mr Ripley*. On the other hand, Graham Greene (another Laski *bête noire*) praised Highsmith for creating 'a world claustrophobic and irrational, which we enter each time with a sense of personal danger'.

The leading characters in Peter Jackson's *Heavenly Creatures* could well have come out of a Highsmith novel, and the film's tone would certainly have offended Ms Laski. But they are real people (no names have been changed) who committed a terrible murder forty years ago in Christchurch on New Zealand's South Island. With a light touch and dark wit, Jackson draws us into their claustrophobic, irrational world, giving the events an almost tragic inevitability.

In 1952, the fourteen-year-old Juliet Hulme (Kate Winslet) met the fifteen-year-old Pauline Parker (Melanie Lynskey). Juliet, a pretty, confident blonde, was English, the daughter of the remote professor Henry Hulme (Clive Merrison), Rector of the local university, and his smart, unfaithful upper-middle-class wife (Diana Kent). Pauline, an awkward, surly, intelligent brunette, was from a lower-middle-class New Zealand family, her mother taking in boarders, her father a fishmonger.

The film first presents the girls hysterically running through a park in

June 1954, the blood of Pauline's mother splattered all over them. But the story really begins after the credit titles when Juliet, as a new girl, is introduced by the headmistress to Pauline's class at a girls' secondary school run on strict English lines. Within minutes, Juliet is correcting the teacher's French, and in the next lesson, an art class, Juliet and Pauline are paired as artist and model. A classic *folie-à-deux* has begun.

The time and place are skilfully evoked – a repressed corner of the Commonwealth, devoted to gentility and dominated by the so-called 'cultural cringe' towards all things English. Equally astute is the way Jackson traces the growth of a dangerously intense, innocently homo-erotic friendship brought out by loneliness and isolation from their uncongenial families. An initial bond is forged by both being excused Physical Education – each had spent long childhood periods in hospital, Pauline with osteomyelitis, Juliet with TB. A shared love of *Biggles* books, Mario Lanza records (fragile 78s) and James Mason films leads on to a collaborative novel set in the cruel, romantic country of Borovnia, where the pair act out violent fantasies as aristocratic lovers. Their families' growing opposition to what they regard as an unhealthy rela-tionship serves only to intensify it. The ghastly climactic murder is their last, insane attempt to prevent being separated.

Jackson and his co-writer Frances Walsh draw extensively on Pauline's intimate diaries, and they take the bold step of bringing to life the mythical Borovnia and populating it with menacing plasticine courtiers, life-size versions of the figurines modelled by the girls. These fantasy sequences, which some viewers may think excessive, are all that this subtle picture has in common with the deliberately gross horror flicks for which Jackson is celebrated.

Jackson elicits performances of frightening depth from his two young actresses. For the most part, everyday reality is presented through their distorted vision, but while the adults are two-dimensional and some-times caricatured, they are not viewed unsympathetically. The death of Pauline's kindly, considerate mother is unbearably painful, not only because of the brutality but also because we are made to feel her shocked incomprehension.

The Shawshank Redemption (Frank Darabont)

The Observer, 19 February 1995

Frank Darabont's *The Shawshank Redemption* is a jail movie in a classic Hollywood mode and is about injustice, hypocrisy and the preservation of personal dignity. His script is based on a rather good Stephen King novella and has two heroes. One is the film's narrator, Red (Morgan Freeman), a middle-aged convict serving a life sentence for murder at Maine's Shawshank State Prison. The other is Andy (Tim Robbins), a young banker given two life sentences in 1947 for killing his wife and her lover. Andy had contemplated the crime but professes his innocence, and the picture covers his twenty years of incarceration, the influence he has on his fellow inmates, and his friendship with Red.

Darabont directs with authority, cutting rapidly when he needs to, but mostly creating a deliberate pace that draws us into an enclosed world of oppressive routine. His touch is firm but supple, and while there's plenty of laughter, it isn't the sort known as comic relief. Freeman makes a substantial figure of the humane, ironic Red, a youthful killer grown into a man of wisdom and probity. Andy is a more complex character, whose mystery and inner life Robbins skilfully projects without making him appear priggish. Andy uses his gifts as a financial expert to manipulate the sadistic guards and the crooked warden ('I had to come to prison to become a criminal,' he remarks), but at times he defies them to his considerable cost. While attaining a form of spiritual transcendence, he shows how humanity can be brought to an uncaring institution, and he proves that hope, friendship and fellow feeling are more important to survival than a brutal Darwinian fitness.

The Shawshank Redemption is a fine example of cinematic storytelling, and it's highly satisfying in the way it fulfils traditional expectations while providing plausible surprises. The casting is immaculate, right down to the last gnarled old convict (there's a marvellous performance from the craggy James Whitmore as the jail's oldest inmate). The British cinematographer Roger Deakins gives the picture a stylish penumbral look somewhere between Gustave Doré and Edward Hopper. Thomas Newman's effective score artfully incorporates a duet from *The Marriage of Figaro* and the Ink Spots' version of 'If I Didn't Care'.

Priest (Antonia Bird)

The Observer, 19 March 1995

Antonia Bird, who shocked audiences with *Safe*, her unflinching look at the plight of London's young homeless, has now moved north to assault us with *Priest*, a film that might well have been called *Last Exit to Bootle*. It is scripted by the eloquent Liverpool writer Jimmy McGovern, author of *Cracker*, and through its themes, setting and casting, *Priest* allies itself to the work of Ken Loach, Alan Bleasdale and Terence Davies, as well as to the TV series spawned on Merseyside from *Z-Cars* to *Brookside*.

I use the term 'assault' as a description, not as a criticism. In treating the priestly vocation, the film seeks neither the austerity of Bresson's *Diary of a Country Priest,* the asperity of Buñuel's *Nazarin*, nor the sentimental pieties of Leo McCarey's *Going My Way*. It begins in fact with a metaphor for its own style. Accompanying the opening credits, an elderly priest (James Ellis, one of the original *Z-Cars* cops) takes a hefty crucifix from his inner city church and carries it across Liverpool as if making the Stations of the Cross. He finally uses it as a battering ram against the graceful palace occupied by the callously indifferent bishop who has put him out to pasture. The subsequent story concerns his replacement, the thirty-year-old Father Greg Pilkington (Linus Roache), a handsome young idealist of conservative views, who rejects the notion of using society as a scapegoat for the ills of man.

Father Greg is put in to assist his diametrical (or dialectical) opposite, the forty-something Father Matthew Thomas (Tom Wilkinson), a radical priest with four years experience of liberation theology in Latin America, an unconcealed contempt for the church hierarchy, a conception of his role as part social worker, part guerrilla leader, and a beautiful black housekeeper (Cathy Tyson), who openly shares his bed. The education of Father Greg proceeds apace as he discovers how limited are his resources in the face of the apathy, hostility and hopelessness of his parishioners. It is a film of ferocious confrontation, both of issues and between people, and one key sub-plot deals with a demonic child abuser whom Greg cannot denounce because he's heard both the man's and his abused daughter's confessions.

On top of all this, Greg is a guilt-ridden homosexual, an aspect of his character only revealed half-an-hour into the film. During an emotional crisis he removes his dog collar, puts on a leather jacket and goes cruising. In a gay bar he picks up the kindly Graham (Robert Carlyle, the Glaswegian hero of Loach's *Riff Raff*) and lust leads, a little too soon perhaps, to love. But an indiscreet public reunion with Graham following another professional crisis brings Greg into the courts, on to the front page of the *Liverpool Echo*, and up before the bishop, his congregation and his own conscience.

Can people be changed by religion without an unjust society being challenged? What should the church's role be in a predominantly secular culture? How are supposedly eternal truths to be interpreted? How different should priests be from their congregation and what is the nature of vocation today? These and other matters are earnestly (and sometimes comically) debated at the kitchen table, in church and on walks round the parish. And when people aren't talking, Bird resorts to rapid cross-cutting. Indeed, what makes *Priest* exhilarating and bearable is precisely its ferocious energy, its decision to let everyone speak their minds and spell everything out in didactic speeches and explosive accusations, and its rejection of subtlety and English understatement. Given these limits, it is admirably acted.

Hoop Dreams (Steve James)

The Observer, 2 April 1995

In the late fifties, following the heart-searching provoked by the launch of the first Sputnik, it seemed certain that American educational institutions would start downgrading sport and elevating academic achievement. In fact, games and athletics have become more significant than ever. Equally, no one would have predicted when Lyndon Johnson embarked on creating his Great Society in the mid-sixties that far from being transformed, the lives of urban blacks would get steadily worse over the next thirty years. Both these disappointing developments lie behind *Hoop Dreams*, one of the best American films of this decade and among the finest documentaries ever made.

Lasting nearly three hours, and the joint work of Steve James, Fred

Marx and Peter Gilbert, the film follows the fortunes from 1987 to 1991 of two black Chicago teenagers, Arthur Agee and William Gates. Both see their aptitude for basketball as a 'ticket out of the ghetto', a way of escaping a world of unemployment, crime and drugs. They dream of being recruited by a leading high school, where decent teaching and superior coaching will bring the academic grades and sporting success that will win them athletic scholarships to a major university.

Following that, there is the National Basketball Association and the prospect of emulating Magic Johnson and Michael Jordan. Of course the majority merely dream, while few of the gifted make it even to college, let alone the NBA.

Hoop Dreams is three things. First, it is an intense human drama that begins with the boys being spotted at fourteen by a scout for St Joseph's, a fee-paying Catholic high school in a well-off suburb. Both have feckless absentee fathers and strong, self-sacrificing mothers who courageously hold the home together through times that are usually bad and often worse. We feel for and suffer for the two families, sharing their hopes and disappointments,

Second, *Hoop Dreams* is about a system involving schools, politicians, the media and sports promoters that stretches from the bottom of society to the top. A healthy, recreational activity has been turned into a brutal business that ruthlessly exploits kids from the age of twelve upwards and corrupts everyone associated with it. I speak with a certain authority, because some years ago my main source of income came from helping semi-literate footballers and basketball players on athletic scholarships make the academic grade at Indiana University by 'assisting' them with their weekly essays and term papers.

At St Joseph's, Gates and Agee become the creatures of coach Gene Pingatore, whose job is to provide a winning team at all costs. As one of the university coaches in the film remarks: 'We've got to fill the arenas to keep our jobs.' When Gates gets into academic difficulty, Pingatore gets special assistance for him from the head of *Encyclopedia Britannica*. Agee, on the other hand, is doing less well beneath the hoops, so Pingatore uses the poor grades to pass him over to a free, all-black inner city school. As Agee's parents have run up debts at St Joseph's, the holy fathers demand payment in full from a family on welfare before they'll release Arthur's records without which he cannot graduate from his new school.

Finally, *Hoop Dreams* is both a microcosm of American society as seen by its less fortunate members, and a metaphor for an aggressive, exploitative way of life that deceives people by playing with their dreams and creating false values. But at the end, after countless vicissitudes, neither boy confronts either disaster or clean-cut triumph. The producers' report on their subjects' situation as of 1994 is better than we might have expected, and far more complicated. Yet for all the cliff-hanging scenes of Arthur and William on the court, ball in hand with seconds left in a needle match, the most memorable and uplifting moment comes when Arthur's mother breaks into joyful tears as she receives her diploma as an auxiliary nurse.

The bluntest comment in the film is made by Spike Lee addressing the high school stars gathered at the Nike All-American Basketball Camp on the Princeton campus to be appraised by university recruiting staffs. 'This thing is revolving around money,' he tells them.

Once Were Warriors (Lee Tamahori)

The Observer, 16 April 1995

Lee Tamahori's *Once Were Warriors* opens on an idyllic New Zealand landscape, a crystal lake beneath imposing snow-capped mountains. This clichéd tourist-office image of the country seems strangely still, almost surreal. The camera then pans to the left, revealing that it isn't a real landscape. It's a picture on a billboard beside a bustling urban motorway that carries noisy, polluting traffic through a depressed Maori ghetto in Auckland, the country's largest city. What we are to be shown by Tamahori and his screenwriter, Riwia Brown (she's adapted Alan Duff's novel), is a New Zealand that lies behind the official face presented to the world.

In the opening reel, the film vividly introduces, first separately, then together, the eight members of the Heke family – *déracinés* working-class Maoris – and locates them in a shoddy milieu vibrant with a danger bred of desperation. They are the imposing, macho Jake (Temuera Morrison), who's just lost his dead-end job; his handsome wife Beth (Rena Owen);

and their five children, two of them infants, the other three teenagers – Gloria, a beautiful thirteen-year-old with literary gifts, and her elder brothers, the surly, forceful Nig, and the withdrawn Boogie, both running with street gangs. Like members of many native populations, American Indians for example, and Australian aboriginals, they have lost touch with their traditional culture without being assimilated into the world of those who dispossessed them. This harsh, almost unbearably painful picture never sentimentalises their situation.

For sixteen years Jake and Beth have cheerfully muddled by. She has put up with his fecklessness and violence, because she loves him and cannot resist his sexual magnetism. There is also her pride. It transpires that Beth is from a regal Maori family and Jake from the former slave class. When she left her tribal settlement to marry him, her parents predicted disaster, and she has been determined to prove them wrong. But this classically hypergamous relationship has bred resentment in Jake and been an additional factor in his disturbed personality. He becomes increasingly abusive towards his wife and children, and a series of crises culminates in tragedy, forcing Beth to desert him and reclaim her ethnic identity.

The brutal, irresistible Jake, boozing with his mates, bringing them home to disrupt the household, is an unromanticised version of Tennessee Williams's Stanley Kowalski. Indeed, there's a close resemblance between *A Streetcar Named Desire* and *Once Were Warriors*, including a major theme of the rape and destruction of innocence. But this is *Streetcar* seen from the wife's point of view, and while it isn't a feminist tract, Beth is presented as a strong, long-suffering woman. Having sacrificed everything to hold the family together, she finally recognises limits to what she should endure. It is her character and behaviour that turn a potentially dispiriting picture into an affirmative experience.

On the other hand, however appalling and inexcusable his actions, Jake emerges as a pathetic, frustrated victim, incapable of understanding and transcending the conditions that have shaped him. Rena Owen and Temuera Morrison give towering performances, almost epic in their intensity, and they head an excellent cast.

With *The Piano*, *Heavenly Creatures* and *Once Were Warriors*, New Zealand is reaching cinematic peaks no one could have anticipated twenty years ago. Of course, the Australian New Wave prompted its antipodean neighbours into creating their own cinema, but now it's the Australians who are in the doldrums. The major pictures of the seventies tackled subjects such as national identity and spiritual transactions with the land. These noble topics have been exhausted or set aside, the pioneer directors now work abroad, and the dominant preoccupations of their successors are the bitter frustrations and small compensations of suburban life in the sprawling coastal cities.

Land and Freedom (Ken Loach)

The Observer, 8 October 1995

The Spanish Civil War is a milestone in the history of socialism and it is appropriate that Ken Loach's *Land and Freedom* should open in the week of Labour's annual conference. The Party's greatest Prime Minister, Clement Attlee, whose 1945 government transformed this country, was very proud when, during his visit to Spain in 1938, the Number One Company of the International Brigade's British Battalion was named the 'Major Attlee Company'. Looking back on his experiences in Spain, Orwell wrote: 'Every line of serious work that I have written since 1936 has been written, directly or indirectly, against totalitarian and for democratic Socialism, and I understand it.'

Scripted by his regular collaborator, Jim Allen, Loach's movie is a visceral, emotional and intellectual experience, and among the finest films of the decade. It begins in 1994 with the death of Dave Carne, an octogenarian working-class Liverpudlian, living alone in a tower block, its hallways daubed with anti-NF graffiti. His granddaughter, Kim, a woman in her twenties, opens a case of his mementoes – press-cuttings, photographs, letters – that take her back to labour history and the Spanish Civil War. Among the souvenirs is a handful of Spanish earth wrapped in a red neckerchief. It transpires that the unemployed David (the excellent Ian Hart), an idealistic member of the Communist Party, made his way to Spain to fight for the loyalist cause, and (as Orwell did) found himself serving with a military group attached to POUM, the Marxist revolutionary group, in Barcelona. With his customary flair for verisimilitude, Loach makes us feel that we are alongside Dave, training with the militia, taking part in battles, thrilling to the comradeship of fellow volunteers united in opposition to fascism.

Like Hemingway's *For Whom the Bell Tolls*, *Land and Freedom* concentrates on one small area of the Civil War and its hero too has a gentle affair with a beautiful Spanish revolutionary (Rosana Pastor). Unlike Hemingway's Robert Jordan (a character written with Gary Cooper in mind), Dave is no handsome Hollywood hero and he does not die with his illusions intact. He sees his democratic militia destroyed by Communists bent on eliminating opponents and troublesome individuals of any political hue in the interests of Stalinist realpolitik.

The film's clever framing device serves several essential functions. First, by showing everything through Dave's eyes, Loach and Allen don't have to deal with the war in its infinite complexity. Second, the movie can switch from incident to incident as Kim sifts through Dave's letters home. Most importantly, the flashback technique links the double learning process of grandfather and granddaughter. In Spain in 1937, David has a painful lesson that leads from naivety to maturity without making him a cynic. He retains his belief in the essential decency of working people and their right to their own destinies, individually and as a community. In Liverpool in 1994, Kim learns a vivid, sobering yet revivifying lesson from her grandfather's legacy. In a moving, affirmative final scene, she reads a poem by William Morris over his grave, drops the Spanish earth onto his coffin and raises the red neckerchief in a salute.

Seven (David Fincher)

The Observer, 7 January 1996

The great detective and the super criminal are complementary figures. Creations of the modern city, they use their understanding of its labyrinthine nature for contrasted purposes. As literary characters both stem from the early nineteenth century, when Poe created the archetypal great detective in Auguste Dupin and Balzac the archetypal super-criminal in Vautrin. At the end of the century, Conan Doyle brought them together as Holmes and Moriarty, and fifty years later Jorge Luis Borges presented them in stark diagrammatic form in his story 'Death and the Compass'. Directed by David Fincher from Andrew Kevin Walker's brilliant screenplay, *Seven* belongs self-consciously to this tradition. I do not expect to see many better pictures in 1996.

The unnamed setting of *Seven* is not a city, but the city, an emblematic metropolis of shadows, unceasing rain and urban decay, its peeling walls exuding millennial pessimism. It's a nightmare version of New York, but a New York that is within a short drive of something resembling the Mojave Desert. A disillusioned, middle-aged homicide detective, William Somerset (a cool, dignified Morgan Freeman), who has one week to serve, is about to hand over to an idealistic young successor, Lieutenant Mills (an edgy Brad Pitt), a newcomer to the city. William Somerset is clearly intended to evoke the worldly-wise Maugham (there's a passing joke about *Of Human Bondage*). Does the name of the hardworking new man hint at Mills of God? The film involves us in this kind of speculation, just as the film's plot directs the detectives to arcane clues. But we don't immediately start thinking like this, because *Seven* initially presents itself as a stylised police procedural thriller with a conventional plot about breaking in a new partner.

Very soon Somerset and Mills are after a serial killer of fiendish intelligence and ingenuity. This also seems conventional material, though extremely well handled. The murderer, however, is a religious maniac, a moralist bent on a sequence of killings based on the Seven Deadly Sins, in which the victims are executed according to their deserts, in obscenely cruel ways. He's a fitting opponent for the formidable Somerset and the headstrong Mills, who need him as much as he needs them as he proceeds to get metaphysical on their asses.

In spotting the first clues, Somerset sets Mills on reading Chaucer, Dante and Milton, which the younger man does by way of students' cribs. He also taps into a covert FBI information bank by which potential criminals can be spotted from the patterns of books they borrow from public libraries, a notion possibly inspired by a line of inquiry employed by Woodward and Bernstein in *All the President's Men*. The portentous mood is always undercut by a steady wit.

Seven is a dazzling movie (if a movie bereft of primary colours can be said to dazzle), and it engages the mind while jabbing the solar plexus. There are chases and fights, but usually what we see is the aftermath of murder, not the act itself. The violence is in our minds as we become involved in a debate about moral decay, evil and retribution. Like *The Usual Suspects*, the less you know about the film the more you'll enjoy it first time around, and I will refrain from revealing a crucial feature that *Suspects* and *Seven* share. Incidentally, although this is an American movie, the production designer, Arthur Marx, is British, and the cinematographer, Darius Khondji (whose recent films include *Delicatessen* and *City of Lost Children*), is French.

Rendez-vous in Paris (Eric Rohmer)

The Observer, 11 February 1996

The oldest of the *Cahiers du Cinéma* critics who made up the French New Wave, Eric Rohmer was the last to establish an international reputation. He was nearly fifty when *My Night with Maud* opened to almost universal acclaim in 1969, and he has kept up a steady output of quiet, quirky films about the complicated romantic lives of the French. *Rendez-vous in Paris* demonstrates that, at seventy-five, his touch is as deft as ever.

Most of Rohmer's characters nowadays are just about old enough to be his grandchildren, yet he neither patronises nor sentimentalises them. All his pictures have been invitations to suffer fools gladly. They may be clever, eloquent, earnest and beautiful fools, but like all of us, they are – in the eyes of the Catholic God who hovers, usually unmentioned, over Rohmer's universe – fools none the less. Shot on 16mm and a minute budget, *Rendez-vous in Paris* is a portmanteau film in which the stories get steadily better.

In the first, *The Seven O'Clock Rendez-vous*, a student discovers her boyfriend is two-timing her and wrongly suspects another man of stealing her wallet. In *The Benches of Paris*, an unnamed woman with a boring technocrat lover has a series of chaste meetings in parks with a handsome literature teacher from the suburbs. She won't go to his place because she can't stand the *banlieue*, and when she decides to leave her lover she also drops the teacher because, as the lover's mirror image, he has ceased to have any significant existence. The third and wittiest story, *Mother and Child 1907*, takes its title from a Picasso painting and centres on an artist who takes a tedious Swede to the Picasso Museum and leaves her, arranging a meeting for the following night. But on his way home he is attracted by a stranger and follows her back to the museum and into an emotional and intellectual tangle.

Rohmer has explored France in a way that no filmmaker has explored Britain – *La Collectionneuse* takes us to the Côte d'Azur, *My Night with Maud* to Clermont-Ferrand, *Pauline on the Beach* to Normandy, and there are films set in Le Mans, Biarritz and beside Lake Annecy. But his adopted Paris is especially close to him, and the three stories of the new film are linked by a girl singing in the streets to the accompaniment of an accordion. This homage to René Clair's *Sous les toits de Paris* invites us to see the film in a cinematic tradition that celebrates the city. The self-consciousness it entails is given an ironic twist when the couple in the central story decide to spend a weekend posing as tourists, meeting at the Gare de l'Est, asking for directions on the Métro and making their way to a hotel in Montmartre. Naturally the plan leads to disaster.

Secrets & Lies (Mike Leigh)

The Observer, 26 May 1996

Mike Leigh's films are so good that you have to see them a second time to realise how well they work. The first time around you are so emotionally involved with the characters that you think you have encountered unvarnished life, almost artlessly conveyed. You don't go away with an image planted in your mind or with memories of a grand landscape or full of admiration for a graceful crane shot.

This has led to Leigh being undervalued as a filmmaker and to his fans almost apologising for there being something uncinematic about his pictures. This is far from the case, though I could not have written this review of his *Secrets & Lies* (winner of the Palme d'Or at Cannes last Monday), which I think is as fine as anything he has done, after a single viewing.

The film's first twenty-odd minutes puzzle the spectator. We ask ourselves who are this battling working-class mother and daughter, Cynthia (Brenda Blethyn) and Roxanne (Claire Rushbrook)? How are they related to the kindly lower middle-class portrait photographer Maurice (Timothy Spall) and his embittered Scottish wife, Monica (Phyllis Logan), and what is wrong with their marriage? And where does the twenty-seven-year-old black optometrist Hortense (Marianne Jean-Baptiste), living alone, her parents recently dead, fit in? As we come to know these people over a period of several summer months, the pieces fall into place. We first come to realise that the slatternly Cynthia is Maurice's unmarried sister, who raised him after their mother's death; that Cynthia's youthful promiscuity (which produced Roxanne) was a search for love and acceptance, and that Roxanne's rebellion (she has dropped out of college to work as a road sweeper) is directed at both her mother for begetting her, and her aunt and uncle for attempting to own her.

Hortense's role crystallises in a beautifully played scene with a perceptive social worker (Lesley Manville). We discover that she was adopted and has decided to find her biological mother (her 'birth mother' as the social worker calls her), who turns out to be white and is indeed Cynthia. What we have here, in effect, is a mixture of Ibsen and Sophocles, of a dangerous Oedipus-like search and of the exposure of the eponymous secrets and lies. As Maurice tells Hortense towards the end, 'You were determined to find out the truth and were prepared to take the consequences, and I admire you for that.' As an optometrist, Hortense's job is to help people see clearly; as a photographer, Maurice's role is to put the best face on life.

These richly three-dimensional characters, so perfectly conceived and played, become intensely real for us, and we observe them change and develop as they confront their real selves. Cynthia's good nature and humour help Hortense overcome her grief, and this new-found daughter encourages Cynthia to achieve a dignity and self-respect that have been denied her. The movie can switch from laughter to tears and back in a second, but it is about the painful human comedy. It isn't satirical in intent, though there are some sharp scenes of Maurice at work with a succession of sitters, whom he coaxes into laughter. And unlike earlier Leigh films there are no malevolent characters. The nearest thing to menace occurs in a slightly puzzling scene in which the former owner of

Maurice's studio, an Ibsenesque figure from the past, returns from Australia a drunken malcontent, and when he departs Maurice remarks: 'There but for the grace of God.' Maurice, the embodiment of decency, can also be sententious.

But Leigh's skill lies not merely in the lines he and his cast write or in the performances he elicits. The extended sequence of Maurice at work is a masterly comic montage. The visual details of dress and décor are impeccable down to the clumsy white phone that Cynthia clutches and the neat black phone Hortense so deftly holds as they converse. The over-furnished home Monica has created to make up for the children she cannot have is contrasted with Cynthia's cluttered house in which Maurice was raised.

Most important, perhaps, is Leigh's unerring sense of where to place his camera. When Hortense and Cynthia first meet they sit beside each other uneasily, framed in a two-shot that is held for about five minutes. They talk self-consciously, rarely making eye contact, their isolation emphasised by the empty tables around them in a drab Holborn café. At the next encounter, however, they're more relaxed, facing each other over the table in an Italian restaurant. Likewise, at the brilliantly orchestrated family gathering, when Hortense comes to meet her new relatives at a twenty-first birthday party Maurice is giving for Roxanne, there is another five-minute take. A static camera frames six people at a garden table so that no one is especially favoured, and we see them socially interact.

The cinematographer Dick Pope uses deep focus so that Maurice, who is at the barbecue behind them, is vividly of the group yet standing apart. After that long take, we cut to the inside of the house for truth-telling and blood-letting, and here Leigh cuts between big close-ups and shots in which a foreground figure is in focus and a second person behind them slightly out of focus. This is masterly moviemaking that never draws attention to itself.

Fargo (Joel Coen)

The Observer, 2 June 1996

Gore, black humour, outlandish violence, eccentric characters, knowing references to old movies, clever manipulations of cinematic genres – these are the characteristics of the films of both the Coen brothers and Quentin Tarantino. Their debut movies (respectively *Blood Simple* and *Reservoir Dogs*) were unveiled to considerable acclaim at Cannes, where they went on to win the Palme d'Or, the Coens for *Barton Fink* (1991), Tarantino for *Pulp Fiction* (1994). They work on the fringe of the American film industry, one foot in the art house, one foot on a rung of the Hollywood ladder. The chief differences between them are that the Coens are more mordant and appear to have cultural roots of a sort absent from the work of Tarantino.

Co-scripted by Ethan and Joel Coen, directed by Joel, *Fargo* is set in the brothers' native Minnesota, home to immigrant Swedes, and – as they explain in the introduction to the published screenplay – to a wintry, tundra-like landscape that recalls the Russia of their grandmother's childhood. Though closely based, they say, on a true story of 1987, *Fargo* essentially reworks their film noir *Blood Simple*, but with greater depth of character and a new respect for human decency. William H. Macy (a David Mamet regular) plays Jerry Lundegaard, an infinitely sad car salesman working for his wealthy, overbearing father-in-law Wade Gustafson (Harve Presnell). Deeply in debt, Jerry hires a pair of seedy out-of-town crooks (Steve Buscemi, Peter Stormare) to fake the kidnapping of his wife.

After a farcical abduction in which the wife runs around the house wrapped in a shower curtain like a stage ghost, tragedy ensues when the kidnappers kill a highway patrolman and two witnesses on a country road. These murders introduce the movie's heroine, the seven-months pregnant Marge Gunderson (Frances McDormand), a small-town police chief. She's happily married to an ornithological painter, whose ambition is to get his painting of a mallard accepted for a postage stamp. The perceptive Marge can interpret clues and track down criminals, but cannot fathom greed or the darker side of human nature.

The beautifully acted *Fargo* is an adroit piece of story-telling, constantly cutting between the desperate Jerry, the patient Marge and the two crooks (one loquacious, one silent). Their paths only occasionally cross. Except for the killers, everyone has a name that ends in Gaard, Son or Kvist, speaks with a singsong Scandinavian lilt, says 'Ja' instead of 'Yeah', and is a stranger to irony. Carter Burwell, the Coens' regular composer, provides a lyrical score with an elegiac melody that suggests a Swedish folk song, and the misty snow-covered landscape gives the picture a pristine, fairy-tale look. Nothing, of course, shows up blood the way snow does, and there is plenty of both. Probably influenced by *On Her Majesty's Secret Service*, when one of Bond's enemies is eaten by a snowplough, the Coens concoct a darkly comic scene in which Marge comes across one of the crooks turning the Minnesota landscape incarnadine as he uses an electric wood chipper to dispose of a body.

Lone Star (John Sayles)

The Observer, 13 October 1996

Among moviemakers now in their prime, the American independent John Sayles is matched only by Bertrand Tavernier for the searching political intelligence he brings to bear on the world around him. Like Tavernier, Sayles has a warm humanistic heart, and since his debut in 1980 with *The Return of the Secaucus Seven*, he has illuminated the contemporary American scene and its recent past in a rare manner.

In *City of Hope* (1990), a complex mosaic movie in the Altman tradition, Sayles anatomised a declining New Jersey town, ending on a howl of despair. In *Lone Star*, he brings a similar technique to bear on a Texas township near the Mexican border, but concludes on a more hopeful note. The interconnectedness of the citizens in *City of Hope* was shown by starting a shot on one person then switching to another as they passed in the street. To show the seamless connection between past and present, the flashbacks in *Lone Star* begin with the camera panning from 1995 to 1957 without a cut or dissolve. This is a film about history, as well as a thriller, and all the violence is in the past.

It begins with two men out in the arid countryside on a deserted army rifle range; it ends with a man and a woman staring at the blank screen of an abandoned drive-in cinema. Between these striking images of nature being allowed to reclaim land on which its despoilers have left strange clues of their presence, Sayles subtly examines the interrelated lives of three families – one black, one Anglo, one Hispanic – over forty years and the way they embody the experience of Texas since the first settlers arrived.

The two men in the opening scene discover a skull, a corroded star and a masonic ring that belonged to Charlie Wade (Kris Kristofferson), a corrupt, racist sheriff hated by the blacks and Hispanics, who vanished in 1957. Wade was succeeded by his deputy, Buddy Deeds (Matthew McConaughey), a legendary lawman who, thanks to his political acumen, was regularly re-elected until his death in 1991, surviving through an era of unprecedented social change. The .45 slug found beside Wade's skeleton may have come from Buddy's Colt. Investigating the murder is the present sheriff who happens to be Buddy's son, Sam Deeds (Chris Cooper). Sam left town to escape his oppressive father and recently returned after his marriage broke up. Also involved are Sam's childhood sweetheart, the schoolteacher Pilar (Elizabeth Peña) and Colonel Del Payne (Joe Morton), the black commandant of a nearby fort soon to be closed. Wade had murdered Pilar's father and persecuted Payne's bar-owner father.

The substantial performances and the patient way Sayles develops his detective story keep *Lone Star* from becoming overly schematic. We are involved in the sheriff's search for the truth and, like a number of recent pictures, the film is a clever spin on the Oedipus myth. There is wit in the dialogue and narrative, and the great pleasure the film gives us comes as much from the issues that are left unresolved as from the overall symmetry.

Michael Collins (Neil Jordan)

The Observer, 10 November 1996

The thin trickle of films inspired by the current Irish Troubles of these past twenty years have all been fictions, dealing mostly with their effects on bystanders and innocents. Now Neil Jordan, who made the best of them, *Angel* and *The Crying Game*, has boldly taken a hold on history with *Michael Collins*. And a pack of historians have tried to take a stranglehold on him and his movie, in the process showing little regard for the value of art, not bringing much credit to their profession.

Appropriately, it is financed largely by Warner Brothers, because this engrossing film, among the best we're likely to see this year, is in the tradition of biographical movies created at that studio in the thirties. The classic Warner biopics eschewed psychological interpretations and focused on a few key years in the lives of politicians, scientists and writers who took great risks on behalf of mankind. Jordan's picture picks up Collins (Liam Neeson) in 1916 at the end of the siege of the Dublin GPO during the Easter Rising; it ends six years later with his assassination by Republican guerrillas in West Cork at the age of thirty-one. We learn little about his early life growing up in the country and working as a clerk in London; the four months in England negotiating the treaty that brought about the Irish Free State (and provoked the subsequent civil war) are handled obliquely in a letter to his girlfriend, Kitty (Julia Roberts), and a newspaper headline. In an intelligent, well-argued diary-essay that prefaces the published screenplay, Jordan explains his decisions.

He has wedded the Warner biopic to something more dynamic, the European political thriller created by Costa-Gavras and Gillo Pontecorvo, and, as an Englishman watching *Michael Collins*, I understood what the French must have felt in the sixties on seeing Pontecorvo's *The Battle of Algiers*.

This film, at once exciting and sombre, presents a man of charm, determination, courage and humanity, constantly on the run. Willing himself towards what he sees as necessary violence to win freedom from an imperial power, Collins finds a ruthlessness within himself and an ability to instil it in others. Neeson's 'the big fella' is charismatic, a leader large in stature and character, but with a sense of inner moral questioning. No actor worries the way Neeson does, and this is a magnificent performance. We can believe that the very force of his personality has converted a trusted policeman in Dublin Castle (Stephen Rea) to the cause, persuading him to risk his life providing valuable intelligence.

Complementing Collins is his friend, the easy-going Harry Boland (Aidan Quinn), with whom he competes for Kitty's hand, and his openness is contrasted with the chilly, Machiavellian Eamon de Valera (Alan Rickman). There's a delicious moment when Dev rebukes the Big Fella for his obscene language at the very moment Collins is freeing him from Lincoln jail.

The movie is good on the way violence breeds violence, how the terror of the IRA leads to the counter-terror of the Black and Tans. In 1916, Collins is inside the GPO as it is being pummelled by British artillery. Five years later, a uniformed Collins, leading the Free State Army and committed to peace and compromise, is giving the order to bombard the law courts occupied by Republicans. The same goes for his own death at the hands of licensed assassins.

The picture has about it a tragic grandeur, an effect assisted by Chris Menges's low-key lighting. In the opening sequence, when a plain-clothes policeman picks out the ringleaders after the surrender at the GPO, the names MacDonagh, Connolly and Pearse evoke that incantation of the executed leaders at the end of Yeats's '*Easter 1916*' – 'A terrible beauty is born,' the poem concludes, and Yeats's oxymoron is echoed in a powerful sequence modelled on the climax of *The Godfather*, in which Collins spends a gentle night with Kitty in a suite at the Gresham Hotel while his killers carry out executions all over the city. A second forceful movie allusion occurs later, an echo of *The Third Man* (another story of friends torn apart, one of them also called Harry), when Harry Boland, having committed himself to the Republican cause, flees through the catacombs and sewers of Dublin, with a reluctant Collins among his pursuers.

Grosse Pointe Blank (George Armitage)

The Observer, 10 August 1997

One of the feeblest forms of humour is to give your protagonist a funny name, then make jokes about it. Naming him Pink, for instance, as the central character of a wacky comedy called *Tickle Me Pink*, or, to give a real example, calling the FBI agents played by Kathleen Turner and Dennis Quaid in *Undercover Blues* Mr and Mrs Blue. *Grosse Pointe Blank* is the story of a deliberately anonymous figure named Martin Blank returning to a high school reunion in Grosse Pointe, a smart lakeside suburb of Detroit. So for me the film was off to a bad start.

However, once you've passed this gross point of no return, it is a cool, ruthless comedy that completes the cultural domestication of a current folk hero, the professional hitman. The wry, self-contained John Cusack, the only person not to overact in *Con Air*, plays Blank, a twenty-eight-year-old assassin, who combines business with leisure when he comes to Detroit to carry out a mob contract on a federal witness and attend an anniversary gathering at his old school. Before going there, he has amusing encounters with his secretary (Joan Cusack) who handles his affairs with no-nonsense efficiency, a professional rival (Dan Aykroyd) who wants to organise an assassins' union, and a shrink (Alan Arkin), who feels so threatened by his analysand that he neither bills him nor takes notes.

Blank, it transpires, left Detroit in a moment of moral panic on the day he graduated, fleeing an alcoholic father and jilting his girlfriend Debi (Minnie Driver) on the eve of the school prom. After army service he became a government killer ('I tested high for moral flexibility') before going freelance. He now wants to use his homecoming as the occasion to turn his life in a different direction. But acting on the principle that naked is the best disguise, he tells Debi and his old schoolmates that he's a professional hitman, which they think is a very amusing explanation for his decade's absence.

As viewed from the air in establishing shots, Grosse Pointe looks like your average cosy, middle-class, Middle American suburb. But on the ground Cusack (who also co-scripted and co-produced) and director George Armitage (who made the bracing *Miami Blues*) show it to be a place unacquainted with the ordinary. Meeting his old English teacher on arrival, Blank has an exchange of jokes worthy of Bob Hope that only concludes when she hears the bell and says, 'They're playing my song.' Debi is a feisty DJ of considerable poise, her father (Mitchell Ryan) is a witty ironist, all Martin's former classmates are wildly eccentric or dangerous.

Meanwhile, four assassins are after him for different reasons, one of them a former terrorist characterised as 'a Basque-whacker from the Pyrenees'. The latter is dispatched with a pen in the neck (a promotional gift Martin had just received from an insurance broker) and his corpse disposed of in the school's incinerator, and the final shoot-out is as extravagant as anything in a John Woo action movie. This subversive, highly enjoyable picture invites us to identify with an unrepentant killer and manages to be simultaneously wild and cool. It is over-egged, but then on the menu at a most unassuming Grosse Pointe diner so is Gatsby's East Egg Omelette.

LA Confidential (Curtis Hanson)

The Observer, 2 November 1997

In his classic *Los Angeles: The Architecture of Four Ecologies*, Rayner Banham claims that 'the splendours and miseries of Los Angeles, the graces and grotesqueries, appear to me as unrepeatable as they are unprecedented'. Yet LA is the city in which, and with which, the movies have grown up, and it has become part of the vicarious experience of everyone who has been shaped by this century. Other cities may be more obviously cinematic, but LA simply is the cinema.

Carved from the best of James Ellroy's quartet of dense crime novels examining the history of post-war southern California through the prism of law enforcement, *LA Confidential* is one of the great movies about the city.

It's the best picture to date by Curtis Hanson, hitherto known as a highly efficient director of anonymous realistic thrillers. The time is 1953, the year in which Raymond Chandler wrote the elegiac *The Long Goodbye*, and Los Angeles is attempting to create a modern, corruption-free police force. The big Hollywood studios are still in business with rosters of contract stars, but television is breathing down their necks. The weekly TV show *Dragnet* (lightly disguised in the movie as *Badge of Honor*) is being made with official cooperation to aggrandise the LAPD.

Meanwhile, McCarthyism still holds sway with the suspicion of homosexuality or left-wing sympathies enough to ruin a career, and *Confidential* magazine is pioneering a new form of prurient journalism exposing the seamy side of Tinseltown life.

The freeways are just about to be built, carving up the city and changing forever its character of interlocking villages. On the criminal front, the mob is up for grabs after the imprisonment of Mickey Cohen, Bugsy Siegel's successor as the Syndicate's local enforcer.

The film's four main characters, each superbly realised, are LAPD cops. Naturally, as we are in 1953, they are white; blacks and Hispanics are suspects to be roughed up or at best patronised. Two of them have been around since before the war – the middle-aged Captain Dudley Smith (James Cromwell), an astute Irishman with a silver tongue and a flexible attitude to the law, and the fortyish Sergeant Jack Vincennes (Kevin Spacey), a debonair vice detective who's in league with the sleazy editor of *Hush Hush* magazine Danny DeVito and is becoming a celebrity as technical adviser to *Badge of Honor*.

The younger cops, both Second World War veterans, are the ambitious, self-righteous thirty-year-old Sergeant Ed Exley (Guy Pearce), a cop's son with a reputation to make, and Detective Bud White (Russell Crowe), a brutal plain-clothes man, a loner with a volcanic temper.

The struggle between good and evil, right and wrong, goes on not between but inside these men. The triumph of the picture is the way they grow and change in relation to the world around them during a period of rapid social change and competing economic forces over which they have no control. 'Why did you become a cop?' is a question they are all asked, and the way they live is their attempt to answer it.

Smith, Vincennes, Exley and White are introduced through an official inquiry into a nasty Christmas Eve incident in which drunken cops beat up three Hispanic prisoners at a downtown police station. They are next drawn together for the investigation of a massacre at a greasy spoon diner, the Nite Owl, where an off-duty cop, a hooker got up to resemble Rita Hayworth, and the entire staff are butchered.

1997   165

The case is investigated and closed as a botched hold-up by three drug-crazed blacks. But it turns out to be a Watergate can of worms that reveals an interlocked network of corruption, and everyone's career is put on the line.

To say more would be unfair, even for those who've read Ellroy's novel and have forgotten his labyrinthine plot. But at the centre of the picture is a stunning sequence, wittily and precisely backed by Kay Starr's 1952 jukebox hit 'Wheel of Fortune'. As she sings, Exley is awarded the Medal of Valor, the ground is being broken for the Santa Monica freeway, Vincennes is back as a *Badge of Honor* adviser after a period of exile, and White is becoming obsessed with a prostitute (Kim Basinger), who resembles Veronica Lake and belongs to a harem of movie-star lookalikes managed by a criminal kingpin with his claws in every pie in town.

LA Confidential is an intelligent, morally concerned movie for adults, and one of the two most entertaining films I have seen this year (Woody Allen's *Everyone Says I Love You* is the other). The script, by the director and Brian Helgeland, has been carefully worked out,

The casting and performances are perfect. And it is beautifully crafted. The same cinematographer, Dante Spinotti, lit a recent crime movie set in present-day Los Angeles, *Heat*, but whereas the stress in Michael Mann's picture is on architectural space and hard bright surfaces, *LA Confidential*, with its diffused light, presents a darker, softer, more intimate city. It is, however, a movie with a precise historical setting, not a nostalgia trip, and as unforgettable as *Chinatown*.

It's a Wonderful Life (Frank Capra)

The Observer, 7 December 1997

Christmas usually means watching *It's a Wonderful Life* on television. This week, for the first time in years, it's back in the cinema in a sparkling new print that does justice to its monochrome beauty. Premiered in the US in December 1946, it marked the return of Colonel James Stewart and Colonel Frank Capra to Civvy Street. It was not, however, especially well received, though its star and director always thought it the best thing they'd done. Not until the seventies, when a new respect for the craftsmanship and artistic sophistication of traditional Hollywood fare developed, was its reputation as the greatest of all Christmas movies established.

The story of George Bailey, the decent small-town guy dedicated to family and community who reaches a point of suicidal despair on Christmas Eve, is in fact *A Christmas Carol* with Bob Cratchit as its central character. But in Capra's version, the Scrooge figure – the wicked banker Potter – is left to go his iniquitous way, unpunished in this life. There is a great deal of anger and frustration in George, and the film revealed for the first time a complexity in Stewart's screen persona that Hitchcock and Anthony Mann were later to exploit. Quite a lot of Stewart's autobiography was also fed in – the heroic flying career (but attributed to George's brother), the devotion to the small-town businessman father, the ambition to be an architect – in the final scene there's even an accordion, Stewart's favourite instrument from boyhood.

The film is marvellously constructed as a narrative, and the town of Bedford Falls is beautifully realised, for which considerable credit must go to the husband-and-wife screenwriting team of Frances Goodrich and Albert Hackett, who wrote the *Thin Man* movies in the thirties before becoming specialists in idealised Americana in such films as *Summer Holiday*, *Father of the Bride* and *Seven Brides for Seven Brothers*. But the movie ultimately belongs to Capra in the deft rhythm of the pacing, the endless little comic touches, the emotional sweep and the Whitmanesque affirmation,

Like *Casablanca*, *It's a Wonderful Life* has entered into the cultural bloodstream. In numerous Christmas movies the film is playing on TV screens (dubbed into French in *Home Alone*), episodes of *Cheers* and *Friends* are built around it, and the two main pictures released this week explicitly refer to it. The first of these, aimed at the seasonal children's market and inspired by Mary Norton's children's novels, is *The Borrowers*, about a family of four-inch-high figures (headed by Jim Broadbent and Celia Imrie) living beneath the floorboards of a middle-class home. The plot turns on a villainous lawyer (John Goodman in great form) bent on taking over the house for an ugly property development, and he's called Potter in homage to the cruel plutocrat played by Lionel Barrymore in *It's a Wonderful Life*.

The Ice Storm (Ang Lee)

The Observer, 8 February 1998

Director Ang Lee and his regular screenwriter James Schamus have always been interested in the tensions of family life, whether in present-day Taiwan or in Jane Austen's England. In the elegant, meticulous *The Ice Storm*, working from a perceptive novel by Rick Moody (a cross between John Updike and J.D. Salinger), they turn their attention on an American family at a precise time and place – 1973. It's the time of sideburns, flared trousers and tight shirts with long collars. A nation nursing an ego badly bruised by the recently ended Vietnam War has just seen a Vice-President forced to resign and now watches a President fighting for his political life. The sexual revolution is reaching Middle America, threatening traditional bonds, offering the illusion of new freedom.

In his poem 'Musée des Beaux Arts', Auden famously observes that 'About suffering they were never wrong, the Old Masters', and praises Brueghel for a painting in which a galleon in full sail and a ploughman working a field go about their business, failing to see, or callously ignoring, Icarus as he plunges into the sea. But the overreaching Icarus, the solitary farmer and the ship's crew are linked forever by their presence in the picture and the poem it inspired, and they lend meaning to each other. And as we look back over our own lives, we see them in relation to the shaping times, and we demand of artists that they relate the private experience to the public.

The Icarus figure in *The Ice Storm* is Richard Nixon, in free fall as the Watergate scandal gathers momentum and constantly on TV in the background. The equivalent of Brueghel's sailing ship and ploughman are the middle-class professional households of affluent exurban New Canaan, Connecticut, drawn together to celebrate Thanksgiving – in particular two families, the Hoods and the Carvers. Ben Hood (Kevin Kline), a forty-year-old Wall Street investment analyst, is having an affair with Janey Carver (Sigourney Weaver), a Mrs Robinson type whose inventor husband is frequently away on business, and his infidelity is devastating his wife, Elena (Joan Allen). Each family has a pair of bright kids in their mid-teens, who get everything except love, attention and understanding. In various ways the children are alienated from their parents, most especially the fourteen-year-old Wendy Hood (Christina Ricci), a self-proclaimed radical who delivers a hilariously politicised grace at Thanksgiving dinner and is thrice caught in sexual experiments with the shy Carver boys.

The period detail is precise, evocative, but far from warmly nostalgic, though the tone is deceptively genial for much of the way. We're inclined to laugh at rather than despise the treacherous pastor, a smooth, long-haired hippie who attends a wife-swapping party, explaining that sometimes 'the shepherd needs the company of the sheep'. The film-makers clearly invite us to compare the Hoods with America's First Family just as, by naming his characters George and Martha Washington, Edward Albee makes *Who's Afraid of Virginia Woolf?* a state-of-the-nation play. Ben's bad faith and self-deception parallel Richard Nixon's; Joan Allen, outstanding as the depressed, deceived Elena Hood, echoes her performance as Pat Nixon in Oliver Stone's *Nixon*; the compromised Ben stumbles across his daughter Wendy wearing a hideous Nixon mask while she's feeling up his lover's fourteen-year-old son. Running through the picture is a succession of images of freezing and thawing, of numbness and warmth, that leads up to the climactic ice storm of the title, when black comedy is shattered by genuine tragedy and lives are utterly changed.

The photography, giving an elegiac feel to the movie, is by Frederick Elmes, who has shot all David Lynch's pictures. The strange, lilting score, its innocent tone disconcertingly at odds with the film's mood, is by Mychael Danna, who again uses early musical instruments the way he did in his haunting music for Atom Egoyan's *The Sweet Hereafter*.

Saving Private Ryan (Steven Spielberg)

The Observer, 13 September 1998

In the spring of 1944, the last thing I saw at night and the first thing I saw in the morning was a giant rectangular National Savings poster on my bedroom wall. In vivid colours it provided what was then called 'an artist's impression' of what D-Day would be like. This great CinemaScope panorama depicted our soldiers pouring out of landing craft and storming up the beach through tank traps and barbed wire. In the foreground German machine guns blazed away while in the air shells exploded and aircraft zoomed. At the top of the poster were the words, 'This Is The Year', at the bottom 'It's Up To Us To Let Em Have It'.

This childhood memory and the emotions of danger, excitement and high patriotism came flooding back as I watched the bravura opening sequence of *Saving Private Ryan*, a war movie that operates according to certain well-established conventions. One of the greatest works of art about World War II, J.D. Salinger's *For Esmé – with Love and Squalor*, written by someone who landed on D-Day and went through five campaigns before VE-Day, jumps from April 1944 to July 1945, leaving the horrors of the war to our imagination. *Saving Private Ryan*, however, is not an exercise in reticence and begins with troops praying and vomiting as they approach the Normandy shore on 6 June 1944. For twenty-five minutes it batters us unceasingly with sights of carnage and sounds of battle directed by Steven Spielberg with the dynamic brilliance that has become his trademark.

Unlike my wartime poster, all these troops are Americans. The only reference to the British involvement is a sneering mention of Montgomery's dilatoriness. Also unlike that poster, there is much mayhem and mutilation. These troops are on Omaha Beach where seas were roughest and the German resistance most intense. Working with hand-held cameras, using desaturated colour and having blood splash on to the lens, the film makes us feel that we are there, or are watching a film made by a combat camera team. Most war movies establish their characters before they go into battle. But like Cornel Wilde's *Beach Red*, which begins with an assault from the sea, *Saving Private Ryan* plunges us right into the fray with only the familiar faces of Tom Hanks as Captain Miller, US Rangers, and Tom Sizemore as the tobacco-chewing

Sergeant Horvath to cling to. The fighting is ferocious, the losses terrible, and we see and are only moderately shocked by angry, exhausted GIs killing German soldiers who emerge from pillboxes with their hands up.

The fighting over, John Williams's elegiac score swirls up as the camera contemplates the aftermath of battle and we see the name 'Ryan S' on a corpse's equipment. We then cut back to Washington DC as a female clerk, dispatching letters of condolence to the families of the dead, notices that three sons of the same Mrs Ryan of Iowa have been killed. A major and a priest break the news to her at a hilltop farm that's shot to resemble Andrew Wyeth's painting *Christina's World*, this century's most celebrated depiction of the US rural idyll. Meanwhile, patriarchal General George C. Marshall decides that the fourth brother, Private James Francis Ryan, somewhere in Normandy with the scattered 101st Airborne, must be brought home alive. Marshall is of course mindful of the deaths in 1942 of the five Sullivan brothers, also Irish-Americans from Iowa, who were drowned at Guadalcanal and who became the subjects of the 1944 film, *The Fighting Sullivans*. But Marshall reads a Civil War letter from President Lincoln to a grieving mother, and Spielberg handles these Washington scenes with a solemnity calculated to prevent us interpreting the top brass's compassion as a public relations exercise.

Captain Miller is assigned to take a handful of men through enemy lines to find Ryan, and *Saving Private Ryan* becomes a mission movie. In mission movies the characters have a limited task to perform – a killing, a kidnapping, a rescue – which briefly makes them something more significant than pawns in an immense, impersonal campaign. Their journey becomes a microcosm of the larger war through which filmmakers can express their attitude to warfare and society, or alternatively just tell an exciting tale. Most of the cynical, despairing movies about World War II made in the sixties and seventies were really about Vietnam, and consciously or unconsciously Spielberg and screenwriter Robert Rodat are using World War II to present an idealistic, upbeat riposte to the most famous Vietnam mission movie, *Apocalypse Now*.

In *Apocalypse Now*, Capt Willard is sent behind enemy lines to kill a renegade American. He leads troops who have no sense of purpose or duty, and at every stage they encounter madness and corruption. After fighting in North Africa and Italy, Miller is as mentally and physically frayed as Willard, but he is engaged in what is essentially a good war.

There is flaccid discussion about the merit of sacrificing several men to preserve one and vice versa. But just as the aim of World War II was to defeat totalitarianism and preserve democracy, so Miller's mission is also pure and positive – to save life. And ultimately most of what happens to Miller is morally affirmative. Almost the only line that could have been spoken by Willard is Miller's unlikely remark after locating Ryan (Matt Damon): 'The world has taken a turn for the surreal.'

The characters are familiar types from the melting-pot platoon – the Hungarian-American sergeant, the backwoods sharpshooter from the Bible Belt, the wise-cracking Casanova from Brooklyn, the compassionate Italian-American, the acerbic Jew, the bookish intellectual getting his first taste of battle, and of course the decent, concerned junior officer played to stereotypical perfection by Hanks. Everything they say, as well as the order in which they die, is predictable, and we are rooting for them all the way, almost cheering as they blow up Tiger tanks and slaughter Germans. Despite the brutal realism with which the climactic battle is conducted, there is no anger in the picture of the sort that jumps from the screen in Robert Aldrich's *Attack* or Sam Peckinpah's *The Iron Cross*.

The picture, in fact, has an optimistic message. 'Earn it,' Miller says to Ryan, but what that 'it' is remains vague. You suppose this injunction is aimed at the audience. Spielberg is telling his fellow Americans to appreciate the sacrifices their forebears have made and to act accordingly. To relate the film to the present, he uses a device he resorted to in *Schindler's List*, another movie that demands gratitude for a rescue mission. *Saving Private Ryan* begins and ends with three generations of a US family visiting a military cemetery in present-day France, the grandfather clearly engaged in an emotional pilgrimage. There is a touching and resonant piece of casting here. Spielberg is a great admirer of Powell and Pressburger, and the elderly veteran's wife is played by Kathleen Byron, who appeared in several of their pictures. In one of them, *A Matter of Life and Death*, she plays the angel at the reception desk who welcomes dead British and US servicemen to heaven.

The Truman Show (Peter Weir)

The Observer, 11 October 1998

One evening in 1763, Dr Johnson and James Boswell stood outside Harwich parish church discussing Bishop Berkeley's theory about the non-existence of matter and that everything in the universe exists only in the eye of the beholder. Johnson struck 'his foot with mighty force against a large stone, till he rebounded from it' and announced to Boswell: 'I refute it thus.'

Truman Burbank, protagonist of *The Truman Show*, a superbly crafted conspiracy thriller that manages to be simultaneously metaphysical, satirical and emotionally engaging, finds himself in a similar situation to Dr Johnson. But in his case, he must prove that the world around him is unreal.

The thirty-year-old Truman Burbank (Jim Carrey) lives in the perfect coastal community of Seahaven with a safe job in insurance, an adoring wife, likeable neighbours and a best friend he's known since childhood. Everything is gauged to keep him where he is – newspaper headlines proclaim Seahaven the most desirable city in America, his favourite TV soap assures him that happiness is to be found in his own backyard, posters stress the dangers of travel, and he has a phobia about crossing water.

But seeds of discontent were sown during his high school years by the lovely Lauren (Natascha McElhone), who was trying to tell him that there was something wrong with his life, before her father whisked her away forever. Eventually he begins to interrogate his fellow citizens and scrutinise his world.

Gradually, subtly, it is revealed that Truman is the only authentic person in Seahaven, which is the world's largest movie set, one of the only two man-made constructions visible from the moon. Adopted by a TV network while still in the womb, he was born on television and for thirty years has been the unknowing central character in *The Truman Show*, a 24-hour-a-day soap opera devised by the reclusive producer Christof (Ed Harris) and broadcast live around the world to an audience of millions.

On the surface, the movie is a clever satire on a manipulative mass culture that has invented orderly dream worlds into which people can escape from their messy, dissatisfying lives. It also resembles sci-fi tales like *Westworld* and *Blade Runner*, that explore controlled environments and the difference between robots and human beings. The film's screenwriter, Andrew Nicol, wrote and directed the cerebral sci-fi film, *Gattaca*. Most significantly, *The Truman Show* is an allegorical work; one of its chief influences is *The Prisoner*, Patrick McGoohan's Kafkaesque TV series of the sixties.

The setting of *The Prisoner* was Portmeirion, the picture-postcard Italian town that Clough Williams-Ellis conjured up between the wars on the coast of North Wales. *The Truman Show* likewise takes up an existing attempt by a well-meaning architect to build an ideal community. The film's Seahaven is the real-life Seaside, a planned community of picket-fenced cottages, a sort of inhabited corner of Disneyland, built thirty years ago in Florida.

The Truman Show explores two themes that run through director Peter Weir's work, the loss of innocence and the nature of the numinous, and while set in the near future, it takes us back to Old Testament concerns. To grow up in Australia, as Weir did, must make you aware of the shallow roots of city life and the power of a religion bred in the desert. The name 'Truman Burbank' suggests the contrasting ideas of a real man produced by a dream factory (i.e. Burbank, the Los Angeles home of Warner Brothers and Columbia Pictures).

His creator is a remote, benevolent despot, and the name Christof brings to mind Christ and Beckett's Godot as well as Christo, the artist who specialises in wrapping up and packaging buildings and landscapes. Seahaven is a bland world of prelapsarian innocence, a modern Eden created by mass culture.

Truman is drawn out of it by an Eve in conflict with a self-appointed God and determined to reveal to him the difference between fantasy and reality. Thus, one aspect of the movie resides in its alternative Creation myth – that mankind was born into and escaped from a soap opera.

This is that rare thing nowadays, a movie that provokes thought and discussion about both current issues and abiding concerns. But it is wittily fleshed out, full of incidental detail, such as that all the advertising in the show is product-placement.

Truman is not a cypher like his mediaeval predecessor, Everyman, and we come to care deeply for him. In an outstanding performance, Jim Carrey plays both with and against his manic screen persona to reveal Truman's inner struggles and the growth of his character, as he becomes aware of a world elsewhere. Particularly moving is the scene in which his 'best friend' (admirably played by Noah Emmerich) says: 'The last thing I'd ever do is lie to you.'

Ed Harris is also first-rate as Christof, the TV magnate as Prospero, a man who can't understand why anyone would wish to live outside his universe and without his blessing. You leave *The Truman Show* not only wishing to see it again, but wanting to have a look at Weir's earlier films.

All About My Mother (Pedro Almodóvar)

The Observer, 29 August 1999

From the start of his career in the early 1980s, Pedro Almodóvar has been fascinated by the Spanish obsession with love and death, with his countrymen's taste for histrionics and emotional extremes, and the traditional rigidity of sexual identity. But until the past couple of years I found his films, brilliantly crafted as they are, tiresomely camp. Until *Live Flesh*, which I consider a minor masterpiece, the only film I'd really admired was the 1985 *Matador*, a schematic thriller about a repressed mother's boy who wants to become a bullfighter, though he can't stand the sight of blood, and confesses to murders he hasn't committed to prove his machismo. *All About My Mother*, which brought Almodóvar the Best Director award at Cannes and should have received the Palme d'Or, is his finest film to date.

This superbly plotted, supremely confident black comedy begins with the senior nurse and single parent, Manuela (Cecilia Roth) watching *All About Eve* on TV with her handsome son Esteban the day before his seventeenth birthday. He wants to become a writer and is engaged on a school project called 'All About My Mother', for which he wants to hear about the father he's never met and about whom he knows nothing.

As a birthday present, he asks if he can attend the closed circuit TV sessions that his mother, an organ transplant coordinator conducts with young doctors, in which she plays the role of the grieving relative of a deceased patient whose organs the hospital is seeking. That night, this scene is repeated for real after Esteban is killed in a road accident while trying to get the autograph of the great actress Huma Rojo (Marisa Paredes) outside the Madrid theatre where she's appearing in *A Streetcar Named Desire*. The second part of the boy's birthday treat was a visit to the play, which has special associations for Manuela, who as a teenager played Stella in an amateur production opposite the Stanley Kowalski of the man who became Esteban's father.

From then on, *All About Eve* and *Streetcar* run through the plot as leitmotifs. Continuing her son's work of exploration, the grieving Manuela returns to Barcelona, which she left pregnant seventeen years before. The train rushes through a long tunnel towards the light; Almodóvar cuts to a shot of the glimmering city from the sky; a taxi takes Manuela past Gaudí's cathedral, but continues on to a suburban waste patch where garish whores parade for kerb crawlers. This, it transpires, is where she once worked, and she meets again her best friend, an ebullient transsexual prostitute (Antonia San Juan) who styles herself La Agrado, 'the agreeable one'.

Manuela discovers that her ex-husband, born Esteban but calling himself Lola after becoming a transvestite whore, has stolen Agrado's savings and left an idealistic nun, Rosa (Penélope Cruz), pregnant and HIV positive. She cares for both of them, and meanwhile she becomes the assistant to Huma, whose stage name (a feminised version of the Spanish for 'smoke') derives from having taken up cigarettes in imitation of her idol, Bette Davis. When Huma's drug-addicted lover is unfit to play Stella in *Streetcar*, Manuela steps in, identifying passionately with the role. Asked if she can act, she replies: 'I can lie very well, and I'm used to improvising.' Inevitably, she's accused of behaving like Anne Baxter in *All About Eve*.

This funny, sad and emotionally generous movie is about love, parenthood, friendship and loyalty, about life, art and acting roles, about re-creating oneself according to one's dreams, and about what, if anything, is truly natural. All the performances are excellent, and the picture is immaculately designed in a manner recalling Douglas Sirk's work at Universal in the fifties. While the three writers specifically cited – Truman Capote, Tennessee Williams, Federico García Lorca – are homosexual, this isn't in a narrow, excluding sense a gay picture. Nor, despite the fact that the only two heterosexual males of any consequence are a boy who dies in the first ten minutes and an old man with

Alzheimer's whose dog takes him for walks, is this a woman's picture, other than in the way it draws on certain Hollywood conventions. The film is, however, dedicated 'to every actress who has ever played an actress' and to the director's mother.

The World Is Not Enough (Michael Apted)

The Observer, 28 November 1999

Pierce Brosnan, the screen's fifth 007, makes his third appearance as the playboy hero of the Western world in *The World Is Not Enough*. He was two years old when James Bond sprang from the pages of *Casino Royale* forty-six years ago. Fittingly, Ian Fleming's first, possibly best, novel was reviewed in *Time* magazine alongside Raymond Chandler's last significant book, the elegiac *The Long Goodbye*. The honourable private eye going down those mean streets was giving way to the secret agent negotiating the labyrinth of the Cold War.

Only gradually did Fleming become a bestselling author, but the Bond cult grew steadily, reaching its apotheosis in the 1961 White House announcement that President Kennedy was a fan, and receiving scholarly validation three years later with Kingsley Amis's *The James Bond Dossier*. Parallelling this was an anti-Bond movement of great ferocity. In 1957, John Raymond's *New Statesman* review of *From Russia With Love* had saluted Fleming as a popular writer of genius. The following year in the same journal, Paul Johnson denounced Bond as a sadistic fascist; his views were widely echoed, one critic going so far as to call Bond 'a blood brother to General Massu', the liberal's current *bête noire*.

This was the atmosphere into which the first Bond movie, *Dr No*, starring the unknown Sean Connery, was released in the autumn of 1962. Although Fleming lived for another couple of years and wrote three further novels, the film of *Dr No* was the point at which Commander Bond passed out of his hands into those of the producers, Harry Saltzman and Albert Broccoli, whose daughter Barbara now manages the franchise. Fleming never achieved his ambition of matching Chandler and writing 'a thriller that was also a work of literature'.

None of the movies based on his books has been as good as his favour-ite picture, Hitchcock's *North by Northwest*. But like Sherlock Holmes, Bertie Wooster and Philip Marlowe, all versions of the English gentle-man created by earlier British public schoolboys, Fleming's hero transcended his creator. Bond has taken on an identity of his own that his manipulators have carefully gauged to fit the times, a process examined in James Chapman's *Cultural History of the James Bond Films: Licence to Thrill*.

Bond has endured. He has fought off imitators like Matt Helm and Derek Flint, cinematic opponents drawn from the novels of Len Deighton and John le Carré, and endless rip-offs, one of them starring Sean Connery's brother Neil. He has survived the disappearance of Swinging London, the decline of patriotism, the challenge of political correctness, the age of safe sex. His first superiors as MI6 chief, Bernard Lee and Geoffrey Keene, were both NCOs in the key Cold War movie, *The Third Man*; the current M, played by Judi Dench, famous for imper-sonating the Queens Elizabeth and Victoria, is a flirtatious and motherly feminist.

But while the Bond movies fed on angst, they dodged the actual conflict itself, preferring to engage with sybaritic megalomaniacs like Ernst Stavro Blofeld of Spectre rather than the real men from Smersh and the KGB. These sinister opponents inhabited underground kingdoms, part rocket silos, part Renaissance palaces, designed by Ken Adam, whose sets and ingenious devices were central to the series. Currently the subject of a major retrospective at the Serpentine Gallery, Adam created the Bond world and his contribution to the series is arguably more important than Connery's.

Until the nineties, the producers employed British journeymen direc-tors. Only in the last decade have they engaged younger men of a more independent disposition – Martin Campbell, Roger Spottiswoode and, for *The World Is Not Enough*, Michael Apted, not that you'd greatly notice the shift.

Bond composed haikus in *You Only Live Twice*, and the films are as precise, formal and witty as those Japanese poems, though rather longer. We expect a rousing pre-credit sequence, and *The World Is Not Enough* provides not one but two. Together they last twenty minutes and probably cost the GNP of an average Third World country. In the first, Bond (an increasingly confident Brosnan) has a lethal showdown in

Bilbao with Swiss bankers whose offices are in the same street as the new Guggenheim Museum.

Two more cinematic firsts of an architectural kind follow in the second pre-credit sequence, a boat chase along the Thames from the new MI6 HQ at Millbank (which is virtually blown apart) to the Millennium Dome at Greenwich.

This is virtuoso stuff, in which two of the movie's strongest actors – Patrick Malahide and David Calder – are casually killed. The audience needs the credits to recover its breath, and of course we're regaled with elegant thematic graphics in the Maurice Binder style (silhouettes of writhing girls and sexy oil pumps, orgasmic spurts of black gold) accompanied by a title song performed by the fashionable group Garbage.

Then M, from her temporary headquarters in a Scottish castle, dispatches Bond to the Middle East to pursue an insane terrorist, the former KGB agent Renard (Robert Carlyle), who's plotting to destroy the essential pipeline being built by Elektra, a plutocrat's daughter (Sophie Marceau). While infiltrating Renard's gang, Bond meets American nuclear scientist Christmas Jones (Denise Richards).

Nothing is as good as those first twenty minutes. There is some creaky plotting, and the post-Cold War villain is nasty in a commonplace way and, being realistically peripatetic, has no need for a subterranean palace to luxuriate in. Desmond Llewellyn's Q prepares to bow out and, somewhat unwisely, is preparing to hand over his workshop to the neurotic John Cleese.

But M is in the field this time, pluckily putting herself at risk; the pace is that of a high-velocity bullet; a buzz-saw hanging from a helicopter, designed to clear forests, carves up buildings and Bond's BMW as if slicing the Sunday joint. Christmas Jones, we learn, is so called in order that Bond, the double-entendre agent, can have the climactic pay-off line: 'I thought Christmas came only once a year.'

The single authentic bit of Ian Fleming is to be found in the movie's title. Though no one explains its provenance, it derives from the last book published in Fleming's lifetime, *On Her Majesty's Secret Service*, in which 007 visits the College of Arms to examine his family tree and is informed that the Bond family motto is 'The World Is Not Enough'.

My advice to the producers of the Bond movies is that they should now acquire the rights to Fleming's *Casino Royale*, disastrously filmed by other hands in 1967, and get the twenty-first century off to a good start by remaking it.

The Talented Mr Ripley (Anthony Minghella)

The Observer, 27 February 2000

Most movie versions of Henry James have been adapted by Europeans or non-Americans. The same is true of another American expatriate, Patricia Highsmith, a great admirer of James. Apart from her first book, *Strangers on a Train* (made in Hollywood by Londoner Alfred Hitchcock and former English public schoolboy Raymond Chandler), the films based on her work have been made by continental directors – René Clément, Wim Wenders, Claude Chabrol, Claude Miller.

Now British writer-director Anthony Minghella has followed up his *The English Patient* with the equally seductive *The Talented Mr Ripley*, the novel Clément filmed in 1959 as *Plein Soleil*.

Highsmith's basic story is simply put and Minghella follows it. A low-born New York charmer, Tom Ripley (Matt Damon), is dispatched by a rich businessman, Herbert Greenleaf (James Rebhorn), to bring his playboy son, Dickie (Jude Law), back from his lotus-eating life on the Mediterranean.

But instead Ripley, envious of Dickie's lifestyle, kills him and assumes his identity. The film is, however, anything but simple and Minghella has taken imaginative liberties with the novel, including making Dickie's death an unpremeditated killing rather than a murder and making Ripley a total stranger to Dickie before their first meeting.

All the scenes in America are contained in a superbly edited sequence that accompanies the opening credits, which begin with the shuffling of various adjectives in the title before arriving at the ambiguous 'talented' to describe the anti-hero.

We're shown Tom mistaken for a Princeton graduate at a smart Manhattan party because of his borrowed blazer; Tom in a different kind of uniform as a lavatory attendant at Carnegie Hall; Tom playing classical piano on stage after the audience has left; Tom being briefed by Mr Greenleaf; Tom learning about jazz as a way of ingratiating himself with the saxophone-playing Dickie; Tom triumphantly sailing out of New York aboard the *Queen Mary* on his first-class, all-expenses-paid trip.

Minghella's own credit comes over the ship steaming down the East River to Europe. Thereafter, Tom is ever present. We see and experience everything from his point of view.

The movie subtly evokes the alluring expatriate world of the late 1950s, when Italy was moving from postwar austerity towards la dolce vita. The rich, young Americans Tom meets and seeks to emulate are Jamesian characters released from Victorian restraints, the girls travelling without chaperones, the boys being aggressively hedonistic.

The mercurial Dickie plays with his affections; Dickie's sensible girlfriend Marge (Gwyneth Paltrow) keeps a kindly distance between herself and the newcomer; Dickie's snobbish friend Freddie (Philip Seymour Hoffman) cruelly patronises Tom; Marge's rich lookalike Meredith (Cate Blanchett) accepts him as an equal because she thinks he's Dickie. Tom, who proclaims his talents for forgery, impersonation and lying, learns that he cannot enter this world as himself. He must transform his identity, changing his clothes and his character.

One is reminded of the passage in *The Rich Boy* in which Scott Fitzgerald tells us that 'the very rich are different from you and me. They possess and enjoy early, and it does something to them, makes them soft where we are hard, and cynical where we are trustful… they think, deep in their hearts, that they are better than we are because we had to discover the compensations and refuges of life for ourselves.' In the movie, Tom is less the casebook amoral psychopath of the novel and more a victim of class in his desire to be 'a fake somebody rather than a real nobody'.

In fact, various key incidents of *The Talented Mr Ripley* – a socially ambitious outsider helped by a rich benefactor, a pregnant, working-class woman, a fight in a small boat that leads to an ambiguous killing, an alluring upper-class woman just beyond the hero's reach – make the picture look like a refracted version of Theodore Dreiser's novel *An American Tragedy*, which George Stevens filmed as *A Place in the Sun*.

In addition, two dramatic traditions merge in Tom – the American fascination with the confidence trickster who can change himself like a social chameleon, and that recurrent story in fact and fiction (*The Return of Martin Guerre*, *Anastasia*, endless westerns) in which someone is transformed by taking on the identity of another, becoming in some ways more real than the person imitated.

Only about an hour in does the film become anything approaching an orthodox thriller, and it continues to grip like a vice as the action moves from San Remo to Naples, Rome and Venice. Ripley emerges as a brilliant manipulator and we share in, positively admire, his criminal artistry, partly because we despise the milieu he has entered.

Having brought out the homoerotic undercurrent in the relationship between Tom and Dickie, Minghella goes on to suggest that bi-sexuality might be a necessary condition to being Ripley. Tom's floating identity is as much a puzzle to him as to us and one of the recurrent images is of Ripley in reflecting surfaces – the water in Dickie's bath, a piano lid, the glazed tiles of a hotel floor, a magnifying shaving mirror – often grossly distorted. In the final shot, a mirror on a swinging door constantly picks up and loses the benumbed Ripley.

There are unforgettable moments in this beautifully crafted movie as there are in *The English Patient*. One thinks of the Hitchcockian *coup de cinéma* that has four swimmers emerge from the sea carrying a Madonna at a religious festival to be followed by a dead body suddenly surfacing beside them. And of Tom at the opera at Rome, watching the duel scene from *Eugene Onegin*, and then discovering that one group of Americans in the audience knows he's Ripley while another believes he's Dickie. It's an intelligent film, carefully cast and immaculately performed.

The Insider (Michael Mann)

The Observer, 12 March 2000

For the best part of a century, the most desirable heroes of American cinema have carried two lethal props – the handgun and the cigarette. Generations of moviegoers have emulated them.

For a year in the Army, I went out each morning with a loaded pistol strapped to my hip, feeling like a gunfighter or a private eye, and for twenty-one years my self-image as a confident adult was largely achieved by having a cigarette between my lips during most daylight hours.

The murderous and suicidal implications of both actions were not lost on me. But they gave me immense pleasure, and I got out of the Army without firing a shot in anger and gave up smoking before my health was permanently impaired.

As a result, I feel a certain ambivalence when invited to join attacks on manufacturers of arms or tobacco. Arms manufacturers tend to use versions of the persuasive speeches Shaw put into the mouths of the munitions tycoon Undershaft in *Major Barbara* and thus are out in the open.

But there can be no forgiving the hypocrisy with which the cigarette bosses defend their product or the ruthlessness with which they deploy their formidable power against critics. This is one of the key subjects of Michael Mann's engrossing political thriller *The Insider*, which pits a troubled scientist against his former employers, one of the top tobacco companies, whose chief executive officers are known as the Seven Dwarfs.

The movie resembles *All the President's Men* and *The China Syndrome* in the way it involves the media manipulating whistle-blowers. Vulnerable people are persuaded to threaten the welfare of themselves and their families by making public evidence that will discredit the forces of the entrenched and powerful.

The contrast between the private citizen and the professional investigator is cleverly spelt out in the opening sequences that crosscut between the lives of two men of probity involved with large corporations – Jeffrey Wigand (Russell Crowe), a chemist with the Brown & Williamson tobacco company, and Lowell Bergman (Al Pacino), a producer for CBS's *60 Minutes*, America's most prestigious TV current affairs show.

Wigand is an apparently happy husband and father of two, living a quiet, golf-playing corporate life of comfort in Louisville, Kentucky. But prompted by professional scruples, he has offended his smooth employers and been fired, though on generous terms that depend on his respecting professional confidentiality. Bergman is a volatile journalist, a creation of the radical sixties, who constantly has big, dangerous stories on his stove.

Currently on the front-burner is an interview between his show's veteran frontman, the seventy-eight-year-old Mike Wallace (Christopher Plummer), and the head of Hezbollah, which we see him risking his life to set up. On the back-burners are investigations of a drug-laundering outfit, the Unabomber, and a technical aspect of the tobacco industry on which he needs expert advice.

The latter brings Bergman into contact with Wigand, and he rightly smells a story about the malfeasance of the tobacco business and the lies about nicotine addiction told on oath before a Congressional committee by the Seven Dwarfs. Bergman believes that in persuading Wigand to testify on the programme he is serving the public and getting the scientist to do what his conscience dictates.

The result is an upheaval that changes the lives of both men. Significantly, on the day when the die is incautiously cast, the *New York Times* lead story is of O.J. Simpson's acquittal, a case of how in America the ruthless, consciousless rich can get away with murder.

The Insider is a dark paranoid thriller, lit by Mann's regular photographer Dante Spinotti in the penumbrous style Gordon Willis developed in *The Godfather* and *All the President's Men*. Danger, real and imagined, lurks everywhere as the tobacco companies seek to silence Wigand. His pension is cut off; the family moves to a smaller house; he finds a job teaching chemistry in a high school. Obscene threats appear on his e-mail, his phone is bugged and he's followed by menacing agents.

When the FBI are called in, they treat Wigand with suspicion, taking away his guns and his computer. It's suggested that the FBI men, expecting to get lucrative security jobs on retirement, are in league with big business. The final straw comes when the tobacco companies set out to destroy Wigand's character by feeding discreditable stories to the media.

Wigand finds himself deserted by his wife and left, like Gary Cooper in *High Noon*, to face his enemies alone. Moreover, back at CBS headquarters in New York, the corporate lawyers are forcing Bergman's bosses to dilute the programme and to omit Wigand's testimony on the grounds that it could involve the network in 'tortious interference' in a contract between others.

Bergman suspects that the real reason is that a high-profile legal action could affect the value of CBS shares on the eve of a lucrative merger. In an electrifying scene, an affronted Wallace turns on an unprincipled, power-dressing lawyer (an icy Gina Gershon) who seeks to mollify him. But by then Wallace has capitulated, if only temporarily, and left Lowell as isolated as Wigand.

The Insider is a movie of the first rank, less flamboyant than Mann's earlier films, but as sombre and realised on the same grand scale and with the same feeling for space. Conflations and fictionalisations have necessarily occurred, but the film avoids triumphalism and the choices that confront Wigand and Bergman are never simplified.

What makes them complex figures (and they are impressively embodied by the ambling Crowe and the balletic Pacino) is that they engage in inner moral debates that their employers dexterously avoid. Yet compromise of a decent sort is given its due in Plummer's formidable, humane and deeply moving performance as Mike Wallace. He has half-a-dozen terrific scenes showing Wallace variously as confident, arrogant, dignified, insecure and contrite.

In one of them, he confronts the implacable Bergman with a *New York Times* editorial accusing CBS of 'betraying the legacy of Edward R. Murrow', and you can see his wrinkled face and self-esteem collapse before the camera's relentless gaze. It's at this point that we remember that Murrow never appeared on air without a cigarette in his hand and died of cancer at the age of fifty-seven after one lung had been removed.

Mulholland Dr. (David Lynch)

The Observer, 6 January 2002

David Lynch's compelling *Mulholland Dr.* is that Hollywood-on-Hollywood movie lurking within every director, but its origins were inauspicious. It began three years ago when ABC-TV eagerly commissioned an open-ended, free-flowing television series along the lines of *Twin Peaks*, hated the pilot and shelved the project. A while later, the French company Canal Plus offered $2m additional financing if Lynch would turn it into a cinematic movie and provide a satisfactory ending.

The title inevitably evokes Billy Wilder's *Sunset Boulevard*, also in the noir mode but far less sinister. Sunset Boulevard stretches across Los Angeles from the Pacific to the old downtown area, passing through Bel Air and Beverly Hills as well as brasher commercial districts. The altogether darker Mulholland Drive zigzags along the crest of the Santa Monica Mountains that divide North and South Hollywood. If you study Ken Schessler's perennial bestseller *This Is Hollywood*, you get the impression that Mulholland is redolent with evil, haunted by the sad and bad spirits of the stars and starlets who have been murdered, committed suicide or participated in orgies this past century.

Mulholland Drive Mansions, Errol Flynn's old place, has a reputation equal in notoriety to the Hellfire Club. The drive is named for

William Mulholland, the ruthless Irish-born engineer who participated in the conspiracy to rob whole inland communities of their water that inspired Chinatown. The dam on nearby Lake Hollywood is named after him, and alongside that is the vast Hollywood sign, from which the twenty-four-year-old British actress Peg Entwistle hanged herself in 1932 when a studio declined to offer her a contract.

This, then, is the brooding setting of a picture that is as nightmarish and blackly comic as anything Lynch has made. It takes place over what appears to be forty-eight hours and, as in *Blue Velvet*, centres on two women, an experienced brunette (Laura Elena Harring) and an ingenuous blonde (Naomi Watts). The brunette narrowly escapes death at the hands of hitmen taking her for a ride on Mulholland Drive; the blonde arrives hopefully from Canada to seek an acting career in what she calls 'the dreamplace'. They meet in an apartment near Mulholland belonging to the ingenue's absent aunt where the brunette has sought refuge when suffering amnesia after the accident in which her would-be killers perished. Time and identity fracture; people seem and, in some cases are, interchangeable. Thus, the flat looks unaltered since the thirties or forties, and the amnesiac brunette decides to call herself Rita after seeing a framed poster for *Gilda* on the wall. Eagerly, the blonde sets out doing auditions and volunteers to help Rita find her true self, using evidence from her handbag.

The women's investigative quest takes them to an apartment block where they discover a decomposing body, to a bizarre Hispanic nightclub called Silencio where everyone mimes to tapes, and into an erotic lesbian affair. Meanwhile, around them swirls a corrupt world of blackmailers, pimps, assassins, agents, directors, disfigured derelicts and hangers-on, who keep crossing each other's paths. A director is forced to give a leading role to an actress chosen by the Mob. In a brilliantly sustained sequence, an inept hitman kills his brother, the brother's secretary and a janitor at a seedy office block.

The sinuous camera constantly leads around menacing corners, and drags us down into lakes of satanic darkness. Death beckons as an end and an escape, and while everything is sharp, super-real, we know that this is a phantasmagoria. We're experiencing the horrors and excitements of somebody's dream, possibly a collective nightmare based on personal anxieties and the gurgling mulch of a community's knowledge of itself.

Curiously, the film that *Mulholland Dr.* most readily brings to mind is the Coens' surreal *Barton Fink*, another story packed with echoes of scrofulous Tinseltown folklore and rumour in which an innocent in Hollywood becomes involved with someone who may be a projection of his anxieties and ends up disillusioned, suicidal, alone. The Coens remained tight-lipped and Lynch is giving nothing away. His own synopsis reads in toto: 'Part One: she found herself inside the perfect mystery; Part Two: a sad illusion; Part three: love.'

How do you judge performances in this context? The two central women – Watts and Harring – bring a certain vulnerable charm to their roles. Some – the eighty-two-year-old Ann Miller, for instance – rely on their familiar faces. Others, keeping a straight face, go with the Lynchian flow.

The Son's Room (Nanni Moretti)

The Observer, 17 February 2002

The Pop painters and Nouvelle Vague directors who emerged in the 1960s now seem more remarkable for their differences than for what at the time appeared to be their similarities. The same is true for the school of humorous Italian actor-directors who turned up twenty years ago, acknowledging the influence of Chaplin and Keaton and inviting comparison with Woody Allen. Maurizio Nichetti initially made the greatest impact with his sweet-natured loser persona in pictures of immense technical virtuosity such as *Volere Volare*, but little of his work has been seen abroad this past decade.

The initially endearing motormouth Roberto Benigni had the highest profile in the English-speaking world, but the brief success of his offensive *Life Is Beautiful* and his egregious behaviour at the Oscars damaged his reputation, perhaps permanently. Which leaves the forty-eight-year-old Nanni Moretti, one of the small chain of beacons reaching from Stockholm to Rome that suggests European cinema is still truly alive.

Moretti is an actor, writer, director, producer and exhibitor. He runs a small cinema in Trastevere in Rome showing independent productions (Ken Loach and the new Iranian moviemakers, for instance), writes and appears under his own direction and produces movies in which he also acts but which others direct.

A wry irony informs his work, and his appearance – slim, handsome, bearded – is unusual for a self-deprecating comedian. He's a man of the Left, fascinated by sport and politics (he's a star water-polo player) and his pictures turn on the relationship between private lives and public events. In two movies he produced and acted in – *Il Portaborse* and *La Seconda Volta* – he played, respectively, a craven career politician and a university professor confronted with the female terrorist who a decade before attempted to assassinate him. The two most recent films he's directed – *Dear Diary* and *Aprile* – are serio-comic documentaries, part-real, part-fantasy, about the state of the nation and his own life.

His new film, *The Son's Room*, starts with the customary light tone of his earlier work, though the larger public world is pretty well excluded. One section of *Dear Diary* was about the year Moretti spent being diagnosed with lung cancer, from which he appears to have totally recovered. A key strand in *Aprile*, interwoven with a movie he's supposedly making and the first election of Berlusconi, was anticipating the birth of his son. The latest picture is about the reaction of a family to a beloved son's death.

Moretti plays Giovanni, a psychoanalyst with a successful practice in Ancona on the Adriatic, a good-looking wife, Paola (Laura Morante), who runs a small art gallery, and two attractive teenage children, Irene (Jasmine Trinca), and Andrea (Giuseppe Sanfelice). The movie begins with a tinkling tune by Nicola Piovani as Giovanni jogs happily along the waterfront with Giuseppe Lanci's crystalline images presenting Ancona as a place as attractive as his compatriot Carlo di Palma makes Woody Allen's Manhattan.

In a series of superbly handled scenes in the consulting room, he treats his patients with amused compassion, some of it arising from his own seeming lack of problems. Without a trace of the maudlin or the sentimental, Giovanni's family get along well, interested in each other's lives and tolerant of their foibles, chatting easily. All is not perfect, of course. Andrea is loved by his father but the lad, though a gifted athlete, almost wilfully refuses to compete. There's also a family crisis when Andrea and a friend are accused of stealing a fossil at school, more a prank than a crime, but serious none the less.

Then halfway through the picture tragedy strikes. Giovanni is called to a neurotic analysand's house and has to cancel a jogging session with Andrea, thus freeing him to go scuba-diving with some chums. In what at first seems a curiously, almost clumsily edited montage, Paola has some sort of collision in a crowd, Irene has a near accident on a motor-bike and Giovanni narrowly misses being hit by a truck, while Andrea heads happily to sea in an inflatable dinghy. Fate can suddenly strike any of us the conjunction of these shots states when they finally register, but in this case it hits Andrea, leaving the family bereft and Giovanni consumed by guilt.

Only gradually do we discover the circumstances of the boy's under-water accident and the slight mystery surrounding it and, in fact, this follows the first necessary details of attending to his death. He's measured for a coffin, which is sealed with a metal cover in a funeral home, the last time the family will see him. Neither parent is religious, but for the sake of a farewell ritual the daughter asks for a mass her brother's friends can attend.

Once these obsequies are over, the family begins to fall apart. The mother stops going to the gallery. With the injunction 'physician heal thyself' hanging over him, Giovanni loses confidence in his therapeutic abilities and decides to abandon his practice.

In a particularly moving scene, he discovers everything in the house that has hidden flaws – a cracked vase, a favourite teapot that has been invisibly repaired. Meanwhile, Irene expresses her unresolved distress through her passion for sport.

Typical of the subtlety underlying the surface simplicity of Moretti's narration is the basketball motif. Irene is first seen at a dinner table talking to her mother about the different sounds a ball makes on a wooden surface and on lino. She's playing on the school court when her father arrives to break the news of her brother's death. At a champion-ship game, she unleashes her pent-up anger by provoking a fight that leads to a month-long suspension. The point at which the family start coming to terms with their loss coincides with her re-instatement as a player.

This coming to terms with Andrea's permanent absence is done quietly, and partly turns on the appearance of a teenage girl Andrea met at a camp and who the family has never previously heard of. Nothing very dramatic happens externally to Paola, Irene and Giovanni, but in their minds and hearts there are healing changes. The experience of this family makes an interesting comparison with Todd Field's recent, equally fine film *In the Bedroom*, where an American family confronts a son's death, but whose members externalise their feelings through an act of extreme violence.

The Son's Room is a remarkable work, thoroughly deserving of the Palme d'Or it won at Cannes last year. The title, *La Stanza del Figlio*, incidentally, has an additional meaning in Italian, 'stanza' being both a room and a unit of verse, thus suggesting a poem or part of a life left standing.

Rififi (Jules Dassin)

The Observer, 18 August 2002

Edward Dmytryk, one of the great Hollywood exponents of film noir, emerged from jail in 1951 after completing an eighteen-month sentence for contempt of Congress as a member of the Hollywood Ten. Disgusted with communism and wanting to get off the blacklist, he immediately appeared before the House Committee on Un-American Activities and named several other Communist Party members, including another leading film noir director, Jules Dassin.

Not wanting to continue the daisychain of confession and betrayal, Jules Dassin went into European exile and, after four years of unemployment, wrote and directed his best-known movie, *Rififi* (*Du Rififi chez les hommes*), one of the greatest crime movies ever made. It's now released in a marvellous, high-contrast monochrome copy with new subtitles that have dispensed with the stupid US slang used in the version released here in 1955.

Cinematic accounts of well-planned hold-ups go back at least to *The Great Train Robbery* of 1903, and the heist movie in its serious and comic form had become a genre well before *Rififi*. Huston's *The Asphalt Jungle* (1950) was clearly Dassin's model, and the great Georges Auric composed the music for both *The Lavender Hill Mob* (1951) and *Rififi*. Dassin later made another highly enjoyable heist film, *Topkapi* (to which homage was made in Brian De Palma's *Mission Impossible*), but *Rififi* remains the high watermark of the genre.

Rififi (underworld argot for a violent confrontation) is, of course, most celebrated for the twenty minutes in which Auric's somewhat excitable music suddenly stops. In silence, punctuated by natural sounds, four professional criminals break into the Paris branch of Mappin and Webb from the flat above and steal 240 million francs' worth of jewellery (or 'ice' as they call the stuff).

This influential robbery scene, however, is only the centre of the picture, and what Dassin did with the Série Noire novel by crook-turned-author Auguste Le Breton is conveyed by François Truffaut's comment that: 'One of the worst crime novels I have ever read Jules Dassin has made into the best crime film I have ever seen.' Dassin created credible three-dimensional figures of his four sympathetic protagonists – the ringleader Tony (Jean Servais with the tired look of a man just out of jail); the two Italians, Mario (Robert Manuel) and the expert cracksman César, flown in from Milan for the job (Dassin himself under the pseudonym Perlo Vita); and Joe the Swede, (Carl Möhner) who has given hostages to fortune in the form of a wife and child.

The first three wear hats and dark suits; the Swede is hatless and dresses in light-coloured clothes. Reflecting Dassin's political situation at the time, they're hard men but bound by a code of honour that separates them from the dishonourable, sadistic crooks who try to rip them off.

Above all, however, there's the semi-documentary realism Dassin developed on American locations (the photographer Weegee was his technical adviser on *The Naked City*). This is a harsh Paris, shot in all weathers and without artificial light, that was to influence Jean-Pierre Melville and the Nouvelle Vague.

A garish nightclub in Montmartre; a rundown café with a poker school in the backroom; the empty streets as the city slowly comes to life at dawn; the crooks' very ordinary flats; the heroes unshaven and dishevelled after a night of crime; the femmes fatales who think 'good behaviour' means deceiving prison governors – the milieu and the people are familiar enough, iconic almost. But, with his eye for the expressive detail, Dassin makes us see it all for the first time.

If... (Lindsay Anderson) & **The Conversation** (Francis Ford Coppola)

The Observer, 2 March 2002

Re-issued in new prints and both winners of the Palme d'Or at Cannes, Lindsay Anderson's *If...* (1968) and Francis Coppola's *The Conversation* (1974) confirm their status as classics, movies of real authority. Seen side by side, they have a surprising amount in common.

Both draw consciously on earlier films by continental directors (and influenced films that followed); both are responses to the political climate of their times yet don't appear dated or trapped in amber; both have rather unusual music. Each of the directors built up a personal repertory company of actors and made a trilogy following the same character over a long period. Anderson uses an English public school, not, like in *Goodbye Mr Chips*, to affirm tradition, but to attack authoritarianism and the way the Establishment rules by dividing and co-opting. His likeable rebels, led by Malcolm McDowell, are romantic anarchists, and a mystical note is introduced by the use of the *Missa Luba* on the soundtrack. Stylistically the movie draws on surrealism and the documentary, reflecting Anderson's attachment to the different cinematic poetry of Humphrey Jennings and Jean Vigo. The climactic assault by McDowell and co from the school's roof is a homage to Vigo's *Zéro de conduite,* and in Pal Gabor's 1971 picture, *Horizon,* a Hungarian rebel goes to see *If...* in a Budapest cinema. A response to the turbulent sixties, the counterculture and the Vietnam War, it was the first film in a trilogy that continued to take the temperature of Britain over the next fourteen years through the picaresque satire *O Lucky Man!* (1978) and the bitter farce *Britannia Hospital* (1982).

The Conversation is a chamber picture made between the first and second parts of Coppola's epic *Godfather* trilogy. Inspired by Antonioni's *Blow-Up,* its protagonist is a San Francisco surveillance expert wondering what he's recorded on tape rather than a London photographer puzzled by the crime he may have captured on film. The picture begins with Harry Caul (Gene Hackman at his self-abnegatory best) and his team taping a man and a woman furtively talking in a crowded San Francisco square, but ironically the first person drawn to our attention is a mime buttonholing bystanders.

This recorded conversation and its meaning will draw Harry into a conspiracy involving corporate skulduggery and murder, and will force him to confront moral decisions about his work.

Like *If...*, there's a documentary side to it in the approach to the security business, but the film is essentially a study in paranoia, a portrait of a guilt-ridden, obsessively private man who believes he's discovered a profession that will provide him with protective colouring and ethical neutrality.

The picture, though long in gestation, was made against the background of the unfolding Watergate affair and is the first of the conspiracy thrillers reflecting that scandal, to be followed by *The Parallax View*, *All the President's Men* and *Three Days of the Condor*. It's suggested that Harry could easily have been one of the White House plumbers.

The Conversation's music is by David Shire, a repetitive piano score like a lounge bar blues version of Erik Satie. But the distinctive quality of the soundtrack derives from one of the cinema's great editors and innovative sound designers, Walter Murch, who pays equal attention to the flapping sound of Harry Caul's plastic raincoat as to the details of the tape recording. For this new print, being shown in an NFT season of pictures from Coppola's American Zoetrope company, Murch has had the chance to restore and enhance the soundtrack, and the result is marvellous to hear.

Adaptation (Spike Jonze)

The Observer, 2 March 2003

The first film of both its writer, Charlie Kaufman, and director, Spike Jonze, *Being John Malkovich* was one of the most breathtakingly original comedies of the late twentieth century, a mixture of Lewis Carroll and Franz Kafka, its protagonist a deranged, idealistic puppeteer. One wondered how they could match it with their next film. The obvious answer, of course, would be a movie about the business of movie-making. But their brilliant *Adaptation* operates at a different level from films such as Truffaut's *La Nuit américaine* or Godard's *Le Mépris* about the dramas attendant upon shooting a movie. It's nearer to Alain Robbe-Grillet's *Trans-Europ Express*, a playful movie that takes us into the mind of a director inventing a plot and characters, though Kaufman and Jonze are concerned with turning someone else's idea into a piece of commercial cinema.

The movie begins with the diffident, fastidious Charlie Kaufman (Nicolas Cage), a lacerating self-portrait, feeling an unwanted outsider on the set of the film he's written, *Being John Malkovich*. He asks himself 'How did I get here?' and the answer comes in the form of a speeded-up documentary of southern California from the birth of time to Kaufman's own birth. He's then offered the job of adapting a bestselling non-fiction book, *The Orchid Thief*, by the *New Yorker* journalist Susan Orlean (Meryl Streep). It's a sensitive, very literary study of the nature of obsession, centring on an eccentric, low-life autodidact in Florida called John Laroche (Chris Cooper), who has gone from one obsession to another, the latest being orchids. While struggling with adapting this intractable material, Charlie discovers that his coarse, ill-educated identical twin, Donald (also Nicolas Cage), is taking up screenwriting. Moreover Donald has developed a popular touch for genre movies under the influence of the celebrated scriptwriting guru, Robert McKee (Brian Cox). Their relationship recalls that of the two brothers, one dedicatedly serious, the other a slob with a gift for cliché, confronting Hollywood in Sam Shepard's play *True West*.

The film is in effect a fiction about real characters – Susan Orlean, John Laroche and Robert McKee actually exist, as of course, does Charlie Kaufman, and there really is an unfilmable book called *The Orchid Thief*. But we have to remember that much of the movie is being filtered through Charlie's troubled mind. Although Nicolas Cage gives a marvellous sense of reality to the often hilarious scenes between the twins, one suspects or infers that Donald is Charlie's extrovert, go-getting doppelgänger. Donald, a stranger to irony, uses Hollywood argot like 'pitch' and 'industry' that causes the discriminating Charlie to flinch; he makes successful passes at girls that Charlie secretly envies and sees no harm in the most egregious professional compromise. The only person who seems to have met both brothers is their agent. There is a typically oblique joke in a remark by Brian Cox as Robert McKee after he has humiliated Charlie at a seminar for doubting the neatness of his theories about dealing with the confusions and vagaries of life. McKee holds up

Casablanca as having the best screenplay ever, despite the fact that it emerged from a series of happy accidents and was still being written during production by at least four writers. When hearing from Charlie that his twin brother attended his course, McKee suggests a collaboration. Julius and Philip Epstein, the two main authors of *Casablanca*, were twins, he says. In fact they were born three years apart.

Adaptation cuts back and forth in time and place between three contrasting milieux – Orlean's poised, superior, self-consciously intellectual Manhattan; the Kaufman twins' slick, hollow show-biz Los Angeles; and the southern blue-collar world of Florida where John Laroche exudes danger and authenticity. All three are wittily observed, and subtly embodied in the performances of Streep, Cage and Cooper. With the lightest of touches, the film discusses ideas about theft, expropriation, passion and obsession. Laroche has stolen orchids from protected areas of the Everglades to satisfy his obsession and in the belief that he can best protect them. Susan has discovered and exploited Laroche, but has also come to envy his capacity to surrender himself so single-mindedly to each successive passionate pursuit. The guilt-ridden Charlie, whose love life is a succession of failures, seeks to preserve the integrity of Orlean's work as a way of proving his own incorruptibility, but finds himself tempted to distort and cheapen it.

As the movie reaches its climax, Donald, with glib principles learnt from McKee, takes command, inventing a plot involving sex and drugs. This, amusingly and frighteningly, leads Charlie into moral and mortal danger. In a calculatedly ambiguous way Charlie Kaufman, the real author of the screenplay, plays games with the audience, as he simultaneously mocks and embraces both melodrama and Robert McKee. His onscreen alter ego seems to preserve his integrity while appearing to satisfy Hollywood. Or should we say his alter egos, because Donald Kaufman is credited as co-author.

Far From Heaven (Todd Haynes)

The Observer, 9 March 2003

Born and raised in Germany, the son of Danish parents, Douglas Sirk was a consummate director of melodramas, and there was much that was melodramatic in his own life. He quit Germany in the late thirties with his Jewish wife, leaving behind a son of his first marriage. This strikingly handsome boy, a child movie star, became a Nazi under the influence of his mother and was killed fighting with the Wehrmacht on the Eastern Front while Sirk was making anti-Nazi movies in Hollywood. This is like the plot of one of the movies Sirk directed at Universal Studios in the fifties before retiring from filmmaking in 1959 and returning to Germany.

These Universal films, starring Rock Hudson, Dorothy Malone, Robert Stack, Jane Wyman and Lana Turner, used the conventions of the women's picture to probe the anxieties simmering beneath the surface of a decade notable for its conformity. Though they were immensely popular, it took some years for Sirk to win critical acclaim for his acute social observation and his expressive use of colour, decor and music.

His influence has been especially acknowledged by two European directors, both gay – Rainer Werner Fassbinder and Pedro Almodóvar. Now one of the leading members of America's self-styled 'New Queer Cinema', Todd Haynes, has made the Sirk pastiche, *Far From Heaven*, his most mainstream work to date. With Steven Soderbergh and George Clooney as executive producers, it is in every respect a magnificently achieved movie.

Like Fassbinder's *Fear Eats the Soul*, *Far From Heaven* is principally inspired by *All That Heaven Allows*, the 1955 Sirk film in which the well-off, recently widowed Jane Wyman forms a close friendship with her gardener, Rock Hudson, and becomes an embarrassment to her children and the subject of malevolent gossip in her New England town. Haynes has set his picture in the autumn and winter of 1957 in Hartford, Connecticut, where Cathy Whitaker (Julianne Moore) is a highly regarded figure in the community. She seems to have the perfect marriage – a handsome, successful husband, two obedient children, a uniformed black maid, a house that exudes what was then called 'gracious living'.

In the background – seen on TV and discussed at cocktail parties – is the enforced integration of high schools and the rioting outside Central High in Little Rock that forced President Eisenhower to intervene. In the foreground, her husband, Frank (Dennis Quaid), is drinking heavily and the kindly Cathy strikes up a friendship with a handsome young gardener, Raymond Deagan (Dennis Haysbert), who has a degree in business and a little daughter.

He happens to be black and tongues begin to wag viciously. It also transpires that Frank is a guilt-ridden closet homosexual and Cathy arranges for him to discuss his 'sickness' with a doctor whose suggestions range from counselling to aversion therapy. What the movie makes abundantly clear is that neither of the problems confronting Cathy can be solved by a little goodwill and understanding. They demand major changes in society and in attitudes towards race and sexuality.

Haynes is, of course, treating directly racial matters that were handled gingerly by films in the fifties, and sexual ones that were approached with immense obliquity by Hollywood. (The American stage was freer, though in Britain serious plays dealing with homosexuality were banned by the Lord Chamberlain.) It was not until *Advise and Consent* in 1962 that Hollywood showed us a gay bar, and the troubled married gay man visiting it had to commit suicide.

But Haynes doesn't preach and he doesn't mock the past. He takes Sirk's style of heightened colour, romantic music and slightly larger-than-life acting to recreate the fifties with affection and understanding. The movie begins with a crane shot, sweeping down from the autumnal trees to close in on Cathy and her happy family as Elmer Bernstein's lush score with its soaring strings and plangent piano plays on the soundtrack. The fin-tailed cars look as if they've emerged from advertisements in the *Saturday Evening Post* .

The costumes (by the great British designer, Sandy Powell) are exactly right. Everyone wears hats over their immaculately coiffed hair. The women's dresses have cinched waists, are made of slightly heavy materials with flaring skirts and, for formal occasions, stiff petticoats beneath. Cathy never goes out without wearing gloves, and there's a different pair in an appropriate colour for every occasion.

The astonishing thing is that for all the obvious calculation and the invitation to admire its virtuosity, Haynes's exercise in postmodernism is as moving and as heartbreaking as the classic women's pictures to which he pays homage. Dennis Quaid catches just the right slightly cowed tone of the fifties organisation man, who had grown up in the Depression, survived the war and is slightly dazed by the affluent society and the threat of nuclear annihilation.

Julianne Moore looks uncannily like her fellow redhead, Pat Nixon, the exemplary perfect wife of the fifties who has sacrificed her identity to her role as homemaker and supporter of her husband. It is a perfect, subtly nuanced performance. I lived in America at the precise time this picture is set and can testify to its uncanny accuracy.

Russian Ark (Alexander Sokurov)

The Observer, 6 April 2003

I have not much liked the two movies of the fifty-year-old Russian Alexander Sokurov that I've seen – the sub-Beckettian *Mother and Son* and his romp in Berchtesgaden with Adolf and Eva, *Moloch*.

But his new film, *Russian Ark*, is a hypnotic work shot in a single, unbroken take lasting ninety minutes as the ghost of an early nineteenth-century French aristocrat walks around the Hermitage Museum and the tsars' old Winter Palace in St Petersburg. He sees, but is seen only occasionally by, a variety of people ranging from Peter the Great to present-day visitors to its art galleries.

Along the way he engages in a debate about Russian culture over the centuries with an off-stage figure, presumably the director himself. This foreign visitor, billed as 'the Stranger', has a striking resemblance to the Swedish actor Erland Josephson, who played the lead in *Nostalgia* and *The Sacrifice*, the last two films by Andrei Tarkovsky, an idol of Sokurov's. Sergey Dreiden may well have been cast in the role for this reason.

This is a virtuoso undertaking involving the German cinematographer Tilman Büttner carrying his Steadicam through room after room for 1,300 metres without stumbling, a cast of a thousand or more (most in costume) performing on cue, a couple of orchestras, numerous changes of lighting.

This breathtaking piece of cinema, infinitely more impressive than any Hollywood hi-tech action movie, has got into the *Guinness Book of Records*. It also has a place in the history of the technical and philosophical development of the cinema.

The cinema began in the 1890s with brief single-shot movies lasting less than a minute. Then the new language of film developed and in the 1920s in the Soviet Union the idea of editing as the essential basis of cinema received a theoretical blessing from Sergei Eisenstein under the name of 'montage'. The concept of montage was accepted by Soviet commissars because of its seeming correspondence with dialectical materialism. It appealed to the movie industry in the West because it allows producers, as well as filmmakers, to re-jig pictures in the editing room. It also makes the censor's job easier.

A counter theory was proposed after the Second World War by André Bazin, co-founder of Cahiers du Cinéma and godfather of the French New Wave. He believed that montage was too interventionist, too destructive of observed reality. He approved of the deep focus and continuous camera movement that he saw in the work of Orson Welles, William Wyler and Jean Renoir. For more than fifty years leading directors have gone in for elaborate long takes as a way of holding our attention as well as amusing themselves, among them Hitchcock (*Rope*, *Under Capricorn*), Angelopoulos (*The Travelling Players*), Welles (*A Touch of Evil*), Polanski (*Cul-de-sac*), Jancsó (*Agnus Dei*), Antonioni (*The Passenger*) and Altman (*The Player*, where the lengthy opening take is accompanied by Hollywood filmmakers discussing the nature of the long take). These directors, however, were limited by the ten minutes of film contained in a normal reel.

Sokurov's picture has been made possible by the invention of the Steadicam in the late seventies, and, more recently, by the development of a high-definition video camera with a hard disc that can record for one hundred minutes.

The question arises as to whether *Russian Ark* is merely a bravura piece of filming that leaves us admiring the cameraman's stamina, the technicians' brilliance, the director's courage and the actors' discipline. The movie is never less than intelligent in its historical debate, is often amusing in a pawky way and is frequently beautiful (especially a scene in which the Russian court receives a petition from the Shah of Persia).

Only occasionally does it touch the heart, as in the sequence of Nicholas and Alexandra taking tea with their children where the clothes, the walls and the furnishings are all white. But none of this is in itself new. Sacha Guitry did something similar in 1954 with his three-hour movie, *Si Versailles m'était conté... (If Versailles could have told me...)*, which featured virtually the whole French acting profession (plus Orson Welles as Benjamin Franklin) to tell the history of Versailles from the age of Louis XIV to the present and was shot in the palace itself. The climactic ball held at the Winter Palace in 1913, with its awareness of marking the end of an era, is inferior in mood, presentation and dramatic depth to the great ball sequence of Visconti's *The Leopard*.

What *Russian Ark* resembles is a historical pageant, a son et lumière show without three-dimensional characters, and rather narrowly focused. Despite the title, it doesn't contain all of Russia any more than a similar treatment of Hampton Court or Windsor Castle would. There's also a total absence of Russian art, as the Stranger himself points out. One supposes a Russian audience would be more involved and affected, especially those people who would like to see Tsar Nicholas II canonised.

Sokurov's chief purpose apparently was to involve the viewer in the continuity of history, in the experience of time itself. He sees the film as being 'shot in a single breath', a term that might be better applied to a line in a poem by Whitman or Ginsberg than to ninety minutes of film. But people must judge for themselves whether this technique leads beyond admiration and into a deeper involvement.

Phone Booth (Joel Schumacher)

The Observer, 20 April 2003

Alexander Graham Bell, the Scot who pioneered the telephone, and Thomas Alva Edison, the American who pioneered the cinema, were born within a couple of weeks of each other in 1847. Their careers became linked through their experiments with recording sound and later through the appearance of phones in films. The sophisticated Italian comedies of the 1930s came to be known as 'white telephone movies', and there are as many telephones as blondes in the films of

Alfred Hitchcock, who began his working life as an employee of the Henley Telegraph Company.

Hitchcock's signature appearance in his first American film, *Rebecca*, has him standing outside a telephone kiosk occupied by George Sanders; during Grant's famous long kiss with Ingrid Bergman in *Notorious* he's conducting a phone call with his boss; the blonde Tippi Hedren is trapped inside a glass kiosk by menacing seagulls in *The Birds*; *Dial M For Murder* speaks, or rings, for itself.

The phone call (remote, but intimate) and the phone booth (private, but public) symbolise aspects of modern life and our relationship to technology, and they're cleverly used in Joel Schumacher's involving thriller *Phone Booth*. Interestingly, though I'm sure coincidentally, the plot is very similar to a 1936 radio play that Patrick Hamilton wrote for the BBC, *Money with Menaces*, in which an apparently innocent middle-class man is led a merry dance around London from phone box to phone box, menaced by an unseen tormentor who turns out to be someone the protagonist bullied at school. When Hitch suggested that he and Hamilton work together, the writer offered to adapt this radio piece. The Master turned it down and they didn't collaborate until *Rope* a decade later. A pity.

Scripted by the gifted writer-director Larry Cohen (whose credits include a movie I haven't seen called *The Man Who Loved Hitchcock*), the Schumacher film stars Colin Farrell as Stu Shepard, an unscrupulous Manhattan PR man very like the slimy Sidney Falco, unforgettably played by Tony Curtis in *Sweet Smell of Success*. Like Falco, Stu is first seen bobbing and weaving through Times Square, fast-talking, glad-handing, making deals on his mobile phone. When he gets to a phone booth on 53rd Street between 8th Avenue and Broadway, he stops to make a call to an ingenuous actress client, whom he's enticing into an affair.

Promising to get her name into the gossip columns, he says: 'The first step on the way to being noticed is to be mentioned.' While he's in the booth, a pizza is mysteriously delivered to him. He rudely rejects it, insulting the delivery boy. Then the phone rings, and a quiet, sardonic voice starts to needle him. 'What do you want?' – 'I want your complete attention.' And this unseen caller gets it, for the next seventy minutes, because he knows everything about Stu and because, from a nearby window, he has a rifle with a telescopic lens trained on the box.

2003

The makers find it necessary to explain why this kiosk – which belongs to the company Alexander Graham Bell created – is being used by Stu. Why isn't he, like everyone else, using a mobile? The answer is that this is one of the last phone booths left in this area of New York and the two-timing PR man doesn't want his wife to see a phone bill listing calls to his lovers.

For over an hour Stu is trapped in the box getting more and more desperate as his level-voiced torturer keeps up the pressure. A trio of hookers try to break in to use the phone, and the plug-ugly doorman from 'Sextuff', the parlour in which they work, comes over with a baseball bat. This pimp figure is killed by the sniper, and the police, the media and Stu's wife arrive on what is now a crime scene. The tension mounts as Stu is forced by the unseen menace to get under the skin of the sympathetic black police captain (Forest Whitaker) in charge of the operation.

Schumacher, cameraman Matthew Libatique and editor Mark Stevens keep the film as tautly wound as a tourniquet. They focus on Stu, but use a split screen and superimposed images to show other people in the street or at the end of the line (though never the sniper). At times, however, it can seem a little fussy.

What gives the film a special interest is the way the phone kiosk becomes a cross between a glass coffin and a confessional. As in Hamilton's radio play, the psychotic manipulator is a moral avenger. He's an angel of death and a self-appointed judge who (not for the first time, he claims) has set out to expose a carefully selected victim's crimes and depredations – making him face up to them himself and to confess them to the world. By the end the deplorable PR man has undergone a nightmarish inquisition and become worthy of our sympathy. For which one of us would wish to undergo the public exposure to which he is treated?

Good Bye Lenin! (Wolfgang Becker)

The Observer, 27 July 2003

There is an insular arrogance in the confident British claim that the Germans don't have a sense of humour. What about the films of Ernst Lubitsch, the plays of Bertolt Brecht or the books of Erich Kästner? And has Britain produced a movie comedy these last few years that compares with Wolfgang Becker's *Good Bye Lenin!?* Set in Berlin in the late 1980s and early 90s, it's an inventive satire on German reunification that cleverly updates Washington Irving's seminal story of amnesia and social sleep walking, *Rip Van Winkle.*

In Irving's 1820 fable, Rip Van Winkle downs a flagon of Dutch gin in the Catskills, falls asleep a subject of George III and awakens twenty years later to discover he's missed the American Revolution and is now a free citizen of the United States. In Becker's movie, an idealistic communist, Christiane Kerner (Katrin Sass, a former East German film star) has a heart attack while watching a demonstration in East Berlin in 1989 and goes into a coma, waking up eight months later after the Wall has come down, Honecker has resigned, capitalism has invaded the East and Germany is on the point of reunification.

While she's comatose in hospital, her grown-up son and daughter have thrown out their old furniture and got new jobs – Alex (Daniel Brühl) has switched from being a TV repair man to selling satellite dishes, Ariane (Maria Simon) has abandoned her studies to work for a fast-food chain. But when Christiane suddenly regains consciousness, the doctor tells Alex that in her fragile state, any small shock could kill her. He thus realises that it would be fatal for her to confront the social and political transformation of the past year.

So Becker and his co-screenwriter, Bernd Lichtenberg, add to the traditional Rip Van Winkle story the ingenious plot device found in George Seaton's film *36 Hours* (inspired by a wartime story by Roald Dahl) and Emir Kusturica's *Underground.* This involves a vast deception by which a false world is created to deceive an innocent person – for malign purposes in *36 Hours* and *Underground*, for beneficent ones here. Alex rapidly restores the family's flat to its GDR dinginess, installs his bedridden mother at home and pretends that all is still for the best in the best of all communist worlds.

This scheme involves him in constant improvisation of a frequently hilarious kind. He hunts in dustbins for old pickle jars and coffee packs of East German brands no longer manufactured. He involves elderly neighbours in his schemes, several of them only too eager to revert to a more certain past, and he bribes kids to dress as Young Pioneers to serenade his mother on her birthday. A workmate with ambitions to be a movie director concocts phoney videos to be shown between old tapes on her TV set.

He delights her by acquiring a Trabant ('After only three years' wait,' she says in wonder) for an outing to the countryside, and when she sees West Berliners in their smart cars in East Berlin, he convinces her they're fugitives from the consumer society. Gradually, the movie takes on a larger dimension as Alex comes to create an alternative history of Germany in which the West is cracking up and the generous East opens its arms to share the idealism which his mother represents.

In this version, there is no brutal triumphalism in which capitalism prevails over an evil empire, but a more just society is created. This is linked, both thematically and dramatically, to the children discovering that their father, a doctor who left for the West in the 1970s because he was persecuted for refusing to join the Communist Party, is living in Wannsee and has remarried. Alex's sister first notices him when he and his family buy a drive-through takeaway at her fast-food place. 'What did you say to Father?' Alex asks. 'Enjoy your meal and thank you for choosing Burger King,' she replies, a line that's funny, sad and deeply moving. This is a remarkable film that makes you laugh and leaves you thinking. It's the work of people who have a great sense of humour. Washington Irving would have liked it.

Pirates of the Caribbean: The Curse of the Black Pearl (Gore Verbinski)

The Observer, 10 August 2003

When movie people speak of piracy nowadays, they mean video pirates making a fortune producing bootleg cassettes and DVDs. No doubt these people are turning a few doubloons putting into contraband circulation *Pirates of the Caribbean: The Curse of the Black Pearl*, the grand summer entertainment named after a popular attraction at Disneyland.

If the public at large don't take these criminals as seriously as they should, it's because filmmakers have spent the past eighty years carrying on a tradition created by Defoe, Scott and Stevenson of romanticising the pirate.

'Swashbuckler' is an onomatopoeic term suggesting the sound of swords swishing and striking shields, and is to movies as geographically distant from each other as *The Mark of Zorro* and *The Prisoner of Zenda* what the sound of ricocheting bullets is to the western. The pirate movie is a sub-genre of the swashbuckler and its first classic came before audiences could hear the swash – the 1926 silent movie *The Black Pirate* starring Douglas Fairbanks Sr, most graceful and spirited of action stars.

A key ingredient peculiar to the pirate movie, experienced through the spectator's imagination, is the tang of salt air and the sea breeze in one's face as the Jolly Roger is unfurled, the sails billow and we embark for the Spanish Main. It is a childhood feeling of freedom, fraternity and irresponsibility.

There have been surprisingly few truly first-rate pirate movies since *The Black Pirate*. The best came in the thirties and forties – Errol Flynn in *Captain Blood* and *The Sea Hawk*, and Tyrone Power in *The Black Swan*, and a couple of versions of *Treasure Island*. And there's been little since Burt Lancaster's tongue-in-cheek *The Crimson Pirate*, made in 1952.

Recently, there has been a string of critical and box-office disasters as bleak as those grinning skeletons stretched out beside empty treasure chests on desert islands: *The Island* (1980), which cost Michael Ritchie the chance to direct *The Right Stuff*; Peter Cook and Graham Chapman's sad spoof, *Yellowbeard* (1983), *Pirates* (1986), which introduced a fifteen-year drought for Polanski; and *Cut Throat Island* (1998), which damaged the careers and marriage of its director, Renny Harlin, and star, Geena Davis. Talk about a curse.

Appropriately enough, a key plot line of *Pirates of the Caribbean* is a curse befalling a pirate ship that has seized a blighted cache of golden medallions given by the Aztecs to Cortez.

The principal screenwriters on this movie, Ted Elliott and Terry Rossio, demonstrated their sly humour with the animated comedy *Shrek* and their knowledge of the swashbuckling genre in *The Mask of Zorro*. And they've cheerfully plundered every decent pirate movie on the Spanish Main, including a little nod towards the scene in *The Crimson Pirate* where James Hayter invented the submarine by using an upturned rowing boat to go underwater.

The movie begins magically with a twelve-year-old girl, the daughter of a British governor in the West Indies, on the mist-shrouded bridge of a British frigate, frightening the sailors by singing a pirate song. Then she espies an umbrella floating past, followed by a lad clinging to some planks, and then a blazing ship, shattered and sinking. From the unconscious boy, she takes a gold medallion bearing a skull that would have him condemned as a pirate.

From this prologue, we cut forward some years. The girl has now grown up to be the beautiful, aristocratic Elizabeth Swann (Keira Knightley), daughter of the governor of Port Royal (Jonathan Pryce), dressed in a hat and gown that make her resemble a younger version of Gainsborough's Mary Countess Howe. The boy has become Will Turner (Orlando Bloom), blacksmith and skilled swordmaker. Very soon, he finds himself crossing swords in the film's first big fight with the fugitive pirate, Captain Jack Sparrow (Johnny Depp), vigorously staged in a blacksmith's forge.

Sparrow has saved Elizabeth from drowning, but has been imprisoned by her suitor, Commodore Norrington (Jack Davenport), a stiff-upper-lip naval officer. The rumbustious Captain Barbossa (Geoffrey Rush) and his crew from the *Black Pearl* attack the town in search of the golden medallion, and Sparrow (his comrade turned deadly enemy), Elizabeth and Will are drawn into accompanying him on a series of voyages and dangerous pursuits.

The three men are the quintessential pirate heroes and anti-heroes. Rush's bearded, pock-marked Barbossa is the duplicitous villain with a monkey on his shoulder and a great line in roaring bombast.

Depp's Sparrow is the sly, charming trickster with a curious cockney accent, a fatalist and a bit of a dandy with bells on the black braids of his beard. In some shots, Bloom (partly because of his neatly trimmed moustache and Van Dyke beard) resembles the young Errol Flynn, and his dashing Will is the clean-cut young man forced into piracy by chance and social exigency. Elizabeth is the intrepid upper-class girl torn between a life of rigid convention and the adventures and freedom offered by an attractive man of a lower class. All four are near perfect.

There is in the course of *Pirates of the Caribbean* everything you'd ask of such a film – sea battles, a sojourn on a desert island, a secret cave full of plunder, a talking parrot, leering sailors with disfigured faces, victories of the outcasts over the agents of officialdom. There is also a horror story in which the cursed pirates are transformed by moonlight into hideous zombie creatures of skull and bones, giving a new meaning to the term skeleton crew.

There are more special effects than in traditional pirate movies and, as usual, there's a great deal of humour, never unintentional. This is the work of people who like pirate movies and don't think the genre beneath them, and it is arguably the best of its kind since *The Crimson Pirate* fifty years ago.

Dogville (Lars von Trier)

The Observer, 15 February 2004

Danish photojournalist Jacob Riis became one of America's most formidable social critics through his reportage in the *New York Herald Tribune* and his 1890 book, *How the Other Half Lives*, exposing the exploitation and appalling conditions of immigrants.

Unlike his fellow Dane, Lars von Trier, Riis had spent time in New York. Von Trier, who does not like travelling, has followed the example of Kafka, James Hadley Chase, Brecht and Sartre and set highly tendentious works in the United States without actually going there. In his long musical, *Dancer in the Dark* (2000), von Trier attacked the American criminal justice system and in his even longer *Dogville*, also made in English, he presents a typical American small town of the 1930s as irredeemably venal and hypocritical. Both films are ludicrous, arrogant, pretentious and naïve. But Dogville is also boldly conceived, genuinely risky and disturbing.

Initially, *Dogville* seems like a miserabilist version of Thornton Wilder's play, *Our Town*, which broke new ground back in 1938 by being performed on a bare stage with a minimum of props and having a folksy narrator called the Stage Manager. Here, the unseen narrator (John Hurt) addresses us on the soundtrack with smooth, orotund ironies and the action takes place on a flat surface (occasionally seen from high above in elegant vertical shots), with the plan of the houses and streets outlined in white paint and a few suggestive props.

The whole area is boxed in by high white walls that stretch up to infinity. It soon becomes apparent, however, that the dominant stylistic and dramatic influence is Brecht with the division into a prologue and nine chapters and the alienating devices that constantly keep us aware that we are watching an instructive spectacle. There is a very different kind of austerity here from the kind of self-denying ordinances von Trier advanced in the Dogme manifesto of the late 1990s.

Dogville is a rundown former mining town in the Depression and initially its inhabitants seem decent enough folk. When the distraught Grace (Nicole Kidman) arrives as a fugitive from her life as a gangster's moll, the town's intellectual, Tom (Paul Bettany), persuades his fellow citizens to give her refuge. They exact payment in the form of services given and briefly take her to their hearts. But, gradually, they demand more and turn against her and she becomes their scapegoat and victim. She is raped, framed, cheated and finally betrayed for what they believe will be considerable financial gain.

Yet this is not merely a fable of human depravity brought about by economic circumstances. The dubious theme of salvation through sexual degradation is repeated from von Trier's *Breaking the Waves*, suggesting some kind of religious thread, and the film turns into a story of revenge and retribution on an Old Testament scale. The director may have been thinking of Dürrenmatt's play *The Visit of the Old Lady*, Samuel Fuller's small-town exposé *The Naked Kiss* and Clint Eastwood's savage allegorical western *High Plains Drifter*.

Von Trier has recruited a remarkable cast of familiar faces, the majority from the States, and those who aren't (Bettany, Kidman, Stellan Skarsgård) seem convincingly American. This gives the movie a superficial authenticity lacking in Brecht's half-dozen plays set in America. There is also a specificity in its references and allusions. Two pivotal figures, for instance, are called Tom Edison Snr and Tom Edison Jnr, suggestive of something morally deficient or enfeebling in the nature of American genius and specifically in the creator of the American cinema. Dogville's one street is called Elm Street, a reference both to a celebrated place of collective cinematic nightmares and to the thorough-fare in Dallas where President Kennedy was assassinated.

Nevertheless, one emerges after three hours feeling that one has seen something abstract, universal in a vague, metaphorical way. And thinking back on the experience – and you do feel you've been through something – I had the uncanny sense not of having been in a cinema but of having watched a curious show that Peter Brook might have mounted in an enormous warehouse in Scandinavia.

Eternal Sunshine of the Spotless Mind (Michel Gondry)

The Observer, 2 May 2004

Films with literary titles like *For Whom the Bell Tolls* and *Gone With the Wind* are mostly adapted from novels, so it's unusual for a movie with an original screenplay to have a title – and a rather beautiful one – like *Eternal Sunshine of the Spotless Mind*. It comes from the *Epistle of Eloïsa to Abelard*, Alexander Pope's poem about the great twelfth-century lovers, who were separated by the church, she incarcerated in a convent, he castrated and appointed abbot of a remote monastery.

In the poem, based on the letters she wrote about her enduring passion, Eloïsa envies the chaste virgins who have no such memories to torment them: 'How happy is the blameless Vestal's lot!/ The world forgetting, by the world forgot:/ Eternal sunshine of the spotless mind!/ Each pray'r accepted and each wish resign'd.'

Directed by Michel Gondry, a filmmaker celebrated for music videos and commercials, the movie concerns love and memory and the pain and happiness they bring, the way people exist in our minds and we in theirs.

But as the screenplay is by Charlie Kaufman, who scripted *Being John*

Malkovich, *Adaptation* and *Confessions of a Dangerous Mind*, the approach to the subject is quirky, witty, elliptical. From one minute to another, or one second to another, we're not sure whether what we're seeing is reality or illusion.

Essentially, it is about a contrasted, or complementary, pair of lovers, Joel (Jim Carrey) and Clementine (Kate Winslet). He's quiet, cautious and introverted, recording the world in an illustrated journal. She's impetuous, extrovert, reckless. They appear to meet, seemingly by chance, one winter's day in the Long Island resort of Montauk. She draws him out, he softens her up and an affair begins. But it transpires that both are, in fact, trying to write each other out of their lives.

There have been a number of recent movies about memories, real and false: Christopher Nolan's *Memento* for instance, and Tim Burton's *Big Fish*. But *Eternal Sunshine* most brings to mind two major John Frankenheimer films of the 1960s, *The Manchurian Candidate* and *Seconds*.

In the former, an American platoon in Korea is kidnapped by the Chinese and brainwashed (a term introduced into English during the Korean War) and the movie opens with a virtuoso sequence where what we see shifts constantly between the distorted worlds perceived by the victims and the reality of their manipulators. This is the visual style pursued throughout *Eternal Sunshine*.

In *Seconds*, an unhappy man learns of a secret organisation that can transform, at a price, his identity and allow him to lead a new life divorced from the past. In *Eternal Sunshine*, there is a similar organisation called Lacuna, housed in a rather messy side-street office and run by the slightly dotty Dr Howard Mierzwiak (Tom Wilkinson) and three skittish, unreliable assistants (Mark Ruffalo, Elijah Wood, Kirsten Dunst).

Lacuna specialises in the selective eradication of memory, specifically in taking away all traces of a particular person through a cross between science and witchcraft. This is done by parcelling up objects that recall that person, then going with a brain scanner to those points in the cranium that have registered this now unwanted figure.

Both the hero and heroine engage Lacuna's services and when Joel asks the insouciant Dr Mierzwiak if such a process can cause brain damage, he is coolly re-assured: 'Technically speaking, the procedure is brain damage.'

As that line suggests, *Eternal Sunshine* is a very funny and unsentimental film, a romantic comedy with absurdist undertones. The serious philosophical and psychological ambitions are kept up its sleeve rather than worn on it. In this, it resembles the now classic *Groundhog Day*. Carrey and Winslet play well together; both are naturally aggressive performers with actively expressive eyes. Wilkinson and his staff at Lacuna are suitably disturbing in their seeming ordinariness. Ellen Kuras's photography and Valdís Óskarsdóttir's editing are highly accomplished and *Eternal Sunshine* fully repays the demands it makes on viewers.

Many, like myself, will want to see the film a second time when the experience is likely to be more relaxing.

The Day After Tomorrow (Roland Emmerich)

The Observer, 30 May 2004

On my way to seeing Roland Emmerich's latest blockbuster, *The Day After Tomorrow*, I found myself humming for the first time in forty years a song from *Blitz!*, Lionel Bart's 1962 musical about plucky East Enders in the Second World War. The show was most celebrated for Sean Kenny's remarkable sets featuring destructive air raids, with St Paul's glowing as a beacon of hope in the background while blazing buildings collapsed all around. This was as near to a disaster movie as any play I've seen, but the song I recalled was an uplifting number, 'The Day After Tomorrow', that looked forward in an optimistic spirit to a free and prosperous post-war world.

The Day After Tomorrow has a lot in common with *Blitz!* in its predictability, sentimentality and depiction of a nation drawn together through a sense of shared peril. But the meaning of its title is the reverse of the wistful tenor of Bart's song. Here on the day after tomorrow most of mankind will be wiped from the earth.

The film's central character, the Washington-based climatologist Jack Hall (Dennis Quaid), has a premonition of disaster in a cliff-hanging opening sequence. Jack finds himself clinging to a fissure that suddenly appears beside a research station in Antarctica. He's persuaded that global warming will bring on a new Ice Age within five hundred to a thousand years unless world leaders introduce immediate reforms. But he's pooh-poohed by an arrogant Vice-President, who places the national economy before unproven anxieties about the environment. Only the British scientist, Professor Rapson (Ian Holm), believes him.

But Hall was being optimistic. A series of freak storms convinces him this climactic transformation will be sudden rather than gradual – possibly in days rather than weeks. He urges an evacuation to the south.

Emmerich's film is based on a book called *The Coming Global Superstorm* by Art Bell and Whitley Strieber which, one supposes, is more sober than the screenplay Emmerich and Jeffrey Nachmanoff have wrought from it. But in the opening scenes they create a convincing, if obviously accelerated, scenario for global extinction that should be – to use a cliché – a wake-up call for humanity.

In the British disaster flick of the 1960s, *The Day the Earth Caught Fire*, coincidental H-bomb tests in the east and west throw the world off its axis and destroy our civilisation. Might the concurrent explosions of *The Day After Tomorrow* and Michael Moore's *Fahrenheit 9/11* throw Bush off balance and save mankind?

Anyway, having delivered his message, Emmerich has to entertain us with all the things we expect from group jeopardy and disaster films, something he has given us before in *Independence Day* and *Godzilla*. The first ingredient is spectacular destruction, which his battalion of special effects experts provide. There is a little problem in making such a film in the wake of 11 September 2001. As the camera pans over the Manhattan skyline, we are only too aware of the absence of the World Trade Center. With footage of the demolition of the Twin Towers indelibly printed on our minds, can we pleasurably anticipate something similarly awful happening to New York for fun?

The answer lies in the fact that no one wrote about 9/11 without evoking disaster movies. Reality and cinema have become one in our media-saturated world. So the audience can gleefully watch a hurricane devastate Los Angeles and see a tidal wave turn Manhattan into a high-rise Venice with a Russian tanker floating down Fifth Avenue. This is followed by a big freeze that covers the city in ice, leaving the Statue of Liberty buried up to her waist.

This sort of cinematic devastation gives us the same kind of satisfaction we get from reading Shelley's *Ozymandias*. The fate of an obliterated

Europe is passed over with little comment. We do, however, see Ian Holm and his two young associates having a final dram – their last toasts are 'To England', 'To mankind', 'To Manchester United'.

The second ingredient of the disaster movie is human interest. We need a small bunch of survivors to identify with, and here that role is assigned to the family of Professor Hall, whose workaholism has led to a separation from his wife and neglect of his teenage son (Jake Gyllenhaal). Naturally the crisis draws them together, and dad undertakes a perilous redemptive journey to rescue the lad, who's taken refuge in the New York Public Library. This provides suspense and humour. The survivors have to keep warm by burning books. But should they throw Nietzsche into the fire?

A third ingredient is the moral dimension, the apportioning of blame, and this usually reflects the temper of the times. The 1936 movie *San Francisco* presented the immoral world of the city before the judgment of the 1906 earthquake and then its subsequent rebuilding. This was equated with the social corruption and financial recklessness that caused the Depression, and Roosevelt's New Deal that was bringing about national recovery. Often there are negligent or hubristic scientists on hand to blame, but in this film they are all good men.

Usually, attendant priests are there to provide a religious message (Spencer Tracy in *San Francisco*, Gene Hackman in *The Poseidon Adventure*) but the references to prayer and God in *The Day After Tomorrow* are perfunctory. In this secular film the faults are laid firmly on the steps of the White House and the bureaucracy serving it.

The Vice-President is a complacent, weaselly figure with a passing likeness to Dick Cheney. The weak, inattentive President always defers to the V-P, but resembles the ecologically minded Gore more than Bush. He is far removed from the President of Emmerich's *Independence Day*, a courageous Gulf War veteran who would now remind us of John Kerry. The movie's best laughs and sharpest ironies arise from xenophobic citizens of the world's remaining superpower having to flee south to save their lives, flowing into Mexico as illegal immigrants.

A disaster movie must also offer hope for the future. *The Towering Inferno* ended with the suggestion that the ruined building be preserved as a monument to the 'bullshit' of capitalism. Here we are consoled by the claim that mankind survived one Ice Age so can get over another.

2004

Sideways (Alexander Payne)

The Observer, 30 January 2005

Many of us grew up regarding pretentious talk about wine with suspicion or derision. We were fuelled by the James Thurber cartoon in which a smug fellow at a dinner table raises his glass and says: 'It's a naïve domestic burgundy without any breeding, but I think you'll be amused by its presumption.' And we laughed along with the bibulous screenwriter Herman Mankiewicz, co-author of *Citizen Kane*, when he left the dinner table of celebrated Hollywood bon vivant Arthur Hornblow to vomit loudly in an adjoining room, and then returned to inform his host: 'Don't worry Arthur, the white wine came up with the fish.'

Jonathan Nossiter's epic documentary, *Mondovino*, may have forced us to take seriously the billion-dollar worldwide wine business and its interlocking culture of growers, dealers, critics and drinkers, but it didn't entirely remove the smiles from our faces.

Now we have Alexander Payne's extremely clever comedy, *Sideways*, a road movie set in California's wine country that will appeal equally to oenophiles and oenosceptics. Like Payne's previous films, *Election* and *About Schmidt*, this new one is co-scripted by Jim Taylor, and again centres on a man of probity, discontented with his life, unhappy in his relationships and living at a distance from a world he distrusts. He's Miles Raymond (Paul Giamatti), divorced, aged around forty, and teaches literature to eighth-grade students in San Diego. He has two obsessions – wine and becoming a published novelist.

Like many people, he has a close friend with whom he has little in common and who came into his life by an accident of propinquity, in this case through sharing a room as college freshmen. The friend, Jack (Thomas Haden Church), is a fleshy, over-the-top actor, once celebrated for playing a doctor in a TV soap opera, and about to marry into a well-off Armenian-American family to rescue himself from impending penury.

The marriage is to take place in a week's time and in lieu of a stag night Miles is taking him on a week's golfing and wine-tasting trip north of Los Angeles. The womanising, extrovert Jack, however, has a different agenda – to get laid once more before marriage and to arrange a one-night stand for the diffident introvert Miles who hasn't had sex since his divorce two years earlier.

To Jack, one wine is much the same as another; to Miles, they are more distinctive than individual people. So, starting with a touching and hilarious visit to Miles's dotty widowed mother, they set about their journey, Miles chatting about wine, Jack chatting up women. Miles finds one wine 'quaffable, but far from transcendental', another 'tight as a nun's asshole, but good concentration'.

They meet two girls – Maya (Virginia Madsen), a waitress who loves wine and is studying part-time for a degree in viticulture, and Stephanie (Sandra Oh), a beautiful, Asian single mother who serves at wine tastings. And they strike up very different relationships with them while drinking great quantities of fine wine. Miles talks with Maya about his novel ('It culminates in a Robbe-Grillet mystery but with no resolution'); they discuss favourite vintages, and a warm relationship develops, though, initially, he goes to bed alone. Jack immediately woos Stephanie with his actorly charm, misleads her about his status and intentions and spends the night with her.

Like a married couple, the depressive, guilt-ridden Miles and the self-deceivingly guilt-free Jack attempt to modify each other's characters and change their lives. But as they squabble, fall out and make up, they need each other just as they are, and Paul Giamatti and Thomas Haden Church turn in performances of complementary subtlety. Payne manages extraordinary changes of pace, combining scenes of contemplation and sadness with moments of high farce that reflect Miles's manic-depressive personality.

There are three especially hilarious moments. First, when Jack's insensitive talk about his friend's ex-wife drives Miles to run wildly through a vineyard downing wine in great gulps. Second, when the news that his book isn't to be published causes him to go berserk at a wine tasting. Third, when he has to retrieve a wallet left behind by Jack after being caught in flagrante by a red-neck husband.

In addition to its wit and insight, *Sideways* is a lyrical film, thanks, in part, to the delightful presences of Virginia Madsen and Sandra Oh, but also to the summer light of the Santa Ynez Valley, nicely caught by cinematographer Phedon Papamichael, and to Rolfe Kent's 1950s-style cool jazz score. There's also the romance of wine itself, caught in a delightful montage of split-screen images as Jack and Miles go on their way around the vineyards, and in the affectionate talk on the subject that includes a particularly affecting speech by Maya that begins: 'I like to think about the life of wine.'

Kinsey (Bill Condon)

The Observer, 6 March 2005

Some years ago, when I was awarded a scholarship to study journalism at Indiana University, my friends suggested I'd been attracted to this particular campus by its institute for sex research whose founder, Alfred Kinsey, had recently died.

Soon after I arrived, there was a message for me to call one of the late doctor's associates. Thinking I was to be interrogated about the sex lives of the British (a project then under consideration), I returned the call, only to discover all they wanted was my opinion on the relative standing of the British newspapers seeking serial rights to the institute's next book.

So while I cannot testify personally as to how the institute's reports were compiled, I can confirm that Bill Condon's *Kinsey* convincingly captures the quiet, conservative Midwestern atmosphere of the campus at Bloomington, Indiana from which sprang the doctor's explosive report on sexual behaviour in the human male and its sequel on the human female.

Condon made *Gods and Monsters*, the excellent picture about the openly gay movie director James Whale. Here he has had the clever idea of bringing together the life and work of Kinsey (Liam Neeson) by using the narrative device of Kinsey answering the questionnaire he devised to interrogate eighteen thousand Americans for his reports. It is also a smart way of introducing us to the industrious three-man team he recruited for his project – Wardell Pomeroy (Chris O'Donnell), Clyde Martin (Peter Sarsgaard) and Paul Gebhard (Timothy Hutton) – who put the questions to him and have their techniques criticised by their mentor.

Condon shows us the growth of Kinsey from a repressive childhood under a deeply religious father (John Lithgow), against whom he rebelled, through his scientific training as a zoologist and taxonomist to his becoming the world authority on the gall wasp.

Kinsey's scientific obsessions are revealed through his collecting a million examples of this minute creature, but classifying them leads him to conclude that 'diversity is life's only irreducible fact'. From this flowed seemingly conflicting impulses – his compassion for the individual and his aim to apply strict scientific methods to the understanding of 'the human mammal'.

In 1922, at the age of thirty and still a virgin, he married Clara (Laura Linney), a gifted student in his zoology class at Indiana University. Their loving marriage, which lasted a lifetime, floundered on their honeymoon. But the practical Kinsey sought medical advice and this led to him teaching a class on sex and marriage at the university.

He wanted to share his liberation from ignorance with others. This, in turn, inspired the research necessary to answer the questions on sexual behaviour his students put to him. The climax, as it were, was the appearance of his first report in 1948, a determinedly unerotic book full of charts and statistics that became a sensational bestseller and led to a permanent change in the way people regard their sexual activities, revealing how widespread masturbation, oral sex, adultery, premarital sex, homosexuality, and even zoophilia were. It challenged ideas of what is 'normal' and the laws and moral codes that seek to enforce that normality.

As Lionel Trilling wrote at the time (in an essay re-printed in his *The Liberal Imagination*): 'The way for the report was prepared by Freud, but Freud, in all the years of his activity, never had the currency or authority with the public that the report has achieved in a matter of weeks.'

This is a fascinating story, told with insight and imagination. It has a quality of intelligence and a readiness to engage with ideas and moral issues rarely found in Hollywood today. At the centre is a towering performance by Neeson, an actor capable of registering pain, heart-searching, doubt and determination at the same time. With his bow tie, tall frame and shock of hair standing nearly upright, he looks like a giant paintbrush.

And by his side is his wife, a deeply moving performance from Laura Linney. Her devotion to him and belief in his integrity helped her endure not only years of neglect and notoriety but also Kinsey's experimentation with homosexuality and masochism in the name of science, and his bizarre encouragement of wife-swapping among his associates.

She even gets to speak the oft-quoted line, which I've always thought apocryphal: 'I hardly see him since he took up sex.'

The film is good on the world of philanthropic foundations and the groves of academe. Oliver Platt gives a charming performance as Herman Wells, the president of Indiana University, a canny operator in the interests of academic freedom, whether in the good days of the New Deal or the dark ones when McCarthyism cast a shadow over the nation. He stood by Kinsey during twenty years of controversy.

What is most remarkable perhaps is the film's mature view of sexual matters, balancing the serious side with its frequently tragic consequences, and the often comical, even absurd aspects. This it does without prurience or smirking. For example, the disturbing inability of the Kinseys to consummate their marriage is followed by a meeting with a doctor that is simultaneously heartbreaking and hilarious.

Love and emotion were matters Kinsey tried to ignore as scientifically unmeasurable. But Condon brings together sexual liberation and love in a final interview with a woman in late middle-age who talks of being liberated by Kinsey and finding late love with another woman. Lynn Redgrave's brief performance of this monologue cannot fail to bring a lump to the throat or tears to the eyes.

A Cock and Bull Story (Michael Winterbottom)

The Observer, 22 January 2006

Sir Arnold Bax, one-time Master of the Queen's Musick, famously said, or rather quoted 'a sympathetic Scot' as saying: 'You should make a point of trying every experience once, excepting incest and folk dancing.' I wouldn't make a large bet against incestuous Morris dancers being the subject of the next picture by Michael Winterbottom, our most prolific, versatile and unpredictable director. His last film was an experiment in assimilating unsimulated sex into a mainstream movie. Before that he made a dystopian science-fiction film; a semi-documentary shot guerrilla-style about illegal immigration from Pakistan to England; a comedy about the Manchester music scene of the 1980s; and two Thomas Hardy adaptations, one of them turning *The Mayor of Casterbridge* into a western.

His latest picture, the dazzlingly clever and often hilarious *A Cock and Bull Story*, is an adaptation, co-scripted with his usual writing partner, Frank Cottrell Boyce (using the joint pseudonym Martin Hardy), of Laurence Sterne's eighteenth-century novel *The Life and Opinions of Tristram Shandy, Gentleman*. There are two kinds of movies based on unfilmable material. The first is of non-fiction works bought by canny producers because of their catchy titles (*Everything You Wanted to Know About Sex* and *Sex and the Single Girl*, for instance) who then hire hacks to create a story.

The second is of seemingly intractable novels – James Joyce's *Ulysses*, William Burroughs's *The Naked Lunch*, John Fowles's *The French Lieutenant's Woman* – that serious artists take on as challenges. *A Cock and Bull Story* belongs to this latter category. It's based on a novel that (as someone says in the film) was 'postmodern' even before there was 'modern'. Under the influence of John Locke's theory of 'the association of ideas' it anticipated Joyce and Virginia Woolf's stream of conscious-ness as well as Jean-Luc Godard's dictum that a film should have a beginning, a middle and an end, but not necessarily in that order.

Winterbottom and Boyce have made a movie about filming *Tristram Shandy*, and Steve Coogan is superb playing three roles – a parodic version of himself, the eponymous narrator Tristram, and Tristram's father Walter, a wealthy North Country landowner. The film-within-the-film faithfully follows the novel's discursiveness and rejection of chronology in the way Tristram tells us his life story and introduces us to various characters whose personal obsessions Sterne calls hobby-horses. The most notable is the retired army officer Uncle Toby (played by Rob Brydon). Assisted by his devoted servant Corporal Trim, he re-creates in the gardens of Shandy Hall famous battles in which he has fought.

The movie does not attempt, in its brisk ninety-five minutes, to encompass the whole novel, nor does it try to find exact visual equiva-lents of Sterne's comic tropes like the black page that marks the Reverend Yorick's death, the asterisks and dashes that conceal and reveal, and the squiggly line made by Corporal Trim with his stick to illustrate the difference between freedom and marital bondage. It does, however, make very explicit the bawdy jokes about Toby's wound in the groin at the Siege of Namur, Tristram's conception and his accidental circumcision as an infant, and the cock and bull story of human and animal insemination that provides the pay-off line for the novel and the title of the film.

For the most part the framing section of the picture unfolds chronologically, the one exception a conventional flashback to the makers emerging from having successfully pitched their project to the financial backers. But of course the idea of the making of a film of *Tristram Shandy* is marvellously absurd. Moreover, the making of this particular film parallels the seemingly anarchic form of the book and mirrors the ideas it contains about the chaos of existence, as well as Sterne's notion that the novels by Samuel Richardson and Henry Fielding that he was mocking were overly neat in their presentation of life and the workings of the mind.

In this sense the movie is different from such celebrated films about filmmaking as Fellini's solipsistic *Otto e Mezzo*, Truffaut's romantic *La Nuit américaine* and Godard's *Le Mépris* where the film-within-the-film is largely a pretext. In *A Cock and Bull Story* Sterne's book is clearly a genuine text. It also differs from the solemn, pretentious film of *The French Lieutenant's Woman*, whose makers believed that they had successfully transformed Fowles's self-conscious novel into a movie by replacing the authorial reflections on literature and Victorian society with comments on the film's themes from the actors. Fowles called the film 'a brilliant metaphor' for his book, but it is an elegant white elephant. Winterbottom and his colleagues don't affect to believe their playful film is successful as a work of art, and paradoxically the implicit recognition of failure is essential to the film's success.

Intelligent, full of sharp observation and good jokes, *A Cock and Bull Story* is that rare thing, a modest tour de force. It begins and ends with extremely funny scenes with Brydon and Coogan, first involved in preliminary rivalry over professional status while being made up, then arguing about their skills as impersonators after seeing the completed film. The music, most of it old and borrowed, plays the rigorously modernist compositions of Michael Nyman against the rich movie themes that Nino Rota provided for Federico Fellini. The conversations and conflicts on the set ring true, while slyly satirising all the people involved. There is a particularly amusing character, an earnest assistant played by Naomie Harris. She's the only person with a true passion for cinema, and her favourite filmmakers are Fassbinder and Bresson. The pivotal presence, however, is Coogan and, as with Alan Partridge, you can never tell where being ends and acting begins. He invents a semi-fictional persona for the movie and joins the filmmakers in sending himself up as insecure, conceited, deceitful, lecherous. It is a brave act in a way, constantly amusing and a generous gift to the audience.

Incidentally, I know of no previous attempt to film Sterne's novel, though there's an arresting scene in Arthur Penn's western *The Missouri Breaks* when a rich Montana rancher, acting like a brutal eighteenth-century squire, returns from the summary execution of a rustler. He sits in his library (he boasts of owning 'eight thousand Texas half-breed cattle and thirty-five hundred volumes of English literature') and says to his daughter, 'Honey, pull down *Tristram Shandy* for me again, would you?'

The History Boys (Nicholas Hytner)

The Observer, 15 October 2006

Most films about schooldays are American and concerned with who'll take whom to the prom, who'll fix the school bully, who'll score the decisive touchdown. Few have much to do with education. Indeed only a couple come readily to mind – the Hollywood version of Emlyn Williams's *The Corn is Green* in which a Welsh miner's son is encouraged to go to Oxford by an inspirational schoolmistress, and of course *Dead Poets Society*. That's why the film version of Alan Bennett's *The History Boys* is special, though certainly not the only reason. It's been thoughtfully brought to the screen with its National Theatre cast intact and with the same director, Nicholas Hytner, who made his movie debut twelve years ago with *The Madness of King George*, based on another National Theatre play by Bennett.

After years of writing and performing sketches for the stage, radio and television, Bennett wrote his first play in 1968, the comedy *Forty Years*

On, which used a minor public school as an image of Britain. Working through parody and pastiche, it reviewed the recent history of the country through a play staged by a rebellious new teacher in defiance of a hide-bound headmaster. *The History Boys* can be seen as a development of this prentice work. Though it's much more elaborately shaped, deeper, and even funnier, it's another state-of-the-nation play using a school as the setting, dealing with the same themes of education, history, class and national identity.

The year is 1983, the setting is now an all-boys grammar school in Yorkshire attended largely by working-class lads, and the piece concentrates on eight bright sixth-formers who have stayed on for an extra term preparing to sit Oxbridge scholarship exams in history. There are the merest glimpses of other pupils, and although in adapting the movie for the screen Bennett has briefly introduced a comic gym teacher straight out of *Kes*, and a dispirited teacher of art history, there are only four significant figures from the faculty. They're the snobbish headmaster (Clive Merrison), a geography graduate of Hull determined to put his school on the map by getting boys into Oxbridge; Mrs Lintott (Frances de la Tour), a sensible traditional history teacher who studied at Durham; Hector (Richard Griffiths), a brilliant, theatrical English master who went to Sheffield University and runs an unconventional general studies class; and Mr Irwin (Stephen Campbell Moore), a Machiavellian recent history graduate brought in on a temporary basis to show the working-class kids how to present themselves and their ideas in a way that will impress (or deceive) Oxbridge dons.

There's no feeling of this being a filmed play (on the stage there was quite considerable use of video material), but the classroom remains central. Except for a couple of deft montages (the boys going to Oxford and Cambridge, the fateful letters from their chosen colleges arriving at their homes) and Hector riding his motorcycle, everything is pedagogically inclined. Though the year is 1983 there's no reference to the Falklands war, unemployment, Sheffield's dying steel industry or the rise of the SDP. But then the picture is as much about Bennett's boyhood and Blair's post-Thatcher world as about the eightees, and there is a despairing coda set several decades later. In fact nothing deflects our attention from the movie's ideas and the central debates about what education is for, who owns history, and in a more general way how we are meant to conduct our lives. This is denser in the stage and radio versions, but Bennett has skilfully pared down the discussions and they remain substantial. In what other recent film has a poem been sensitively dissected the way Hardy's *Drummer Hodge* is here by Hector and a pupil?

There is no doubt about where Bennett's sympathies lie, and the production designer, John Beard, has served him and Hytner well. The caricatured headmaster's study is packed with cups, shields and other trophies of his school's success. The sensible Mrs Lintott's history room has maps and dynastic charts on the wall. The general studies wall is covered higgledy-piggledy with hundreds of postcards of art ancient and modern and portraits of Wilde, Joyce, Orwell, Betjeman, Bette Davis, Jack Hulbert and numerous others, including several of Charles Laughton with whom the fat, gay, histrionic Hector evidently identifies. They reflect his mind, methods and ethos as do the endless quotations he swaps with his class, the games they play, the delight they take in jokes, in learning, in life. Irwin, a man of mystery and deceit, has no office, no hinterland; he's a moral and social chameleon.

On its way to the screen Hector's role has been somewhat diminished and Irwin has become less sinister, his future as a revisionist historian and a political spin doctor toned down. The play's sexual politics, mostly concerned with frustration and discontent, are now more prominent. Hector practices grope therapy on pupils who ride pillion on his bike, and thus blights his professional future. The most sensitive of the boys, Posner (beautifully played by Samuel Barnett), confides in the closet gay Irwin: 'I'm a Jew. I'm small. I'm homosexual. And I live in Sheffield. I'm fucked.'

Posner loves the saturnine Dakin, the only sexually experienced member of the class, and serenades him with the Rodgers and Hart song 'Bewitched', which restores the original gay intention of Hart's lyrics. The manipulative Dakin not only toys with the affections of Posner, Irwin and Hector, he blackmails the headmaster over his lunges at the school's flirtatious girl secretary. As for the forthright Mrs Lintott, who's as much a reflection of Bennett as Hector is, she recalls her first pizza at Durham more vividly (and fondly) than her first experience of sex.

Approaching the film version I feared that the acting, so wonderful on stage, might be overly theatrical. This is not the case. The performances are nicely toned down. That the headmaster remains two-dimensional is not Clive Merrison's fault. I also worried that the boys would look too old when scrutinised in close-up. This too hasn't happened. They look just right and just as scruffy in their uniforms as teenagers ever were. Of course they're cleverer, wittier, better informed than grammar-school boys were in my day. But there's a moment when the assured Dakin is embarrassed and humiliated to discover he's been mispronouncing the name of Nietzsche that rings absolutely true. It brought back painful memories I've been trying to suppress all my life.

Flags of Our Fathers (Clint Eastwood)

The Observer, 24 December 2006

The most famous photograph of the Second World War is the one taken by the Associated Press cameraman Joe Rosenthal on 23 February 1945. This iconic image depicts six US servicemen (five Marines and a sailor) raising Old Glory atop Mount Suribachi on the fifth day of the costly thirty-six-day battle for the Japanese island of Iwo Jima. Its impact on the American public was immediate and it became the centre of a massive bond-raising campaign for a nation brought to the edge of bankruptcy by the war. The three surviving flag-raisers – John 'Doc' Bradley, a naval medic, and Marine privates Ira Hayes and Rene Gagnon – were flown home to appear at large-scale rallies and to be promoted as national heroes. That is the background to Clint Eastwood's magnificent *Flags of Our Fathers*, which he has co-produced with Steven Spielberg.

The film is based on a book of the same name by James Bradley, son of 'Doc' Bradley, who died in 1994, and the project follows the same form as *The Longest Day* and *Tora! Tora! Tora!*, which looked at both sides of respectively the Normandy landings of 6 June 1944 and the 7 December 1941 attack on Pearl Harbor. In this case, however, there are two films, and the one from the Japanese point of view, *Letters from Iwo Jima*, will appear next year.

Shortly after belatedly attaining stardom in the late sixties, Eastwood made, back-to-back, *Kelly's Heroes* and *Where Eagles Dare*, action yarns that glorified the Second World War. Early in his career Spielberg made *1941*, a broad comedy about the Californian response to the prospect of a Japanese invasion after Pearl Harbor, followed by the adventure story *Raiders of the Lost Ark*, where the two-fisted Indiana Jones confronts the German army. Both have come a long way since then, and *Flags of Our Fathers* is a film of great power, sadness, complexity and insight.

Back in 1962, twenty-nine cinéastes replied to an American film journal's questionnaire on war and the cinema. Among the most interesting responses was François Truffaut's. 'It seems to me that war films, even pacifist, even the best, willingly or not, glorify war,' he said. 'A film that truly shows war, battles, almost necessarily exalts war – unless it is a matter of parody... The effective war film is often the one where the action begins after the war, when there is nothing but ruins and desolation everywhere... War should not be shown as an accepted fact, inevitable, imponderable, but rather as a human decision, made by a small group of men... After having shown those who give the orders, one should show those who receive them, and their reactions (the simple soldiers).' Clearly Eastwood, Spielberg and their screenwriters, Williams Broyles Jr and Paul Haggis, have pondered these points in approaching what is still generally thought of as a 'good war' and a 'just war', regarded as necessary and entered into reluctantly by a citizens' army.

The movie alternates between three points in time. The first is the invasion of Iwo Jima and the bloody battle that ensued between the carefully concealed Japanese in their network of underground emplacements and the dangerously exposed US soldiers making their way up from the beaches. Shot in desaturated colour on bleak, black landscapes in Iceland, this is an all-male story of courage and comradeship, of terrible pain and dubious sacrifice, and is as effectively cruel and remorseless as the Normandy landing scenes with which *Saving Private Ryan* opens. It begins with a troubling image of a soldier falling overboard from a troopship on its way to Iwo Jima. His comrades laugh, sure that he'll be picked up. But he's expendable, left to drown as the fleet sails on. Soon hundreds of his comrades will be sent to their deaths. The last image of life on Iwo Jima is of a group of GIs running into the sea, relaxing playfully together, an innocently homoerotic time out of war, which brings to mind one of the most famous poems of the Second World War, F.T. Prince's *Soldiers Bathing*.

The second strand is on the home front to which Bradley (Ryan Phillippe), Hayes (Adam Beach) and Gagnon (Jesse Bradford) return as exploited heroes. This part is political, satirical and bitter. The media start to question the authenticity of Rosenthal's photograph, just as Robert Capa's comparably iconic picture of a Republican soldier at the moment of death in the Spanish Civil War has undergone similar scrutiny. Pictures do not lie, but they don't quite speak for themselves, and the provenance of the Iwo Jima photograph is complicated, though in no way dishonourable. The blood that is the one primary colour on Iwo Jima is matched by the bright lipstick of the girls who are around as the three are drawn into a publicity machine, re-enacting the flag-raising in stadiums, meeting the recently elevated President Harry Truman, feted by (to use Stanley Baldwin's famous phrase) hard-faced men who were doing well out of the war. Bradley takes it in his stride. Hayes, a Native American of the Arizona Pima Indian tribe, having found pride and comradeship in the Marines, never wanted to become involved in this publicity campaign and slides into the alcoholism that will end his life. The extrovert Gagnon thinks his role in this enterprise will ensure him a postwar career and happily joins in the PR charade.

The third point of time is the postwar America in which the three attempt to adjust in their different ways. 'Doc' Bradley, the most normal, embarks on a quiet suburban life as, ironically enough, a mortician. He keeps in touch with the relatives of dead comrades, and retains that silence about his experiences that Hemingway described in his great 1925 story *Soldier's Home*, which contains the mortifying line: 'By the time Krebs returned to his home town in Oklahoma the greeting of heroes was over.' Gagnon, a somewhat surplus figure on Iwo Jima, was given numerous cards by super-patriots promising him lucrative demob employment. He runs into brick walls and ends up as a janitor.

Most tragic is Ira Hayes. He took to drink on the bond-raising tour, incurred the wrath of senior officers for disgracing the Marine Corps, and was sent back to the front. He'd almost certainly have died had not atom bombs been dropped on Hiroshima and Nagasaki, thus preventing the Armageddon that would have accompanied the invasion of mainland Japan. He became a drifting, guilt-ridden drunk and went to an early grave in 1955 on his impoverished reservation. He was to enjoy a certain posthumous fame in John Frankenheimer's 1960 TV film *The American* (played by Lee Marvin), the 1961 film *The Outsider* (impersonated by Tony Curtis), and through Peter La Farge's 1964 protest song, 'The Ballad of Ira Hayes', a major hit for Johnny Cash, though banned as unpatriotic by numerous radio stations. It's good to see his emblematic life brought to the attention of a new generation, and he's admirably impersonated by the Canadian Indian Adam Beach. In Frankenheimer's TV film, Hayes is seen staggering around the set of the 1949 John Wayne movie, *Sands of Iwo Jima*, unable to distinguish Republic Studio sets from wartime reality. Eastwood's film borrows this device as the drunken Hayes has traumatic flashbacks during re-creations of the flag-raising at bond-selling rallies in 1945.

Flags of Our Fathers is touched by greatness. It argues that soldiers may go into battle for country and glory but they always end up fighting for the survival of themselves and their comrades. The elegiac, melancholy music is composed by Eastwood himself and is far from being martial or triumphalist.

Letters from Iwo Jima (Clint Eastwood)

The Observer, 25 February 2007

Clint Eastwood's account of the 1945 battle for Iwo Jima from the viewpoint of the Japanese defenders complements *Flags of Our Fathers*, his film about the American invaders and the way the iconic photograph of Old Glory being raised on Mount Suribachi was exploited for patriotic ends in the States. It isn't the first movie about the war in the Pacific to be made in Japanese and directed by an American. That was the bizarre *Saga of Anatahan*, the true story of Japanese sailors shipwrecked in 1944 on a remote island and holding out for seven years, refusing to believe Japan had lost the war. Made in 1953 by Josef von Sternberg on sets in a Japanese studio, it received limited distribution and is rarely revived.

Both Eastwood pictures are masterpieces of humanist cinema, forming a magnificent diptych. They're about glory and heroism and bring into question both concepts, centring on a bloody, costly battle for a barren, waterless island of rock and black volcanic sand that happens to be part of the Japanese empire. *Letters* is framed by the discovery of a cache of letters hidden in 1945 and exhumed sixty years later. They symbolise the burial and retrieval of the past, one of the film's subjects, and as they float down at the end, slow motion is used for the only time.

Unlike *Flags of Our Fathers*, which centres on the experience of three US soldiers who participated in the flag-raising, *Letters* pays equal attention to General Kuribayashi (a towering performance from Ken Watanabe) and his staff and to several lowly conscripts, most notably Private Saigo (Kazunari Ninomiya), a baker in civilian life. Both men are realists, aware that defeat is imminent. But the general, a concerned leader and professional soldier, knows that honour dictates that he must die, while the private is determined to see his wife and baby daughter again.

The film opens with Kuribayashi's arrival, his disgust at the lack of co-operation between the services, the foolish conduct of zealots and the unimaginative plans of defence. Instead of meeting the inevitable invasion on the beaches, he builds a labyrinth of tunnels in which his army lives like burrowing animals. As a result, the battle is extended from the three days anticipated by the Americans to more than a month.

The movie is doom-laden and non-triumphalist, with a plangent score co-written by Eastwood's son Kyle, and characteristically dark cinematography. The flashbacks to Japan involving Saigo and a former military policeman, who's been dispatched to the front line as a punishment for an act of kindness, do not reflect happier times. They show the madness of war fever on the home front.

Kuribayashi's flashbacks to when he studied with the US army in the late 1920s are brightly lit to express his love of the States and the hopes he had for harmonious relations between Japan and America. A major symbol is the pearl-handled 1911 Colt pistol he's given by American colleagues as a farewell present at Fort Bliss, New Mexico. His troops believe he's taken it from a US soldier he's killed, and it ends up as a souvenir in the possession of a GI.

The battle scenes are brilliantly handled, and what we best remember are moments of horror: a mass suicide of trapped soldiers killing themselves with hand grenades, for instance, and matching scenes of an injured American being bayoneted by his Japanese captors and two Americans casually killing a pair of Japanese POWs. Yet there are also moments of kindness and dignity as when the general plans for the baker's survival, and a moving encounter between Baron Nishi, the Japanese equestrian star who won a gold medal at the 1932 Olympics in Los Angeles, and a dying marine he saves from his angry men.

The film is based on a scenario by Paul Haggis, who co-scripted *Flags*

of Our Fathers and won an Oscar for *Million Dollar Baby*, but the carefully organised screenplay is the work of Japanese-American writer Iris
Yamashita, a discovery of Haggis's. It is a fine piece of work, though
there are inevitably numerous scenes and incidents familiar from other
pictures. Indeed the war movie, whatever its setting, is part of a genre
that has its roots in the Trojan War. The film it most brings to my mind
is John Ford's poetic, beautifully understated *They Were Expendable*,
released just after the end of the Second World War, and also a case of
victory in defeat, in that instance of US sailors fighting a rearguard
action during the Japanese invasion of the Philippines in 1942. Both
raise our respect for the human spirit and enhance our understanding of
what it means to live and to die.

How violent taboos were blown away (*Bonnie and Clyde* forty years on)

The Observer, 26 August 2007

Bonnie and Clyde opened in London forty years ago, which is to say
exactly at the halfway point between the present and the coming of
talking pictures in 1927, and it now stands as a landmark in cinematic
history in several ways, not least for its legacy of screen violence. The
reception here was largely positive, and I've rarely sensed such excitement at a press show as that morning at the Warner Leicester Square
(now the Vue). At the reception afterwards everyone was eager to meet
its star and producer, Warren Beatty – hitherto thought of as a light-
weight figure, despite two doom-laden roles in Robert Rossen's *Lilith*
and Arthur Penn's Kafkaesque *Mickey One*. He glowed with modest
confidence as praise was heaped on him, and spoke of the brief battle
he'd had with Warner's British press department over the title. On the
weekly bulletin of previews sent to critics it was listed as *Bonnie and
Clyde Were Killers*. Apparently the publicists believed people would
think it was about Scottish rivers. 'OK,' Beatty claimed to have said,
'Let's call it Bonnie and Clyde aren't Rivers.'

He won the day, and within weeks Bonnie and Clyde were better known than Al Capone. Georgie Fame's song 'The Ballad of Bonnie and Clyde', written after seeing the film, was top of the charts and performed on TV by a chorus of boys and girls toting machine guns and wearing 1930s gear. 'The Speakeasy Look' and 'The Bonnie Parker Look' began to appear in the fashion pages.

Apart from the title, the British distributors were unsure what audience to target. So they took a two-pronged approach. The London posters depicted a black-and-white photograph of the Barrow gang posing with guns beside a 1930s car, accompanied by this text: 'Clyde was the leader. Bonnie wrote poetry. CW was a Myrna Loy fan who had a bluebird tattooed on his chest. Buck told corny jokes and carried a Kodak. Blanche was a preacher's daughter who kept her fingers in her ears during the gunfights. They played checkers and photographed each other incessantly. On Sunday nights they listened to Eddie Cantor on the radio. All in all, they killed eighteen people. They were the strangest damn gang you ever heard of.' Outside London, another poster featured a crude drawing of Bonnie and Clyde firing machine guns with the caption: 'They're young! They're in love! And they kill people! The most exciting gangster film ever made.'

Among the things that thrilled us at that time were the film's sudden changes of mood from farce to tragedy, from social observation to shocking violence, as the Barrow gang robbed banks around the depressed American southwest of the 1930s. It was a piece of Americana treated in the style of the French New Wave, and it is significant that the screenplay was written on spec by two movie buffs, Robert Benton (who'd grown up around Bonnie and Clyde's Texas stamping ground) and David Newman, who'd never made a film. They worked as editors at *Esquire*, then the hippest magazine in the States, and their job was to create new fashions and cultural games for smart people to play and discuss – things like the 'In and Out' game for instance, something called 'the new sentimentality', and a piece of cod sociology, 'the McLandress dimension', a way of assessing the self-regard of public figures, which J.K. Galbraith devised for them under the pseudonym Mark Epernay. 'Like millions of you,' they subsequently wrote, 'we were riding the crest of the new wave that had swept in on our minds, and the talk was Truffaut, Godard, De Broca, Bergman, Kurosawa, Antonioni, Fellini and all the other names that fell like a litany in 1964, along with the sudden and staggering heights of rediscovery around the pantheon people – Hitchcock, Hawks, Ford, Welles and the rest.' Subsequently they brought in the then unknown Robert Towne as 'script adviser'.

Benton and Newman offered the script first to Truffaut and then to Godard, both of whom liked it but for different reasons had to back out; but not before giving them some input. Thus the Nouvelle Vague borrowings from Hollywood returned to roost at Warner Brothers, when Beatty took up the project and brought in his friend Arthur Penn. Penn was a director with a TV and stage background who'd made some distinguished but not especially popular films and had a reputation for his sensitivity towards actors.

Boldly Beatty surrounded himself with fresh faces. Gene Hackman was cast as Clyde's older brother, the extrovert Buck Barrow. Estelle Parsons was brought in to make her first Hollywood appearance as Buck's neurotic wife. The quirky Michael J. Pollard made his name as the gang's driver, C.W. Moss. Above all there was Faye Dunaway, making her debut as Bonnie Parker. She became a star the moment she cast eyes on Beatty's Clyde, the man who'd sweep her out of West Dallas into a world of romantic violence. Beatty gave the production designer Dean Tavoularis (later to design the *Godfather* trilogy) and costume designer Theodora van Runkle (her credits would include *Bullitt*, *The Godfather: Part II*, and *New York, New York*) their first major assignments. Only veteran cinematographer Burnett Guffey had a serious track record.

As a major genre the gangster movie had flourished in the early thirties, the coming of sound having made possible the necessary screeching of tyres, rattle of machine guns and snarled dialogue. But the enforcement of the Hays Office Production Code after 1934 had tamed filmmakers. An edict was issued that insisted that the law enforcers be made the heroes (James Cagney switched from mobster to FBI agent in *G-Men*), and another that no film should be based on a celebrated gangster. However, from the late fifties there had been a cycle of low-budget crime films about famous criminals of the interwar years, including *Al Capone*, *The Bonnie Parker Story* and *Baby Face Nelson*, and two streams developed. One dealt with organised crime among urban professionals from ethnic backgrounds in the Prohibition era. The other centred on disorganised country crooks from poor white backgrounds in the Depression, who were in thrall to Hollywood pictures.

These parallel cycles culminated in 1967 with the simultaneous release of *The St Valentine's Day Massacre* (Roger Corman's only film for a major studio) and *Bonnie and Clyde* – the former sombre, factual; the latter lyrical, legendary. These two threads have continued up to this day, with most of the 1970s school of filmmakers working in one stream or the other – Robert Altman's *Thieves Like Us* (from a novel inspired by the lives of Bonnie and Clyde), Scorsese's thirties film *Boxcar Bertha* and John Milius's *Dillinger* on one side, Coppola's *Godfather* trilogy and De Palma's *The Untouchables* and *Scarface*, on the other.

It was immediately apparent to most people that *Bonnie and Clyde* was a zeitgeist picture, reflecting a troubled America tormented by an impossible war in Vietnam – riots in the black ghettos; campus demonstrations; draft card burning; military recruits fleeing to Canada. The hope that died with the Kennedy assassination is echoed in the peeling posters of Roosevelt and the New Deal on walls that the Barrow gang pass by. It was a time of violence and disruption, and the following year there came the assassinations of Martin Luther King and Bobby Kennedy, and the tempestuous Democratic convention. This of course brings us to the central controversy engendered by *Bonnie and Clyde*: that it glorified violence and its perpetrators.

Bosley Crowther, influential critic of the *New York Times*, let go with both barrels on 14 August, attacking the acting, direction and script: 'This blending of farce with brutal killings is as pointless as it is lacking in taste, since it makes no valid commentary on the already travestied truth. And it leaves an astonished critic wondering just what purpose Mr Penn and Mr Beatty think they serve with this strangely antique, sentimental claptrap.' He concluded indignantly, 'This is the film that opened the Montreal International Festival!', thus echoing an incident of twelve years previously when Clare Booth Luce, US ambassador to Italy, intervened to prevent *Blackboard Jungle* being shown in competition at Venice. Crowther was not alone. Among others, *Time* magazine's anonymous reviewer dismissed the movie out of hand as 'a strange and purposeless mingling of fact and claptrap that teeters on the brink of burlesque'. But there was a backlash. Ten days later Andrew Sarris in the *Village Voice* wrote of *Bonnie and Clyde* as 'the subject of a Crowther Crusade that makes the hundred years' war look like a border skirmish'. Crowther was retired the following month. Another Crowther opponent, Pauline Kael – then forty-eight and a recent arrival in New York from San Francisco – wrote a long piece in praise of the film (reprinted in her book *Kiss Kiss Bang Bang*) that was rejected by the *New Republic* as overly enthusiastic, but accepted at the *New Yorker*. She became the *New Yorker*'s regular film critic for the next twenty-four years, changing the face of film criticism and transforming that journal's approach to the cinema. In the mid-1970s she left to become a script adviser to Warren Beatty at Paramount, but returned to the *New Yorker* after a few months. As significant as her article was *Time*'s recantation in December, with a specially commissioned *Bonnie and Clyde* painting by Robert Rauschenberg on the cover and a story by Stefan Kanfer calling it the movie of the year.

Beatty's model for a shoot-out was the scene in George Stevens's *Shane* in which gunslinger Jack Palance guns down the hapless Elisha Cook Jr in the mud outside the town's saloon. Repeating this exponentially, *Bonnie and Clyde* upped the ante on screen violence overnight. The film's various transgressions were made possible by the appointment the previous year of Jack Valenti, former special adviser to President Johnson, as the new president of the Motion Picture Association of America. He'd immediately replaced the old Production Code with a certification system.

But if *Bonnie and Clyde* had brought European art cinema into the Hollywood bloodstream (the Alain Resnais-influenced *Point Blank* appeared a few months later), it opened the floodgates for forms of violence ranging from the sturdily moral to the wholly gratuitous. Sam Peckinpah, not previously noted for ultra-violence, picked up the slow-motion finale of *Bonnie and Clyde* (which itself had come from Kurosawa) and used it throughout *The Wild Bunch*. This was soon followed by his own *Straw Dogs*, Kubrick's *A Clockwork Orange* and Siegel's *Dirty Harry*. They made screen violence a topic of international debate that has stretched down the years to Quentin Tarantino's *Reservoir Dogs* and beyond. In a thoughtful *New York Times* piece on the *Bonnie and Clyde* anniversary, the paper's film critic A.O. Scott shows sympathy for his most famous predecessor: 'We've become pretty comfortable watching the infliction of pain, and quick to laugh it off,' he writes. 'Don't misunderstand me: I still get a kick out of *Bonnie and Clyde*, but it's accompanied by a twinge of unease, by the suspicion that, in some ways that matter and that have become too easy to dismiss, Bosley Crowther was right.'

Oddly, *Bonnie and Clyde* had a benign influence that's quite the opposite, introducing the American public to the European avant-garde.

To keep themselves in the right mood while writing their script, Benton and Newman played Lester Flatt and Earl Scruggs's bluegrass record 'Foggy Mountain Breakdown', and eventually decided to use their music for the whole film. This was widely imitated, with Johnny Cash appearing on the soundtracks of both John Frankenheimer's *I Walk the Line* and Sidney J. Furie's *Little Fauss and Big Halsy*, and Tammy Wynette becoming world-famous through Bob Rafelson's *Five Easy Pieces*. Thus country music was brought to the intellectuals. The climax was reached at the bicentennial in Altman's *Nashville*, where the home of country music and its performers became a symbol for America itself.

There Will Be Blood (Paul Thomas Anderson)

The Observer, 10 February 2008

This film is Paul Thomas Anderson's first since the curious Adam Sandler comedy *Punch-Drunk Love* five years ago. Dedicated to his mentor, Robert Altman, it's inspired by a long-forgotten novel, *Oil!*, written in 1927 by the muckraking socialist author Upton Sinclair, now known largely for *The Jungle*, his fictional account of the appalling conditions in the Chicago meat-packing industry that in 1906 led to crucial legislation. The film's resonantly Old Testament title comes from the seventh chapter of Exodus where God, via Moses, orders Aaron to smite the waters so that 'they may become blood; and that there may be blood throughout all the land of Egypt'. In the context of the film this biblical blood is oil, the contaminating element dealt in by its forceful central character, the demonic Daniel Plainview (Daniel Day-Lewis), oil tycoon and upholder of untrammelled capitalism.

In early twentieth-century California, Plainview is set up against a young, charismatic preacher, Eli Sunday (Paul Dano), fanatical creator of the Church of the Third Revelation. The ironic name 'Plainview' is given to a seemingly benevolent straight dealer who operates covertly, and the preacher's name inevitably evokes Billy Sunday, the most celebrated tub-thumping American evangelist of his day, a man in league with capitalism. In this parable, realistic in its depiction of everyday life and symbolic in its force, oil and fundamentalist religion are conjoined as conflicting and symbiotic elements of our time.

This hugely impressive film begins in the deserts of the American Southwest, and no words are spoken during the first twenty minutes as a lone prospector digs deep down underground. He's like some mythical figure in his determination, endurance and suffering, and his exertions are accompanied by an extraordinary score by the British composer Jonny Greenwood of Radiohead that's dissonant, occasionally lyrical, and uses strange combinations of strings and percussion. He draws on Bartók, Stravinsky, Messiaen and Arvo Pärt and right at the end of the movie calls in Brahms. When the prospector strikes silver and is stretched out with a damaged leg in an assay office, we learn his name when he signs a form 'Daniel Plainview'.

He uses his money to switch to oil drilling and eventually strikes it moderately rich and adopts the baby son of an employee killed down a well. Surrogate fathers of a dubious nature recur in Anderson's work – the porn movie producer played by Burt Reynolds in *Boogie Nights* for instance, or Philip Baker Hall's gambler-assassin in *Hard Eight* – and Plainview is another example. Ten years later, established in the oil business, he uses this sweet-natured lad, whose milk he once laced with whiskey, as a front of warmth and respectability while gulling poor Californian farmers out of their land.

One of his targets is the dirt-poor Sunday family who live on oil-rich land which becomes the basis for Plainview's fortune. But in the process he enters into financial obligations to the local population – schools, roads, water – and promises Eli Sunday backing for his fundamentalist church. This early rural California in 1911 is beautifully realised. It shows the far West in the process of change – moving from the horse to the automobile – and the local station and rundown township look like sets from *Bad Day at Black Rock* and *Once Upon a Time in the West*. But it isn't an idyll. Men die as the oil gushes forth, Plainview's adopted son is seriously injured during a drilling accident, and little trickles down to the poor.

We gradually realise that Plainview and Eli are in their different ways deranged, and each is out to control or destroy the other. Initially the oilman seems a reasonable, ambitious entrepreneur, neatly dressed, always wearing a hat and tie, smiling seductively, speaking quietly and precisely. But the measured cadences, the drawn-out vowels, the sharp consonants reminded me strongly of someone, and I suddenly realised it was John Huston as Noah Cross, the ruthless Californian plutocrat and robber baron in *Chinatown*. Plainview refuses to be intimidated by or to strike bargains with competitors, but there is something much more than greed or independence in his character. 'I don't like to explain myself,' he says, 'I hate people… I have a compulsion to succeed… I want to earn enough to get away from everyone… I see the worst in people and things.'

Is this the product of a psychosis or is it what unbridled capitalism in its extreme form does to its exponents? Are such people and their visions necessary for human progress? Anderson's film and Day-Lewis's performance, magnificent in their horrific, near-operatic grandeur, offer no easy answers. This is a deeply pessimistic, at times puzzling film, and it seems to lack a political dimension central to Upton Sinclair's life and work. Organised labour was a significant force in the American West in the early twentieth century, often involved in violent conflict.

This has largely been ignored by Hollywood, and recently only the independent producer-director John Sayles has shown interest in it. In 1927, the year Sinclair wrote *Oil!*, Louis B. Mayer created the Academy of Motion Picture Arts and Sciences as a company union to keep labour organisers at bay. In 1934 when Sinclair ran for Governor of California on the EPIC (End Poverty in California) ticket, Mayer and the other studio bosses conspired with Hearst's newspapers and radio stations to defeat him in one of the dirtiest political campaigns ever mounted. Sinclair lost to a time-serving Republican non-entity and Mayer famously remarked: 'What does Sinclair know about anything? He's just a writer." It would be good to see him honoured this year by the academy Mayer created.

In Bruges (Martin McDonagh)

The Observer, 20 April 2008

Playwright Martin McDonagh, author of *The Lieutenant of Inishmore*, makes his feature debut as writer-director with *In Bruges*, a stylish, funny, exciting thriller in a tradition of tales about professional assassins that goes back through Tarantino's *Pulp Fiction* (1994) and Pinter's *The Dumb Waiter* (1957) to Hemingway's *The Killers* (1927). It centres on two Irish hitmen, the edgy young novice Ray (Colin Farrell) and the reflective, more experienced Ken (Brendan Gleeson). They've been sent by their London boss, Harry (Ralph Fiennes), to await their next assignment in the quiet, beautiful, medieval Belgian town of Bruges (known to its Flemish citizens as Brügge).

The time is Christmas (carols and seasonal decorations abound), there's a chill in the air, snow is on the way, Bruges's famous canals are shrouded in mist. Ken takes the opportunity for sightseeing. Ray is bored stiff and burdened by the guilt of accidentally killing a child while carrying out a recent contract to murder a priest (an uncredited Ciaran Hinds) in London.

They engage in philosophical conversations about life and their bizarre profession, which are even funnier and more scabrous than the exchanges between Samuel L. Jackson and John Travolta in *Pulp Fiction*. There's a marvellous row with a family of obese American tourists. Ray meets a pretty Dutch girl, who's working for a film company that's in Bruges to make a dream sequence paying homage to Nicolas Roeg's *Don't Look Now* and featuring an aggressive American dwarf.

Drugs enter the equation, sudden outbursts of violence ensue and then the menacing Harry arrives with homicide in mind. Looking at the array of weapons offered him by a Russian mafioso, Ray says: 'All I want is a normal gun for a normal person.'

McDonagh's plotting is fiendishly clever, his dialogue crashes in on us like a tide throwing nails ashore with each wave and his black humour is laced with serious moral issues. Farrell, his eyebrows constantly wrinkling like a pair of leeches limbering up for a fight, Gleeson, the ultimate principled hitman, and Fiennes, the family man as sadistic killer, have rarely been better. The violence is extreme, the blood flows as thick and dark as the city's canals and the picture could well have been called

Brügge Mortis. My favourite joke is Farrell's remark about the nature of Purgatory while looking at Hieronymus Bosch's *The Last Judgement*: 'It's when you're not really bad and not really good – like Tottenham.'

Gone Baby Gone (Ben Affleck)

The Observer, 8 June 2008

Crimes involving children touch on our deepest emotions, and though we've seen numerous films about infant abduction over the past fifty years, ranging in tone from *Seance on a Wet Afternoon* to *Murder on the Orient Express*, the subject is peculiarly affecting at the moment in the light of the publicity given to the cases of Shannon Matthews in Dewsbury and Madeleine McCann in Portugal. In fact, the British release of Ben Affleck's directorial debut *Gone Baby Gone*, a thriller centring on a child abduction in Boston, has been held up for more than six months because of the McCann affair. To add to the anxiety, there is a striking physical resemblance between Madeleine McCann and the film's four-year-old Amanda McCready.

This thoughtful, highly accomplished film is set in the south Boston suburb of Dorchester, initially settled in the seventeenth century by Puritans from the west of England, and now largely working-class with a core population of Irish-Americans. From the opening montage of gnarled faces, badly dressed, overweight folk of different nationalities huddled together, sitting on stoops, ambling around the streets, of walls covered in graffiti, decaying buildings, liquor stores, the viewer gets a sense of both vigour and aimlessness, of dilapidation and vibrancy. All this suggests that the film's makers know this world. Indeed, Ben Affleck and his co-writer Aaron Stockard grew up in blue-collar Boston and they've adapted a novel by local writer Dennis Lehane, author of *Mystic River*, who was brought up in Dorchester and was seven when his fellow Irish-American, the prolific George V. Higgins, put Boston on the crime fiction map in 1972 with *The Friends of Eddie Coyle*, later filmed starring Robert Mitchum.

Gone Baby Gone is based on one of Lehane's novels featuring Patrick

Kenzie (played by the director's brother, Casey Affleck) and Angie Gennaro (Michelle Monaghan), both aged around thirty and from working-class, Catholic backgrounds, running a small-time private detective agency from the modest apartment they share. Within minutes of the opening, they're hired by Bea McCready (Amy Madigan), the bitter aunt of the abducted Amanda, to use their knowledge of the neighbourhood and its protective ways in order to assist the police in finding the missing child.

Bea despises the child's neglectful single mother, Helene (Amy Ryan), who, it transpires, is a heavy-drinking, cocaine-sniffing low-life with serious underworld connections and by any normal standards unfit to be in charge of a child. Bea's husband Lionel (Titus Welliver) is an ex-convict and reformed alcoholic, who apologises for his sister. 'Helene's got emotional problems,' he explains. 'She's a cunt!' says Bea.

Patrick and Angie's investigations begin in a saloon Helene frequents, where they're treated with contempt and suspicion by the Irish-American barflies, who unwisely make homophobic jokes about Patrick's baby face and threaten him. That's a big mistake, leading to the most electrifying bar-room scene since Eddie Murphy confronted the redneck in *48 Hrs*.

They then, in another mordantly funny, edgy scene, join forces with two cops working on the case for the chief of the city's crimes against children division, Captain Jack Doyle, an Irish-American name but played by the dignified, paternalistic Morgan Freeman. These middle-aged plainclothesmen are an established team of 'good cop' Nick Poole (John Ashton) and 'bad cop' Remy Bressant (Ed Harris), the former Greek-American, the latter of French extraction from Louisiana, and in uneasy alliance the foursome follows a series of leads.

The files of known sex offenders get them nowhere, but a big-time drug dealer, who may have employed the child's mother and her lover as drug mules, becomes a prime suspect. A rendezvous with possible abductors goes tragically wrong and the case is apparently over. But the quiet, conscience-stricken, guilt-ridden Patrick can't let go, and he sets about looking for another abducted child, with horrific consequences.

The film has a sinuous, labyrinthine plot and what begins as a combination of police procedural thriller and private-eye mystery turns into a complex moral fable about the conflict between what appears morally right and what society deems to be lawful. Is there a case for bending the law in the interests of some higher purpose, and who is in a position to make such decisions? This becomes the motor of the plot and a question for debate. It is also a matter of style, as Affleck uses frequent aerial shots of Boston to suggest some higher, God-like view of the human events, often cruel, brutal and arbitrary, being enacted down there in the bars, tenements, mean streets and back alleys.

In some ways superior to Scorsese's not dissimilar *The Departed*, *Gone Baby Gone* is a compelling film, the dynamic action sequences alternating with contemplative moments. It's acted with an extraordinary intensity by an exceptional cast and superbly photographed by John Toll, a cinematographer most commonly associated with epic and lyrical pictures like *Braveheart* and *The Thin Red Line*. Particularly good and present in every scene is Casey Affleck, who was Oscar-nominated last year for another difficult role as the killer in *The Assassination of Jesse James by the Coward Robert Ford*. His Patrick Kenzie is a man driven by his religious upbringing and personal moral sense to do what is right, whatever the consequences.

Yet, never knowing whether he has fulfilled this aim, he's neither saintly nor priggish. As Patrick says early on in his voice-over commentary: 'When I was young, I asked my priest how you could get to heaven and still protect yourself from the evil in the world. He told me what God said to the children: We were sheep among wolves. Be wise as serpents yet innocent as doves.'

The Visitor (Tom McCarthy)

The Observer, 6 July 2008

In the difficult years since 9/11, Hollywood has courageously, if not always successfully, ventured into the public sphere, making movies which engage with the politics of the Middle East, the role of the CIA in international politics and corruption in the corporate world. In the meantime, America's independent moviemakers have (with a few exceptions, most especially John Sayles) retreated into a private world of idiosyncrasy and personal relationships unconnected to the public life and its moral demands. In March 2004, I identified writer-director Tom

McCarthy's debut *The Station Agent* as embodying all the formulaic aspects of what I called the independent cinema's 'inaction movie': suicide, despair, alienation, eccentric outsiders coming to decaying regional backwaters. However, I still regarded it as 'a film of considerable quality... worth attending to'.

Now, in his belated second film, *The Visitor*, McCarthy (who during these past four years has acted in such notable mainstream movies as *Flags of Our Fathers*, *Syriana* and *Good Night and Good Luck*) brings together the private and public worlds in the story of the middle-aged New England economics professor Walter Vale. He's played by the excellent sixty-year-old character actor Richard Jenkins, whose expressively pitted face and balding head are familiar to moviegoers from several dozen appearances as cops, businessmen, political functionaries and other professional types, though few people could put a name to him before the TV series *Six Feet Under*. Now he is impressively centre stage, figuring in all but two sequences of the movie.

Vale is a reticent, vaguely depressed man, no longer much interested in his teaching job at a university in Connecticut where he seems on good terms with neither pupils nor colleagues. The certificates on his office wall show he has degrees from the University of Illinois and Boston University (sound enough but not exactly Ivy League). The use of Tipp-ex to change the date on his syllabus suggests he's been teaching the identical course year after year. He wears tweed jackets and shirts with buttoned-down collars and drives a Volvo estate, a signifier in the movies that the owner is reasonably well off, cautious and calculatedly unflamboyant.

We learn slowly and bit by bit, as we would of a withdrawn but not unfriendly neighbour, that he's a widower, his wife was a musician, his son lives abroad and the book he's supposed to be writing is unlikely ever to be finished.

Compelled to represent his department at a developing countries conference in New York, Walter goes for the first time in a year or so to his Manhattan apartment. He's shocked to discover that it's occupied by a Syrian musician, Tarek Khalil (Haaz Sleiman) and his Senegalese girlfriend Zainab (Danai Gurira), a jewellery designer, both Muslims. They've rented it in good faith from a Russian conman, but after getting over the fact that Walter isn't an intruder, they're eager that he shouldn't report the matter to the police.

It transpires that they're not only illegal occupants but illegal immigrants. Sympathising with their predicament, he invites them to remain as his guests until they find somewhere else to stay. Thus Walter, the detached authority on developmental economics and the problems of Third World countries, suddenly finds that his dry academic pursuits have become acutely personal.

Tarek is open, friendly, trusting and introduces Walter to the djembe, the West African drum he expertly plays in a fusion jazz group. This provides a bond between them and puts him in touch with a liberating form of music, a valuable source of therapy for the repressed Walter. Zainab, on the other hand, is suspicious, reserved, taciturn and initially unresponsive to Walter's kindness. This is what saves her from Tarek's fate. One day, while accompanying Walter on the subway, Tarek is picked up by plainclothes officers of the NYPD and drawn into the Kafkaesque world of the immigration people.

From the colourful bustle of Manhattan, he's transported to the blank, anomic area of Queens where he's incarcerated in a windowless correctional centre. Fear of being arrested themselves prevents Zainab and Tarek's mother (Hiam Abbass), who now lives in Michigan, from visiting him. So Walter remains his only link with the outside world. All else is set aside as he finds Tarek a lawyer and cares for his mother and Zainab. Ironically, the strain enables him to relax.

There is, course, a limit to what Walter can do. Patience is recommended and except for two brief explosions of impotent anger, one on Tarek's part, the other on Walter's, there is no emotional grandstanding. And the film is essentially open-ended. Walter ends up despairing of a faceless bureaucracy that has derived further justification from the 'war on terror'. At the same time, his friendship for these three strangers has renewed his sense of social responsibility and broadened his feeling of humanity.

There are wonderful moments in this oblique, understated picture: the shocked Zainab's first appearance, discovered in the bath at Walter's flat like Goldilocks in the three bears' home; Tarek taking Walter to jam with fellow drummers in Central Park; a trip on the Staten Island ferry when Tarek's mother, Zainab and Walter talk about the Statue of Liberty, Ellis Island and the Twin Towers. But above all, *The Visitor* is a film that hangs together as a whole, the images carefully framed, scenes constantly echoing each other, and it is memorably acted by all four principals. A great injustice would be done if Richard Jenkins were not to get an Oscar nomination for this performance.

Man on Wire (James Marsh)

The Observer, 3 August 2008

The distinguished documentary producer Simon Chinn got the idea for *Man on Wire* while listening to a 2005 edition of *Desert Island Discs* featuring Philippe Petit – probably the only tightrope walker to have appeared on that programme, though he is no ordinary funambulist. He's the Frenchman who, on 7 August 1974, strung a two-hundred-foot-high wire between the Twin Towers of the World Trade Center and then walked along it, 1,368 feet in the air. This astonishing story takes us off in so many directions, and the film does its subject full justice.

In movie titles, the word 'tightrope' usually has a metaphorical meaning. The title of Elia Kazan's 1953 *Man on a Tightrope* refers not to one of his acrobats but to a Czech circus owner trying to stay in business in a vindictive communist state. Clint Eastwood's *Tightrope* is about the precarious balancing act of a New Orleans homicide cop. As it happens, the world's most powerful man was walking a tightrope the week Petit staged his famous 'coup': in the White House, Richard Nixon was swaying and then fell in the last scene of the Watergate drama.

Tightrope artists in the movies embody physical risk and are variously attractive, entrancing or sympathetically comic. In the first category is the kindly, whimsical wirewalker who wins the heart of Gelsomina in Fellini's *La Strada*, such a contrast to Anthony Quinn's brutal strong-man. In the second category is the beautiful Pia Degermark, the tightrope walker who runs off with the married Swedish aristocrat in *Elvira Madigan*. Among several comic tightrope scenes the greatest is Chaplin's in *The Circus*.

The World Trade Center never endeared itself to the public. The Twin Towers became a poor substitute for the Empire State Building in the first remake of *King Kong*, and housed the headquarters of the ruthless branch of the CIA pursuing Robert Redford in *Three Days of the Condor*. More important, they represented the hubris that drove architects to construct ever larger skyscrapers. Built in the financial hub of capitalism, the towers were subject to a fire in 1975 and a bomb attack in 1993, before the catastrophe that helped define the experience of our new century.

It is to the credit of *Man on Wire*, directed by James Marsh – a British filmmaker with a particular interest in the American scene – that except for an ironic glimpse of Nixon's 'I am not a crook' speech on a TV screen, audiences are left to make their own connections. The Nixon speech is crucial to Philippe Petit's activities because, as we learn, the Frenchman was a wild rebel, disowned by his family, and his numerous skills as a street entertainer include picking pockets. Of his long-contemplated assault on the Twin Towers he says: 'It may have been illegal, but it wasn't wicked or mean.' He regards himself as an honourable prankster and adventurer, a confederate of Robin Hood, Raffles and Batman, living out his dreams and providing vicarious excitement for the rest of us.

Using interviews old and new, newsreel material, still photography, home movies, discreet documentary reconstructions and voiceover narration by several participants, *Man on Wire* unfolds in two parallel narratives. The first is what happened on that liberating day of 7 August, 1974 after Petit and his team, a pair in each tower, went through the last stages of rigging the equipment and staging the walk.

The second is the story of Philippe's life from the moment as a teenager when, in a dentist's waiting room, he saw an artist's impression of what the completed World Trade Center would look like. He forgot about his toothache, quietly ripped out the picture and made it his ambition to walk from one tower to the other of this still uncompleted building.

There is a further cinematic connection. Petit loved heist movies and this is a benign version of *The Asphalt Jungle*, *Rififi* or *The Lavender Hill Mob*, as Philippe draws together a trusted gang – first of French friends, then an Australian recruit and finally several key Americans. Two earlier capers test the gang's central core: a 1971 walk between the spires of Notre Dame in Paris and another, two years later, between the north pylons of the Sydney Harbour Bridge, from which he gained experience and possibly finance as well. After the Australian triumph, he picked the pocket of the arresting officer.

The conspirators are a colourful, articulate crowd and there is the necessary moll, Philippe's girlfriend Annie, to provide romantic interest. There is also the question of who will crack up. Philippe is a self-dramatising character with a touch of the winsome young Jean-Louis Barrault (especially from *Les Enfants du paradis*) as well as of Hollywood tough guy Kevin Bacon. The bizarre details of the gang's casing of the Twin Towers (at one stage disguised as a French TV crew making a documentary), finding an inside man to join the operation and then pulling off the job, could have been invented by screenwriters, but life itself (with a little nod to the cinema) wrote this wonderful script.

Petit had a false pass in the name of 'Philip Asher' and a crutch that led everyone to facilitate his progress, rather like the assassin in *The Day of the Jackal*. The job would be less easy now and unlikely to result in such public pleasure and official forgiveness. Yet even then, there was the imminent prospect of Petit being dislodged by a police helicopter. Anyway, it's a terrific story about courage, obsession and friendship, cleverly and economically told, and a bit of a trial for acrophobes. And there's an excellent score drawing on Beethoven, Satie, Grieg, Vaughan Williams and Michael Nyman, including themes from his soundtrack to *The Draughtsman's Contract*. Perhaps the film's most haunting image is a photograph taken at an angle from beneath the tightrope. Petit lies on the wire, an airliner passes above. Suddenly two events – one sublime, the other horrendous – are surreally merged.

The Wrestler (Darren Aronofsky)

The Observer, 18 January 2009

One of the most popular characters in Hollywood and American popular culture is the hard man, over the hill in some sport, his body shattered, his life in tatters, trying to make a comeback in the boxing ring, the rodeo corral, the football arena or, as in *Slap Shot*, on the rink of a minor ice hockey league. This folk hero has been played at various times by Robert Mitchum, Robert De Niro, Paul Newman and Charlton Heston. Perhaps the finest, slimmest example is John Huston's *Fat City*, where Stacy Keach works as a casual labourer in rural California, living in a flophouse, his girlfriend an alcoholic floozie, and dreaming of returning to the ring.

Scripted by Robert Siegel and directed by Darren Aronofsky, *The Wrestler* touches most bases of the genre. The hero Randy 'the Ram' Robinson (Mickey Rourke) is a professional athlete far beyond his prime, his marriage a distant memory, his twentysomething daughter Stephanie (Evan Rachel Wood) long estranged and despising him. His current romantic interest is Pam Cassidy (Marisa Tomei), a stripper in a cheesy New Jersey bar, and he lives in a trailer park.

But Randy practises a sport – low-grade professional wrestling – that is widely regarded with derision as phoney, fixed, a form of inferior theatre that offers no hope of real glory. In *Requiem for a Heavyweight* (a.k.a. *Blood Money*), the washed-up pugilist played by Anthony Quinn loses his last fight to Cassius Clay and ends up experiencing the ultimate degradation of donning a ridiculous costume to become a wrestler. When the Coen brothers want to see their idealistic left-wing playwright Barton Fink humiliated, they have a Hollywood studio boss assign him to writing a wrestling picture for Wallace Beery. The fight between Orlando and Charles in *As You Like It* and the naked encounter between Rupert Birkin and Gerald Crich in *Women in Love* are among the few serious engagements with wrestling in literature.

So Randy is at the bottom of the pile in a disreputable subculture, and it takes considerable talent to make an audience believe in his professional pride and to respect him as a figure with a tragic dimension. Yet Aronofsky, Siegel and the fifty-two-year-old Rourke succeed. An opening montage of stills and posters establishes the Ram at the height of his fame in the late eighties, performing in Madison Square Garden and big city venues.

We first see him twenty years later, wearing frayed jeans, a mane of hair (much of it golden extensions) flopping over his shoulders, fighting at weekends in sleazy New Jersey halls while doing manual work in a supermarket during the week. He's a broken man, yet still something of a legend among fellow fighters and older fans. Everything is fixed beforehand between the fighters, who, under it all, have a weirdly tender regard for each other, but the fans bay for blood and it's provided for them.

The fights might be choreographed, but they involve real pain and physical damage and Randy can trace his career through the scars and weals that cover his body. At first glance, he looks in good shape, but he has to be bound up and fed steroids. His face is a wreck from violence, booze and incautious living. He cuts a corner off a razor blade so that at a dramatic moment in the ring he can covertly cut his forehead to drench his face in blood. In the worst of the fights, he and a friendly opponent roll in barbed wire and glass and attack each other with staple guns and thumb tacks. The ring looks like an abattoir as they leave in search of medical attention.

Randy is a generous, kindly, child-like figure, who enjoys playing Nintendo wrestling games with kids and can't understand why they'd like to move on to games involving the war in Iraq. But everything he does goes wrong. He seeks a reconciliation with his daughter, who's probably lesbian, and after a deeply moving day out with her at a dismal, denuded coastal resort, he screws it all up by getting drunk.

Pam the stripper is touched by him but can't include him in her plans to change her life. After collapsing in the dressing room following a particularly arduous fight, he has open-heart surgery that leaves the biggest wound of his career and he's told never to go into the ring again. He takes what he believes to be a proper job, charming little old ladies from behind the deli counter of a supermarket. Then he suddenly rebels against its petty nature, deliberately jamming his hand on the bacon slicer to get the blood spurting again and decides to go back to the ring. A twenty-year return bout in Delaware with an old antagonist, a buffoon bully called the Ayatollah, is irresistible. Outside the ring, he's nobody. In it, he's a sort of hero to blue-collar no-hopers. He needs their applause and adulation, even though they know it is all a bloody farce.

The outstanding work by director of photography Maryse Alberti captures the world Randy lives in – the forbidding wintry exteriors, the dark interiors of bars and trailers, the harsh strip lighting of changing rooms and supermarkets. Through his body movements and subtle facial expressions, Rourke reveals the pride, the hopes, the inner pain of this tormented man, and he moves from the pathetic to the tragic.

In a final speech, we are seeing not just the Ram attempting a comeback, but Rourke talking about his own career and his struggle with his wild, self-destructive, self-despising character. It is a mighty performance and is followed by an affecting Bruce Springsteen song over the final credits specially written for the movie and expressing Randy's defiant spirit. It's far removed from the self-aggrandising, self-pitying 'My Way'. Nearer, in fact, to a blue-collar 'Non, je ne regrette rien'.

2009   247

Antichrist (Lars von Trier)

The Observer, 26 July 2009

What do you do if you're a young film director seeking worldwide recognition, but live in a small country with a language spoken nowhere else? Well, you could emigrate to America as several Scandinavian directors have done. But Lars von Trier, at fifty-three the oldest enfant terrible in the business, has a phobia about travelling. So after he decided to stay put in Denmark, his basic strategy was to make most of his movies in English, becoming, as it were, the dark side of Abba, and then turning his modest productions into big events by attracting public attention, creating gossip, causing outrage, provoking discussion.

Following those earlier self-publicists, Erich von Stroheim and Josef von Sternberg, he awarded himself an aristocratic 'von' (though he must have been furious when the latest edition of Ephraim Katz's *Film Encyclopedia* included the entry 'von Trier, Lars. See SWEDEN'). He created news when he launched a cinematic movement, Dogme 95, and he changes style with each movie: the last one released here, the business comedy *The Boss of It All*, was shot with a computer making decisions about lighting and camera movement.

In May, his latest picture, *Antichrist*, was called the most shocking movie ever to be shown at Cannes. When it opened in Stockholm last month, he gave an interview to the glossy Swedish magazine *Filter* in which he calls Ingmar Bergman a stupid pig ('ett dumt svin'). Well, *Antichrist* certainly isn't a uniquely shocking film (Oshima's *Ai No Corrida*, for instance, and Haneke's *The Piano Teacher* were more troubling in their time).

It is, in fact, a gripping poetic allegory that follows Coleridge's *Kubla Khan* and such pictures as Buñuel's *Un Chien andalou* and Louis Malle's *Black Moon* in drawing directly on its author's subconscious. Von Trier wrote it as a way of dealing with a deep depression and it's clearly based on the mental turmoil of being brought up by parents committed to communism, naturism and atheism and his recent conversion to Catholicism. It's also much influenced by the austere, deeply religious movies of Denmark's greatest director, Carl Dreyer, whose *Gertrud* von Trier helped restore, and the mystical films of Andrei Tarkovsky, who made his final film in Swedish exile and to whose memory *Antichrist* is dedicated.

Shot on location in the forests of North Rhine-Westphalia, the film is set, so one infers from an address on an envelope, in the Pacific Northwest of the United States and it unfolds in four chapters, framed by a prologue and an epilogue. In the prologue, shot in slow-motion black and white, a married couple played by Willem Dafoe and Charlotte Gainsbourg make passionate love in the bathroom of their fourth-floor apartment. Their little son, Nick, opens the gate of his cot, sees the primal scene as he passes the open bathroom door and climbs on to a table beside a window, knocking over three figurines stamped 'Grief', 'Pain' and 'Despair'. It's snowing outside and he falls from the window to his death in the street below, his woollen rabbit falling with him. The only thing on the soundtrack is an aria from Handel's pastoral opera *Rinaldo* and the sequence has a terrible beauty.

The first chapter, 'Grief', begins with Nick's funeral, the one time we see anyone other than his parents – who are never named, so I'll call them Dafoe and Gainsbourg. Dafoe is a psychotherapist and he attempts to allay his wife's guilt over the boy's death by more or less taking her on as a patient. He tries to trace the roots of her fears and discovers that chief among them is the dark forest that surrounds their holiday cabin, which they call Eden.

She'd been there with Nick the previous year, working on a historical study called *Gynicide*, a word new to me and apparently used in the States by feminist critics to mean the destruction of women both by themselves and through the influence of men. She'd abandoned this book and later, when the couple arrive at Eden, Dafoe discovers the text with its medieval illustrations of witches being executed and dismembered.

The film opens like Nicolas Roeg's *Don't Look Now*. When the couple get to Eden for the next three chapters – 'Pain (Chaos Reigns)', 'Despair' and 'The Three Beggars' – it starts to resemble those eco-horror movies that followed in the wake of Hitchcock's *The Birds*. Nature itself turns against the couple: animals (a fox who utters a couple of words as creatures do in fables, a miscarrying doe and a raven) and the very forest become a source of palpable terror.

The woman is suspicious of the therapeutic games her husband devises and even of therapy itself. We sense she feels she is a victim of both society and nature. The tension mounts in the confined, decaying cabin and escalates into terrible violence that involves the much publicised scenes of an attempted emasculation and a self-inflicted clitoridectomy.

2009

Starting with the title, which suggests some titanic conflict between forces of good and evil, *Antichrist* is full of religious symbols and biblical references. Central is the notion of Eden, of original sin and feminist problems with this creation myth, but there's also the grindstone that Gainsbourg bolts to Dafoe's leg (far more painful than hanging it round his neck) and her statement that 'nature is Satan's church'. And, of course, Dafoe is famous for playing Christ in Scorsese's controversial *The Last Temptation of Christ*.

Like the films of Dreyer, Tarkovsky and Bergman, *Antichrist* is something to be experienced rather than understood, at least at a first viewing, and it concludes in the visionary epilogue on a tone of tragic tranquillity. It's a solemn work perhaps, but forceful rather than hectoring, and is performed with an involving commitment and moral conviction by Gainsbourg (who won the best actress award at Cannes) and Dafoe. The cinematography is by Anthony Dod Mantle, the Danish-based British cameraman who did a remarkable job on a couple of Dogme movies, and received an Oscar for *Slumdog Millionaire*. *Antichrist* confirms that he is a cinematographer in the class of Sven Nykvist.

The White Ribbon (Michael Haneke)

The Observer, 15 November 2009

Numerous novelists, dramatists and filmmakers have been attracted to the period immediately preceding the outbreak of the First World War to give their work a touch of nostalgia, irony or historical resonance.

J.B. Priestley, whose life had been transformed by his experiences on the Western Front, was among the earliest with his 1934 play *Eden End*, set in 1912 Yorkshire. Isabel Colegate's novel *The Shooting Party* (filmed by Alan Bridges in 1984) takes place at a grand country house in 1913. István Szabó's movie *Colonel Redl* cuts straight from its eponymous anti-hero's death to the Austro-Hungarian army going into battle, though it was as early as 1916 that the Austrian wit Karl Kraus launched one of the last century's greatest clichés by having a newsboy enter a Viennese cafe shouting: 'Extra! Extra! Archduke Ferdinand assassinated in Sarajevo!'

Austrian filmmaker Michael Haneke uses this historical setting in his masterly *The White Ribbon*, winner of this year's Palme d'Or at Cannes. It isn't, however, until more than two hours into his picture that its timespan is revealed as being from the early summer of 1913 to August the following year. The neat, north German Protestant village has a timeless quality that, with the absence of motor cars, gas and electricity and the reliance on horse-drawn transport and rather primitive bicycles, suggests a feudal community at any time in the late nineteenth or early twentieth century.

At the top of the pile is the Baron, owner of the land and principal employer. Attached to his estate is a burly Steward, and the chief figures in the village are the stern Lutheran Pastor, the Doctor and the thirty-one-year-old Schoolteacher, who is insecure, immature and the only unmarried one among them. Everyone else works on the land and one thinks of them all as archetypes, capitalised as representatives of their social positions. The film's narrator, actually that familiar figure 'the unreliable narrator', is the Schoolteacher. From his infirm voice, we infer he's looking back on the events from old age and thus endowing them with special significance, though this is not spelled out.

The Schoolteacher interweaves two narrative threads. One is personal, lyrical and nostalgic: he has fallen in love with the shy new nanny caring for the Baron's three children. The other, dominant thread is a series of apparent accidents and atrocities that occur in the village, beginning with the Doctor being seriously injured when his horse is tripped by a wire strung between two trees near his house. It continues with a farmer's wife falling to her death through rotten floorboards at a sawmill owned by the Baron. Then the cabbages on the Baron's land are destroyed with a scythe, there are two brutal abductions, a barn is burnt, a caged bird spiked by a pair of scissors and so on. Only in a couple of cases do we see what happens and who the perpetrators are.

As with Haneke's *Code Unknown* and *Hidden*, an air of mystery hangs over the movie and isn't explicitly resolved. It's never, however, less than lucid. Revenge is one possible motive and the children, who move around together in a conspiratorial manner rather like the blond children in the British horror flick *Village of the Damned*, are involved in some way. Indeed, one of them claims to have dreams that foresee the atrocities, but the visiting police can't decide whether she's overheard some plotting, is mentally disturbed, or has psychic powers.

The White Ribbon is a spellbinding movie, as exciting as a thriller, which, indeed, it resembles. Among other things, it's about an unjust social system yoked to a repressive society that is morally and physically disintegrating, though no one's prepared to confront it. The Baron tyrannises his young Italian wife as if it were his right, until she rebels against a world 'blighted by malice, envy and brutality'.

In the name of his narrow religion, the Pastor thrashes and humiliates his children, forcing the two older ones to wear the eponymous white ribbons of purity to keep them aware of their sinfulness (the girl's pride, the boy's masturbation). The Steward, craven servant of the Baron, behaves violently towards his sons. The Doctor's transgressive conduct involves his daughter and the midwife. Yet despite all this, Haneke's cool movie never lacks conviction or edges into melodrama.

The picture is shot in a harsh, elegant monochrome and resembles Carl Dreyer's *Days of Wrath* and *The Word*, both set in similarly austere northern European Lutheran communities. But the picture it most reminds me of is Fassbinder's elegant black-and-white *Effi Briest*, a faithful adaptation of Theodor Fontane's classic 1895 German novel about the subjugation of a young woman by her aristocratic husband.

Another work that comes to mind is *Spring Awakening*, Frank Wedekind's sensational play about sexual suppression in pre-First World War Germany. Wedekind's subtitle, *A Children's Tragedy*, is echoed by Haneke's *A German Children's Story*.

In an interview in *Sight & Sound* magazine, Haneke mentions his admiration for Fontane and he also refers to another influence, the great photographer August Sander who in 1910 from his base in Cologne set about producing a taxonomy of German faces and archetypes that he called *People of the Twentieth Century*. He began with farm workers as they're closest to nature. The riveting faces in Haneke's film have an uncanny resemblance to Sander's.

The final long-held shot is an unforgettable tableau of the villagers gathered in a small, bare church just after the outbreak of war, a portrait of a nation on the point of history. Luther's 'A Mighty Fortress Is Our God' is being played on the organ, and the camera is viewing the congregation from the position of the altar, as if God himself is observing and interrogating his creations.

Me and Orson Welles (Richard Linklater)

The Observer, 6 December 2009

It is difficult to recapture the excitement Orson Welles generated fifty years ago among cinephiles and serious theatregoers. When George Coulouris joined the Bristol Old Vic Company in 1950 after a lengthy sojourn in the States my fellow sixth-formers and I were thrilled beyond measure to have in our city an actor who'd played Mark Antony opposite Welles in the Mercury company's fabled 1937 modern dress production of *Julius Caesar* and had a leading role in *Citizen Kane*. Yet none of us had seen *Citizen Kane* which had been out of distribution since shortly after its opening in 1941. We only knew Welles through a few film appearances, most notably *The Third Man*, and his reputation for brilliance, wit and innovation, and what a few years later we'd learn to call charisma. Satyajit Ray said that one of the great regrets of his life was being out of Calcutta when *Kane* had its brief three-day screening there; one of mine is queuing at a London theatre in 1951 to see Welles in *Othello* and failing to get in.

This exhilaration came back to me this week while seeing Richard Linklater's engrossing film version of Robert Kaplow's charming novel about a fictitious eighteen-year-old schoolboy briefly becoming a member of Welles's Mercury Theatre in 1937. In a very personal way, the experience was enhanced by the curious fact that much of the film was shot in a theatre in Douglas, Isle of Man, where I spent several summers in the earlier 1940s.

The film is presented through the eyes of Richard Samuels, a bright high school senior from New Jersey, in love with theatre, cinema, literature, radio and popular culture, attractively played by Zac Efron, star of the *High School Musical* series. One day he crosses the Hudson to look around Manhattan. First he meets in a music store Gretta Adler (Zoe Kazan), a deeply serious girl his own age with literary ambitions. Then he strikes up a conversation with actors outside the Mercury Theatre on 41st Street, which has just been taken over by Welles's company after their departure from the government-sponsored Federal Theatre. Suddenly Welles himself arrives, immaculately turned out in a homburg and three-piece suit, and he engages in badinage with his actors and the naïve, fearless Richard. The upshot is that after cross-questioning the teenager, the mercurial and capricious head of the Mercury hires Richard to play Brutus's young servant Lucius in the play that is scheduled to open in a week's time.

Welles hands him over to his attractive young assistant, Sonya (Claire Danes), to be inducted into the ways of the company. She's a sophisticated, highly ambitious young woman, determined to use anyone to get ahead in showbusiness, her immediate aim being to get a job with David O. Selznick, Hollywood's hottest producer. She stands in contrast to Gretta, the idealistic writer, and together they represent key facets of the 1930s. Meanwhile, Welles in his role of teacher takes Richard under his wing, demanding he accompany him on his money-making trips to radio stations, using an ambulance to make his way through the traffic. There's a marvellous scene of Welles arriving just in time for a broadcast, largely unacquainted with the script and taking off into an eloquent improvisation that baffles, infuriates and then impresses his fellow actors.

Linklater's film is about the education of a suburban boy in the ways of the world, and the dramatic core is a realistic and persuasive account of the making of the Mercury's *Julius Caesar* and of the outrageous Welles at work. The modern dress production, with its dark green uniforms and Sam Browne belts, raised-arm salutes and a Caesar with a strong resemblance to Mussolini, is designed to make audiences think of Italy and fascist dictators. But Welles himself, playing Brutus, the intelligent, conscience-stricken liberal, is something of a dictator in the way he savagely cuts Shakespeare's text (re-arranged and pared down to ninety minutes), orders everyone around, and takes credit for his collaborators' work.

Never before have I seen a theatrical production so brilliantly re-created, and for this major credit must go to the British cinematographer Dick Pope, who makes us feel we're there on the historic night. But at the end the show belongs to Christian McKay, the fourth and best actor to play Welles on screen. When we first see him the resemblance is merely passing, but after five minutes we think we're in the presence of the arrogant, irresistible young Orson himself, such is the accuracy of the body language, the facial expressions and above all that resonant voice, purring and booming. When after the first night curtain he asks, 'How the hell do I top this?', the complexity of his future life flashes before us. Most of the other performances are convincing – Ben Chaplin as the perennially pessimistic Coulouris, Leo Bill as the puckish Norman Lloyd, and James Tupper as the suave lady's man Joseph Cotten, who figures in a lovely joke when in an ironic re-enactment of the most famous image from *The Third Man* he emerges as eavesdropper from a pitch-black doorway. The one real failure is a miscast Eddie Marsan, a specialist in sad losers, as Welles's closest associate and equal, the haughty, confident John Houseman, one of the great figures of the twentieth-century arts.

A Prophet (Jacques Audiard)

The Observer, 24 January 2010

Born in Paris in 1920, Michel Audiard was a prolific screenwriter and sometime director from the 1940s until his death in 1985. Only marginally associated with the Nouvelle Vague through a couple of pictures he wrote for Philippe de Broca and Truffaut's former assistant Claude Miller, he worked in mainstream French cinema on a wide variety of popular films and co-scripted some of the best thrillers of the day. His son, Jacques Audiard, followed him into the business and was in his forties when he directed his first film, *See How They Fall*, in 1994. Now with *A Prophet*, his fifth movie as writer-director, he's established himself not only as a far more distinctive movie-maker than his father but as a leading figure of his generation.

All his films are elaborately constructed, deeply ironic stories about crime and character. In what is still in some ways his most subversive work, *A Self Made Hero*, a devious young man takes advantage of the social chaos of the last days of the Second World War to reconstruct himself as a hero of the Resistance.

His new film is a violent prison drama, set in contemporary France, in which the central character undergoes a process of self-discovery and self-creation when he's sentenced to six years for an undisclosed crime. He's an illiterate orphan, Malik El Djebena (Tahar Rahim), born in France to Arab parents, his back and face bearing scars that testify to a life of violence, and it's his first time in an adult jail. Within minutes of arriving in the yard, he's beaten by other prisoners and his shoes are stolen. He then becomes the servant of a middle-aged Corsican gangster, César Luciani, who virtually runs the jail and is played with ferocious intensity by Niels Arestrup, the hero's sleazy father in Audiard's last film, *The Beat That My Heart Skipped*.

César gives Malik the choice of either killing Reyeb, a gay Arab who's shortly to give evidence in a mob trial, or be killed himself. The boy discovers there is no possible appeal to the indifferent, corrupt authorities. Reyeb treats him decently but in a terrifyingly protracted killing Malik cuts him up with the safety razor he's been taught to conceal in his mouth. He's learnt his first lesson and is taken under the bat-like wings of the brutal César, becoming his eyes and ears when he eventually reveals that he's secretly learnt Italian and Corsican.

Over the next six years of claustrophobic incarceration, Malik is given increasingly greater responsibility and through string-pulling with the authorities César gets the boy special twenty-four-hour leaves. These are ostensibly to prepare him to take his place again in everyday society but in fact they're to run criminal errands. Meanwhile, Malik has found two other mentors. The first is Ryad, an Arab prisoner with terminal cancer, who encourages him to study languages and economics, and they remain in touch when the older man is released. The other teacher is Jordi, a gypsy who handles the prison's drugs and controls a gang smuggling hash into France from Spain.

To the violent fury of César, who expresses his anger by nearly scooping out the boy's right eye with a spoon, Malik also works with Jordi in his brief absences. But there's no stopping him. Malik steadily leaves his mentors behind as he learns to play both sides against the middle, to manipulate racial tensions, to engage in the financial long game, to act as ruthlessly and decisively as his enemies, but always to postpone revenge until it helps advance business.

Eventually, he's smart enough to get himself deliberately put in solitary for forty days while everyone on the outside and inside is tearing each other apart. To Audiard, the film's title is intended to suggest that Malik is a man of the future, but in a quite literal way an Arab gangster heading an underworld mob in Marseilles actually thinks Malik has supernatural gifts of prophecy.

The movie has an intense, gut-tearing reality and we see Malik change mentally and physically as the months and years pass. He develops and matures in this school for criminal education rather than moral rehabil-itation, a place that is a paradigm of modern society and of capitalism at its most nakedly competitive.

This is an outstanding contribution to a great tradition of prison movies that goes back eighty years to MGM's original *The Big House*. It's the second fine French example this past year, after the two-part *Mesrine*, though, unlike the heroes of that picture, no one here bothers to escape as they know they can just as easily conduct their business from inside.

A Prophet, with its series of social and political lessons learnt and put into practice, resembles a play by Bertolt Brecht from which the ideolog-ical signposting and scaffolding have been removed. It is thus fitting that the final credits are accompanied by 'Mack the Knife', Brecht and Weill's great song from their allegory of crime in Victorian England, *The Threepenny Opera*. But it's not the upbeat concert version of Louis Armstrong or Bobby Darin. It's a tough, harsh performance by the country singer Jimmie Dale Gilmore, one of the best I've heard.

A Single Man (Tom Ford)

The Observer, 14 February 2010

Christopher Isherwood was one of the great prose writers of the twenti-eth century, a man of complexity, honesty and wit, and the fashion designer Tom Ford, making his carefully stylised directorial debut, has done an altogether admirable job of bringing to the screen what many regard as his best novel.

Born in 1904, Isherwood grew up with the cinema, was fascinated by the relationship between literature and the new medium, and his most famous line occurs in his most celebrated book, *Goodbye to Berlin*: 'I am a camera with its shutter open, quite passive, recording, not thinking.' Over the years he worked frequently on movies (his masterly novella, *Prater Violet*, was based on his experience of co-writing the 1934 Berthold Viertel film *Little Friend*), and when he and W.H. Auden left Britain just before the outbreak of the Second World War, Auden settled into the literary world of New York while Isherwood travelled west to be close to Hollywood and to California-based students of eastern religions.

Isherwood touched on Hollywood in *The World in the Evening*, his first novel set in America, and satirised it in the adaptation of Waugh's *The Loved One* that he made with Terry Southern, which he spoke of as his most enjoyable experience in the cinema. He can be spotted as a party guest in his friend George Cukor's final film, *Rich and Famous* (1981). *A Single Man*, however, published in 1964, while as semi-autobiographical as the rest of his fiction, has no reference to Hollywood. Its background is a very specific time in America: the Cuban missile crisis of October 1962 when the nation seemed on the brink of annihilation, but before the escalation in Vietnam and the social and sexual revolutions of the 1960s. And its setting is that rootless, lotus-eating southern California, where conformity and eccentricity painfully coexist and where anything seems possible. Several generations of British homosexuals, from the film director James Whale in the 1930s through Isherwood in the 40s, to the screenwriter Gavin Lambert and the painter David Hockney (both close friends of Isherwood) in the 50s and 60s, found a liberating freedom there.

The central character is the openly gay George Falconer, a fifty-eight-year-old British exile and professor of literature at a middling Los Angeles university, living a few minutes from the beach since 1938. He's played by Colin Firth with an unforgettable intensity. Observing the world through horn-rimmed spectacles in an apparently detached, ironic, quizzical manner, he's a camera with its shutter open and appears as coldly fastidious and un-Californian as his immaculate suit, white shirt and tie. But George, like Isherwood at that time, is concealing an inner turmoil. Isherwood was worried about losing his young partner, the American painter Don Bachardy and thinking of a move back to England or to the more relaxed San Francisco. George is in a state of anguish over the recent death in a car crash of Jim (Matthew Goode), his lover of thirteen years, whose family ignored George's existence. He also finds increasingly infuriating both the homophobia of the political right and the bland understanding of middle-class liberals, and regards his time as a teacher wasted on a new generation of shallow students.

The action takes place in a single day, Isherwood arriving at this day-in-the-life form after re-reading Virginia Woolf's *Mrs Dalloway*, which was in turn inspired by James Joyce's *Ulysses*. Of the films based on these novels, Ford's is, I think, the best, though Isherwood's often savage social criticism – of university life, the straight world and cultural homogenisation – has been considerably softened up. A central theme is ageing and mortality, the inevitability of one's own death and that of those you love.

When the book appeared in 1964 the novelist and critic Stanley Kauffmann noted in his perceptive review striking resemblances between *A Single Man* and Thomas Mann's *Death in Venice*, and he even suggested it might well have been called *Death in Venice, Cal.* This dramatic thrust has been further emphasised by Ford and his screenwriter David Scearce, borrowing, consciously or unconsciously, from a French movie dating from around the same time as Isherwood's novel, *Le Feu follet*, where the protagonist, at odds with a distrusted world, carries with him everywhere a Luger, with which he proposes to commit suicide. Likewise, George has a gleaming black revolver that he similarly fetishises, buys bullets for and thinks of using.

While engaging in reveries and flashbacks, George goes about his business as a teacher, conducting a class on Aldous Huxley's *After Many a Summer* and challenging his students to think about conformity and prejudice. He has two particularly remarkable encounters, one with an old friend, the other with a young student. The old friend is Charley (the excellent Julianne Moore), an English divorcee considering returning to London, with whom he has an extended, boozy dinner. The student is a sensitive outsider, the insecure bisexual Kenny (Nicholas Hoult). Both penetrate George's carapace, bringing out a frankness and vulnerability he's tried to conceal.

Exposed to searching close-ups throughout, Colin Firth gives the performance of his career as George, and subtle, and sometimes not so subtle, gradations of colour and visual texture reflect and complement his changing moods as the day goes on. This is a self-conscious, superbly crafted, deeply felt movie. It's not a gay film but the story of a gay man, a single man in several senses, but also everyman in the way we respond to him, as we do to Clarissa Dalloway or Leopold Bloom.

2010

Toy Story 3 (Lee Unkrich)

The Observer, 18 July 2010

As always, the generous gang at Pixar films offer excellent value, starting with the usual bonus of an animated short as a curtain raiser for the feature. In this case it's the delightful, five-minute *Day & Night*, directed by Teddy Newton, who worked on *The Incredibles*, *Ratatouille* and the magnificent Pixar short *Presto*, which accompanied *Wall-E*. Two amorphous, asexual creatures – like cartoon ghosts – confront each other against a flat, black background. One, it transpires, is the surly Night, the other the cheerful Day. Within the outline of each two-dimensional figure we're shown 3D images of the world in sunlight and moonlight, of Las Vegas neon-lit by night and under blue skies by day. The pair mime their challenges and at the end come to accept their happy, complementary roles.

The charming, semi-abstract whimsicality of *Day & Night* puts us in the right mood to encounter for the third time, and in unobtrusive 3D, the toys we first met in little Andy's nursery back in 1995. In that early episode, which began a new classic era of animation, the devoted cowboy Woody (voiced by Tom Hanks), representative of the Old Frontier, is challenged for supremacy by the astronaut Buzz Lightyear (Tim Allen), boastfully confident avatar of the boldly-going New Frontier, who doesn't believe he's a toy. (Buzz Aldrin, the second man to set foot on the moon, once threatened to sue Disney over the film but eventually thought better of it.) In the even better *Toy Story 2* (1999) we have the theme about kids getting tired of their early nursery favourites, and there is some remarkable satire when Woody is kidnapped by a ruthless dealer in vintage toys and his mates come to the rescue.

The truly wonderful *Toy Story 3* completes the trilogy. It's set on the eve of the seventeen-year-old Andy's departure for college and sees him clearing his room for his little sister. Andy decides to take Woody with him and put the other toys in the attic. But the bags get confused. All except Woody are sent to the Sunnyside Daycare Centre, which they regard as total rejection. This place is ruled over by the apparently benevolent, strawberry-scented Lotso 'Huggin'-Bear (Ned Beatty), who's accompanied by the mute Big Baby, and the tone suddenly gets seriously dark in the manner of *Dead of Night* and *Child's Play*, where the dolls are possessed by evil spirits. Lotso, a tragi-comic figure, has become an emotionally twisted sadist as a consequence of thinking himself abandoned. He's turned the daycare centre into a penitentiary run by the convicts, a parody of a Hollywood prison film, as chilling as Dickens's Dotheboys Hall or *Pinocchio*'s Pleasure Island. Also present at Sunnyside and cleverly used are a reunited Barbie and Ken, the former very amusingly becoming a liberated woman, recognising the preening Ken's limitations and giving a speech reminiscent of the founding fathers. The dogged Woody comes to the rescue, but before all is resolved there are chases and cliff-hanging escapes, and Buzz is first reprogrammed as a militarist and then as a dashing, Spanish-speaking gallant.

The earlier films bring lumps to the throat by evincing a conventional nostalgia for childhood but without resorting to characteristic Disneyesque sentimentality. *Toy Story 3* achieves the same results by showing Andy moving towards an emotional maturity. In the course of the film Andy and his toys develop in different ways as he passes on to a further stage in his life, understanding that his old, somewhat battered, deeply faithful companions are best cared for by a younger generation. It is a reflection of the hold that the Old West still has on American life that Woody should be the token toy he takes along with him – rather more endearing to me than Sebastian Flyte taking his teddy bear Aloysius with him to Oxford in *Brideshead Revisited*.

Seeing *Toy Story 3* and Christopher Nolan's *Inception* within forty-eight hours of each other was to be made aware of two things. First, that there are good reasons for being alive in these dismal days of the second decade of the twenty-first century. Second, there are areas of popular culture where whatever is the diametric opposite of dumbing down is at work, and that those who respect the intelligence and tastes of the general public are being rewarded for their confidence. On a slightly different but not dissimilar note, it was pleasing to see at the end of *Toy Story 3*'s final credits that seventy-two babies were born to members of the production team while the film was being made.

The King's Speech (Tom Hooper)

The Observer, 9 January 2011

W.H. Auden wrote his poem 'September 1, 1939' while sitting in a New York bar: 'Uncertain and afraid / As the clever hopes expire / Of a low dishonest decade.' *The King's Speech* takes a rather different view of Britain and the 1930s, though it's not entirely inconsistent with Auden's judgment and isn't in any sense what is sneeringly called heritage cinema. It is the work of a highly talented group of artists who might be regarded as British realists – Tom Hooper directed the soccer epic *The Damned United*; Eve Stewart was production designer on Mike Leigh's *Topsy-Turvy* and *Vera Drake*; Jenny Beavan was responsible for the costumes worn in *Gosford Park* and *The Remains of the Day*; the cinematographer Danny Cohen lit Shane Meadows's *This is England* and *Dead Man's Shoes*; Tariq Anwar's editing credits range from *The Madness of King George* to *American Beauty*; and the screenplay is by the British writer David Seidler, who co-wrote Coppola's *Tucker: The Man and His Dream*.

The film is the private story of a famous public man, King George VI (known in his family circle as Bertie), the woman who loved him and became his queen, and the innovative Australian speech therapist Lionel Logue, who helped him control and come to terms with the stammer that had tortured him since childhood.

The social and political background, acutely observed and carefully woven into the film's fabric, is the Depression at home, the rise of fascism abroad, and the arrival of the mass media as a major force in our lives. Central to the dramatic action are four crucial incidents: the death in 1936 of George V, the first monarch to address his subjects via the radio; the accession to the throne of his eldest son as Edward VIII and his almost immediate abdication in order to marry American double divorcee Wallis Simpson; the crowning of his successor, George VI; and finally, in 1939, the outbreak of a war for which the king and queen became figureheads of immeasurable national significance alongside their prime minister, Winston Churchill.

Although the film involves a man overcoming a serious disability, it is neither triumphalist nor sentimental. Its themes are courage (where it comes from, how it is used), responsibility, and the necessity to place duty above personal pleasure or contentment – the subjects, in fact, of such enduringly popular movies as *Casablanca* and *High Noon*. In this sense, *The King's Speech* is an altogether more significant and ambitious work than Stephen Frears's admirable *The Queen* of 2006 and far transcends any political arguments about royalty and republicanism.

The film begins with a brief prologue in which both Bertie as Duke of York (Colin Firth) and his contemporary audience endure agonies of embarrassment as he attempts to deliver a speech at Wembley Stadium during the 1924 Empire exhibition. The rest takes place between 1934 when his wife (Helena Bonham Carter) arranges for him to see Logue, the unorthodox therapist (Geoffrey Rush), and shortly after the beginning of the war when he makes a crucial live broadcast to the world from Buckingham Palace, with Logue almost conducting the speech from the other side of the microphone.

Helena Bonham Carter is a warm, charming, puckish presence as Elizabeth, very much aware of her royal status when first approaching Logue using a pseudonym. Michael Gambon is entirely convincing as George V, a peremptory man irritated by the increasing demands of democracy; having been neglected by his own father, he's incapable of expressing love for his sons. Guy Pearce is equally good as the selfish, wilful future King Edward, the movie's one truly despicable character, whose mocking of his brother's stammer places him beyond the pale. Derek Jacobi does a neat turn as Cosmo Lang, the Archbishop of Canterbury, pillar of the establishment, at once dictatorial and obsequious.

The movie, however, ultimately turns upon the skilfully written and impeccably played scenes between Firth's Bertie, initially almost choking on his stammer but trained to insist on court protocol, and Rush's Logue, the informal, blunt-speaking Australian, whose manners are as relaxed as his consulting room in Harley Street is modest. The interplay between them resembles a version of *Pygmalion* or *My Fair Lady* in which Eliza is a princess and Henry Higgins a lower-middle-class teacher from Sydney, and they're just as funny, moving and class-conscious as in Shaw's play. There are also, one might think, benign echoes of Prince Hal and Falstaff from *Henry IV*.

Across a great social gulf they become friends, the king gaining in confidence and humanity, deeply affected by the first commoner he's befriended. But to the end there remains the need to preserve a certain distance.

The film is not without its odd faults, the truly annoying one being the representation of Winston Churchill (Timothy Spall) as a supporter of George during the abdication. In fact, his intrigues in Edward VIII's cause nearly ruined his career. In his biography of Churchill, Roy Jenkins remarks that 'had Churchill succeeded in keeping Edward VIII on the throne he might well have found it necessary in 1940 to depose and/or lock up his sovereign as the dangerously potential head of a Vichy-style state'.

But overall the film is a major achievement, with Firth presenting us with a great profile in courage, a portrait of that recurrent figure, the stammerer as hero. He finds as many different aspects of stammering as the number of ways of photographing sand explored by Freddie Young in *Lawrence of Arabia* or John Seale in *The English Patient*. And as they did, he deserves an Oscar.

The Fighter (David O. Russell)

The Observer, 6 February 2011

In the 1890s, the reputation of the cinema was seriously, possibly permanently, tarnished in the eyes of moralists and opinion-formers through the movie pioneers' preoccupation with filming prize fights, then as now regarded as an unrespectable activity. The fascination continued as Hollywood turned the noble art into the subject of a movie genre and a metaphor for social struggle and for life itself.

Every comedian from Chaplin to Jerry Lewis went into the ring at some time or other, and most stars found themselves putting on the gloves or playing managers and trainers. The best boxing movies have been about defeat, whether glorious or abject, about the loss or retention of dreams. The least interesting have been triumphalist stories that culminate in championship fights.

There have been fewer boxing films in recent years, probably because of the lessening of interest in the sport, and the only two made this century that immediately come to mind are both biographies of boxers whose careers follow a familiar dramatic arc in overcoming adversities and setbacks to win major titles. The first is Michael Mann's *Ali* (2001), featuring Will Smith as Muhammad Ali, the other Ron Howard's *Cinderella Man* (2005), starring Russell Crowe as the Depression-era fighter James Braddock.

Now there's David O. Russell's *The Fighter,* in which Mark Wahlberg plays 'Irish' Micky Ward, who was still taking serious punishment when Mann's biopic was released. If Ward's name is less familiar to most filmgoers, it's because Ali and Braddock were heavyweights and undisputed champions. Ward was a welterweight (in the crucial fight that provides the climax for the picture, both he and his British opponent, the Liverpool-born Shea Neary, weighed in at 10st 6lb) and won a World Boxing Union title which is far from undisputed.

Micky Ward's story, however, if the screenplay by Scott Silver, Paul Tamasy and Eric Johnson is anything to go by, is quite as extraordinary as the others with as many low points, though fewer major high ones. The most frequently quoted line of late twentieth-century poetry is probably the opening of Philip Larkin's 'This Be the Verse': 'They fuck you up, your mum and dad'. Had he lived to see *The Fighter*, Larkin would have found it necessary to add the line: 'And so do your older brother and sisters.' Because the movie is about a classically dysfunctional family that is pulled apart by internecine violence of a physical and emotional kind, then drawn together by an against-the-odds boxing triumph.

The film begins in 1993 in the run-down, post-industrial town of Lowell, Massachusetts, where the handsome, withdrawn, quietly spoken twenty-seven-year-old Micky's career has stalled after early success and he's working as a road paver. Divorced and with limited access to his little daughter, he's a warm-up fighter, a stepping stone for the careers of more promising pugilists on the way up. His extrovert half-brother, Dicky Eklund (Christian Bale), is an infinitely worse case. Dicky is a drunken, womanising crackhead who calls himself the 'Pride of Lowell' and lives off the memory of the night when he floored the titleholder Sugar Ray Leonard, though most people think Leonard slipped. Dicky has persuaded Micky that his role as trainer is essential to the younger brother's success, just as their strident, domineering mother Alice (Melissa Leo) is convinced that he owes everything to her determined management.

In fact, they are a pair of albatrosses around his neck, crippling handicaps who are destroying his career. Standing on the sidelines are Micky's six sisters and half-sisters, foul-mouthed harridans with that hard, prematurely aged look of poor, hard-drinking, heavy-smoking women. There's also a cowed father trying to help his son but terrified of his wife and of the chorus of harpies she leads.

The group dynamics of this rowdy household are handled by director Russell with great unpatronising skill in his best film for years, though his most conventional. Into this ménage comes Charlene (Amy Adams), a tough barmaid at a local saloon, who once had an athletic scholarship to university but dropped out. She's a spirited woman, who gives as good as she gets, and believes she can free Micky from his family shackles. Her uphill struggle appears to be helped when the self-deceiving Dicky is jailed for fraud, assault, theft and attacking the police. He emerges from prison a different, improved man but still a danger to the diffident, dithering Micky.

This is a frighteningly funny, oddly touching movie that never flinches from or attempts to sentimentalise the grotesquely embarrassing Dicky or to turn Micky into a liberated spirit. Both Wahlberg and Bale are excellent in their different registers, as are Melissa Leo and Amy Adams as the differently calibrated women. Bale, Leo and Adams have rightly received Oscar nominations and this is indeed an actors' film that draws its power and moral energy from the interaction of this ensemble. It's more about family than boxing and what's worth bearing in mind is that after the climactic fight, handled with traditional triumphalism à la *Rocky*, Micky had three murderous encounters with the late Arturo Gatti, all ending with both in hospital. A shot of the real Micky and Dicky included in the film's final credits shows what havoc twenty years in the ring can wreak on a man's face.

NOTES FROM THE DREAM HOUSE

Kes (Ken Loach)

The Observer, 11 September 2011

Back on the big screen in a new print that serves well the excellent naturalistic photography by Chris Menges (whose first feature film this
was), the seventy-five-year-old Loach's 1969 masterpiece of social criticism and humanist cinema is at the centre of the current well-deserved
celebration of his fifty years as a film-maker. David Bradley is wonderful
as the semi-literate Yorkshire schoolboy from a sink estate who shows up
the inadequacy of the educational system by mastering a complex book
on falconry to train a kestrel that becomes a symbol of freedom and
spiritual affirmation in a world of cruelty and willed indifference. The
bird's destruction and burial are as tragic, affecting and socially mean-
ingful as anything in twentieth-century art. I note new riches every time
I see this film (for example, the noble kestrel is found nesting high in an
old ruin from pre-industrial days), as well as happily revisiting such
familiar ones as the contrasted teachers, played by Colin Welland and
Brian Glover, and the terrible comedy of the innocent boy accidentally
beaten by the stupid, vindictive headmaster. The only film I rate more
highly is his Spanish Civil War picture, *Land and Freedom*.

Sherlock Holmes: A Game of Shadows (Guy Ritchie)

The Observer, 18 December 2011

A crippled veteran, returning to London from Afghanistan and forced to
live on a small pension, finds a flatmate who turns out to be a drug
addict. They become close friends and this other man eventually tells the
ex-soldier that Britain is heading for disaster but will emerge 'a cleaner,
better, stronger land' and suggests they rush to the bank to cash a cheque
before its signatory reneges. The subject of this highly topical story is, as
you've probably guessed, Dr John H. Watson, narrator of the Sherlock
Holmes stories. He's well played by Jude Law in Guy Ritchie's second
Holmes movie as a sensible, intelligent, reliable chap, even if he too

readily explodes or expostulates when confronted by his flatmate's outrageous behaviour.

But while the film's art director and costume designer give us an attractive version of late Victorian society, Robert Downey Jr's Holmes is from the end of the next century. His stubble is not even of the designer kind, his dress what passes now as 'smart casual'. The introspective, contemplative, ratiocinative, philosophic aspect of Holmes gets obscured as Ritchie turns him into a twenty-first century man of action in the mould of Indiana Jones and Daniel Craig's ultra-tough James Bond. We know that Holmes practised the martial art known as baritsu, but Downey has the fighting skills of an SAS trooper, the agility of a trapeze artist, the stamina of a long-distance runner and the physique of a man with a personal trainer. Like Bond, he endures pain and torture as he's beaten by thugs, injected by deadly poisons and suspended by a meat hook stuck into his chest.

The background mood is right, a complacent, seemingly optimistic 1890s bustling with energy, but with something dangerous rumbling underneath that is more than the tube station being built near 221B Baker Street. A vast conspiracy is being launched by the great mathematician Professor Moriarty, but only Holmes can do the maths necessary to realise that all the bombings and assassinations around Europe are part of the Napoleon of crime's plan to foment war between France and Germany. The aim apparently is to make the professor rich through his recently established control of armament factories that will eventually fulfil his megalomaniac ambitions. But while the intrigue is persuasive and related to many of the concerns of *fin-de-siècle* politics and the melodramatic literature of the period, the nonstop action is very much of our current cinema. The movie begins with a vast explosion in Strasbourg followed by similar pyrotechnics in London, Paris and Germany, which punctuate endless chases, fights on trains and battles that result in a body count that anticipates the world war Holmes seeks to avert.

The frenzy is actually increased by the device of sudden flashbacks using high-speed editing to explain how the great detective-chessmaster had anticipated, then executed, a succession of clever moves that resulted in the violent triumph we've just witnessed. There is not, however, too much time in this high-octane narrative for the development of character. Naturally, the women don't get their due. Irene Adler (Rachel McAdams), the love of Holmes's life, appears fleetingly. In a major comic coup that makes the audience draw its breath and laugh heart-lessly, Holmes throws Watson's wife from a train as it crosses a viaduct at night. Noomi Rapace, the striking heroine from *The Girl With the Dragon Tattoo*, stalks mysteriously through the picture as a fortune teller as if she'd been told to think she's appearing in the gypsy encampment sequence in *From Russia With Love*. The three Ms – Moriarty, Moran and Mycroft – come out rather better.

The screenwriters, Michele and Kieran Mulroney, have drawn on Conan Doyle's novel *The Valley of Fear* for Moriarty's character and background, and on the story *The Final Problem* for the film's climactic encounter between Moriarty and Holmes at an anachronistically named 'summit conference' beside the Reichenbach Falls. And Jared Harris plays him as a ratty or foxy type, rather different from the gaunt senior undertaker depicted by Sidney Paget in *The Strand Magazine*. The ex-army marksman turned assassin Colonel Sebastian Moran is a forceful presence as played by Paul Anderson. Stephen Fry has the right portly build and detached manner for Holmes's older brother, the establish-ment fixer Mycroft (a part in which Christopher Lee was wholly miscast in Billy Wilder's Holmes movie). He is, however, embarrassing when conducting a breakfast-time conversation with Watson's wife while naked, and he introduces an unnecessarily camp element by addressing Holmes as 'Sherly', presumably a reference to the famous 'and don't call me Shirley' joke in *Airplane!*. Hans Zimmer's melodramatic score incor-porates arias from Mozart's *Don Giovanni* and a jaunty Morricone theme from *Two Mules for Sister Sara*.

Watching this movie, I was constantly thinking of my friend and colleague, the brilliant wit, critic, novelist, translator and *pasticheur* Gilbert Adair, who died ten days ago. Especially his postmodern trilogy of parodic detective stories which conclude at a Sherlock Holmes con-ference in Meiringen, where Adair himself plunges into the Reichenbach Falls with his own central character. Adair calls his non-canonical Watson narratives 'Schlock Holmes', but the final book in his series, *And Then There Was No One*, contains the best Holmes pastiche ever written, a thirty-page re-creation of *The Giant Rat of Sumatra*, a tale referred to by Watson in *The Adventure of the Sussex Vampire* and called 'a story for which the world is not yet prepared'. I must declare a slight personal interest here, as there's a pretentious movie critic in the book called Philippe Françaix.

Meet Me in St Louis (Vincente Minnelli)

The Observer, 18 December 2011

This week we have a welcome rerelease of *Meet Me in St Louis*, which opened in America sixty-seven years ago this month. It was the first truly great movie from the Freed unit, the MGM department specialising in musicals and headed since 1940 by Arthur Freed, who wrote some of the best songs of the 1920s and 30s and produced several of the finest films of the twentieth century.

Freed acquired Sally Benson's series of *New Yorker* stories about the delightful middle-class Smith family proudly living in 1903 St Louis and looking forward to the following year's World's Fair but not to a proposed move to New York. He assembled the writers, composers, designers and cast, including the virtually unknown Vincente Minnelli, and told studio boss Louis B. Mayer: 'I want to make this into the most delightful piece of Americana ever.' He achieved his aim with a movie that defines perfection, as it captures the spirit of hope and anxiety that informed the last years of the Second World War, when it was made. It's a film whose four parts cover the seasons from summer to spring but is truly a film for all seasons and all time. Each chapter is preceded by a tintype of the Smith's idyllic suburban house that turns from sepia to tinted to ravishing Technicolor. The combination of new numbers such as 'The Trolley Song' and old music-hall favourites such as 'Down at the Old Bull and Bush' is beautifully judged. The title song that opens the film is picked up by different members of the family as they go around the house, a device borrowed from Hollywood's first great musical, Mamoulian's *Love Me Tonight* (1932).

The casting is flawless, starting with Leon Ames as the gruff, devoted Edwardian paterfamilias and Mary Astor (the definitive film-noir femme fatale in *The Maltese Falcon* three years before) as mother. Judy Garland has never been more spirited or more poignant ('Have Yourself a Merry Little Christmas' is up there with 'Over the Rainbow' and 'The Man That Got Away'). Margaret O'Brien has never been more tolerable, and the film makes her the instrument of the family's dangerous id as she tends her terminally ill dolls, embarks on a disruptive Halloween spree and decapitates the snowmen she'll have to abandon if the family leave their beloved St Louis for New York. When fellow MGM executives demanded to know the source of the film's dramatic conflict, Freed replied: 'Where is the villain? Well, the villain is New York!'

Once Upon a Time in Anatolia (Nuri Bilge Ceylan)

The Observer, 18 March 2012

Turkish filmmaker Nuri Bilge Ceylan initially trained as an electrical engineer and worked as a commercial photographer until becoming a full-time director. Now in his early fifties, he's one of the most significant moviemakers to have emerged this century, an original figure in his own right and a major force in reviving a belief in the kind of serious, ambitious, morally concerned European art-house cinema that was taken to new heights by Bergman, Tarkovsky, Antonioni and Angelopoulos in the 1960s and 70s.

In the films that established his reputation – *Uzak*, *Climates* and *Three Monkeys* – Ceylan used pared-down narratives with long takes and sparse dialogue to explore the ethical dilemmas of middle-class Turks, studying the social and geographical contexts of their personal lives and the larger world that is shaping them. There is always, however, a mystery about his characters. This derives in part because Ceylan refuses to provide intrusive exposition. More significantly, it arises from his generous invitation to audiences to make up their own minds about what they are seeing.

His finest work to date, *Once Upon a Time in Anatolia,* is a carefully controlled masterpiece. As the title suggests, it's a sort of fable with a very specific location in the Asian part of his native land. It's also (and the title inevitably evokes Leone's two violent classics) an exercise in popular genre cinema, in this case the crime scene investigation picture. The themes are universal and it could be reworked without much difficulty on the steppes of Russia, in the hill country of Texas or the desert of Rajasthan – anywhere where people get casually killed and other people come together to tidy up the mess.

A brief pre-credit sequence shows three men drinking at night in a dilapidated garage on the edge of a town. They are, as it gradually transpires, the perps and their victim. After the credits have rolled, three vehicles – two battered saloons and a military-style Jeep – snake their way across a bare, rolling landscape at night, their smallness and vulnerability emphasised by the widescreen. They stop beside the road and some of the passengers step out, two of them handcuffed. We might guess they're a band of mafiosi about to kill and bury some transgressor. In fact, the reverse proves to be the case. The handcuffed men are murder suspects accompanied by the police, a quartet of paramilitary gendarmes, a couple of gravediggers, a public prosecutor and a local doctor. They've confessed to their crime and are being brought to the countryside to locate the place where their victim is buried.

A body is needed to complete the investigation and it is supposedly to be found near a fountain beside a bridge not far from a lone tree situated a little further from the road. It's as if Vladimir and Estragon were accused of killing Pozzo or Lucky. But the chief suspect, Kenan, cannot or will not identify the place, and for most of the film the characters are literally and figuratively in the dark as they drive around the frozen wintry heath.

At first, the dozen all-male characters are anonymous, obscure figures. But as they bicker and banter about getting the routine job done and going home, they become individuals with hopes and fears and part of a contested hierarchy. Naci, the police chief, burns on a short fuse and has a sick child in need of constant medication. His driver, nicknamed Arab Ali, has a passion for food. The sergeant of the gendarmerie wants official credit for his role in the search. Prosecutor Nusret wears a smart overcoat, white shirt and tie and a decent suit and needs to get back to Ankara without getting caught up in any serious breaches of protocol.

He's a vain man, identifying the corpse when it's eventually exhumed as looking like Clark Gable and recalling that as a university student he was nicknamed 'Clark'. His constant urination leads the cops to suspect he has prostate trouble. Doctor Cemal turns out to be a city man, once married to a beautiful woman, childless, sceptical, observant, thoughtful. Keeping his own counsel, and possibly a larger keeper of consciences, he meditates on fate and the significance of individuals in the larger scheme of things. Cemal resembles Anton Chekhov and doctors in Chekhov's work. All this is revealed gradually, subtly, as if we were there in the community.

Along the way, we learn about corruption, neglect, inefficiency. The gravediggers haven't brought a pick. No one has remembered to take a body bag. The police cars are poorly maintained. The driver doesn't have a map. When they put in for a rest at a village to get tea from the mayor, the electricity fails and we discover no official has visited this place for years. Yet it is there that the suspects have an epiphanous encounter with the mayor's daughter that provides the investigation with a major gear change.

The visit to the countryside is beautifully lit by Ceylan's regular cameraman, Gökhan Tiryaki, and has a resonant soundtrack of natural noise ranging from wind in the trees to overweight coppers in creaking car seats. It's followed by a lengthy coda back in the small town where the killing occurred and an autopsy takes place. Here, the doctor emerges as the dominant figure. But daylight brings not an expected clarity but further obfuscation. The case appears to have greater complexities than we'd supposed, and we realise we've been watching a thriller as challenging as Antonioni's *Blow-Up* and Haneke's *Hidden*. As a character casually observes early on, we might remember this seemingly insignificant evening later in life as an anecdote that begins: 'Once upon a time in Anatolia...'

Ted (Seth MacFarlane)

The Observer, 5 August 2012

To some, comedy is a funny business; to others it's no laughing matter, and critics from Aristotle to Eric Bentley have attempted to explain and define it. Pauline Kael's review of *The Sting* set out to explain why it was neither funny nor entertaining; the left-wing theorist and cultural historian Raymond Williams once told the readers of the *Listener* that Rowan & Martin's TV show *Laugh-In* was unfunny. They were as unpersuasive as the British Council lecturer who tried to convince an audience in Tirana that Norman Wisdom isn't funny.

Woody Allen offers two definitions of comedy in *Crimes and Misdemeanors*, both ways of mocking the dislikable TV star played by Alan Alda and through him the celebrated writer Larry Gelbart, on whom the character is based. The fact is that the only definition of comedy is something that makes you laugh, and there's no gainsaying laughter.

These observations are provoked by some very sniffy and patronising reactions to the calculatedly provocative film *Ted*. It's the big-screen debut as director, co-writer and co-producer of Seth MacFarlane, author of the popular, envelope-pushing American TV series *Family Guy* and *American Dad*. I found this weirdly disturbing movie funny in both of the senses referred to in the 1945 British film *The Rake's Progress*. Told by her suave English lover Rex Harrison that she's funny, the Austrian refugee Lilli Palmer asked: 'Funny ha-ha or funny peculiar?'

Ted opens in 1985 in a wintry Boston so full of violence and prejudice, narrator Patrick Stewart tells us, that a Jewish kid immediately joins a band of Irish-American antisemites in tormenting the film's lonely eight-year-old hero, John Bennett. John gets a large teddy bear for Christmas, christens him Teddy and wishes that he could come to life. Which he does, not as an imaginary friend of the kind we all have had or as an invisible rabbit like Harvey, but a real-life 'thunder buddy' to console him at anxious moments. Ted immediately becomes a national celebrity, and in a glorious montage we see his rise to fame, his scabrous repartee causing Johnny Carson to collapse with laughter on his TV talk show. But as with everything else the audience gets bored with the novelty of a talking bear and Ted's popularity is short-lived.

By the time the film's title comes up after the pre-credit sequence, Ted's a nobody and we jump to the present where the thirty-five-year-old John (Mark Wahlberg) is stuck with his friend for life, the cynical, disenchanted Ted, watching TV and getting high on marijuana. By this point, Ted has become real to us, a foul-mouthed, acerbic, wisecracking ex-celeb. His face is immobile, but his voice (provided by Seth MacFarlane himself), eyes and body language are frighteningly human, a triumph of digitally created image-making. John is in a dead-end job with a car-hire company, and Ted is as demanding of his attention as Kenneth Halliwell was for Joe Orton's in *Prick Up Your Ears*, though the nature of their intense friendship is far from gay as Ted is obsessively heterosexual. A triangular relationship is completed by the sensible, high-flying business woman Lori (the delightfully confident and puckish Mila Kunis), who, after four years of going steady, is tired of John's devotion to Ted and his inability to commit.

The crunch comes when Lori and John return from a dinner celebrating the anniversary of their first date to find Ted carousing with three hookers, one of whom has defecated in the corner of the living room after playing truth or dare. The bear must go, and he's found a job at a supermarket where his every outrageous depredation is followed by a forgiving promotion. But he constantly leads John astray, most notably attracting him to an orgiastic party attended by their hero, the minor movie star Sam Jones, who played Flash Gordon in the 1980 film version of the comic strip. The two are enthralled by the popular culture of the 1980s, and Ted has an encyclopaedic knowledge of films and TV.

MacFarlane never stops providing Ted with suitably offensive one-liners: the bear, for instance, talks of suing the toy manufacturers Hasbro for not giving him a penis, and dismisses an unattractive, overweight little boy with the line: 'Back off, Susan Boyle'. And Wahlberg plays along beautifully, at one point reeling off a couple of dozen names for trailer-park girls in answer to a quiz question from Ted. Eventually the writers stumble somewhat while seeking dramatic closure, but they never lose our attention.

Ted belongs to a long line of stories dealing with disconcertingly half-human creations, with pets and toys brought to life, which reaches from *Pinocchio* down through the ventriloquist's dummy in *Dead of Night* to Spielberg's *AI* and Chucky, the malevolent doll in *Child's Play*, alleged by the prosecution to have influenced James Bulger's killers.

Behind this lies Sigmund Freud's division of the psyche into the id, ego and superego. Ted is the id, the area of the instinctual, the libido, the dark, destructive elements of ourselves. John is the ego, mediating between the id and reality but all too easily distracted. Lori is the superego, the conscience, the controlling part of the mind, the parental sense of responsibility.

So in effect we can read *Ted* as not merely a comedy of growing up, or refusing to move on from adolescence, but as a psychological fable about the continuing struggle to become a mature person. Of course, Ted would have something sharp to say about that.

How Hitchcock's *Vertigo* eventually topped the *Sight & Sound* critics' poll

The Observer, 5 August 2012

In the early 1950s, the British Film Institute was transformed by Denis Forman and Gavin Lambert. Forman was appointed director of the BFI in 1948, and one year later he invited Lambert to edit what Lambert recalled as 'the institute's terminally boring magazine *Sight & Sound* and bring it back to life'. Both left the institute in 1955, Forman to help create Granada TV, Lambert to become a Hollywood screenwriter and novelist, and by then the National Film Theatre had been established on the South Bank, and *Sight & Sound* had become one of the world's pre-eminent film journals.

Among Lambert's innovations was a worldwide poll of critics to vote each decade on the top ten films of all time, an immense undertaking that utilises the resources of the BFI and depends on the authority of *Sight & Sound*. The results of the seventh and largest poll were announced on Wednesday to a gathering waiting with bated breath at the now rather grand BFI Southbank complex (formerly the National Film Theatre), and they're published in the redesigned September edition of *Sight & Sound* (in 1952 a quarterly costing 3/6 [17½p], since 1990 a monthly now priced at £4.50).

In 1962, when there were few books on the cinema, no film schools, and virtually the only way to see a movie was in a picture house or at a film club, all ten films were in black and white. Six were silent (two of them by Chaplin), Robert Flaherty's tedious *Louisiana Story* was the single docudrama, and there were just two postwar movies, Lean's *Brief Encounter* and De Sica's *Bicycle Thieves*, a key movie in the influential neo-realist style.

Fifty years later, with film schools everywhere and 115 years of movies easily available to scholars and fans alike, the only surviving film from the first list is Dreyer's *Joan of Arc*, one of three silent pictures. The most surprising inclusion is the documentary *Man with a Movie Camera* by the Soviet theorist who styled himself Dziga Vertov (Russian for spinning top). Vertov's film is as dazzling, obscure and avant-garde as on the day it was made, and somewhat less accessible than such masterly movies as *On the Waterfront* and *12 Angry Men*, photographed in

America by his brother, Boris Kaufman. The 1962 list represented the orthodox canon of that day. The ten top films chosen in 2012 by 846 critics (of whom I was one) are the tip of an iceberg formed by the 1,045 nominated movies, and they reflect a new orthodoxy of sorts. Over six decades a new cinematic canon has been developing and changing, and it is less fluctuating and more conservative than one might have predicted.

Neo-realism has come and gone, as has the new Italian cinema that followed in the form of Antonioni's *L'Avventura*, which in 1962 got on the list in second place a little less than two years after being greeted with uncomprehending derision at Cannes. Ingmar Bergman, too, has also been and gone, possibly because votes were divided between a string of his masterpieces. The same is true of the French new wave, with neither Truffaut nor Godard reaching the top ten. Japanese cinema was unknown until *Rashomon* took a major prize at Venice in 1951 and helped heal the wounds created by the Second World War. Since 1962 every poll has featured Kurosawa, Mizoguchi or Ozu, with the last named now in third place with *Tokyo Story*, one of the most affecting movies of family life and ageing ever made.

In 1962, *Citizen Kane* suddenly took over the first position, with Renoir's *La Règle du jeu* close behind. Then, in 1982, Hitchcock's *Vertigo* joined the list after spending years out of distribution and available only in bootleg prints. This year, not entirely surprisingly, it became substantially pre-eminent. All three movies were box-office failures in their day, and it needed the polemical magazine *Movie* in the early 1960s to establish the reputation of Hitchcock as a personal director of great depth rather than just the 'master of suspense', which he called himself, or merely a gifted entertainer, which was *Sight & Sound*'s view of his achievement. The first book on Hitchcock in English was by a key *Movie* contributor, Robin Wood, published in 1965 and initially reviewed by a single national paper, the *Observer*.

The thirty pages the September *Sight & Sound* devotes to the poll make for a fascinating read. So many of the great masters – Wilder, Lang, Eisenstein, Peckinpah, Almodóvar, for instance – fail to make the cut, though in some cases only just. There's not a single twenty-first-century picture in the new list. The nearest any gets is Wong Kar-Wai's *In the Mood for Love* at 24, and David Lynch's *Mulholland Dr.* at 28. Since 1992, the critics' poll has been accompanied by a parallel top ten chosen by directors, which also contains nothing from this century. Interestingly, Michael Mann picked two pictures from the twenty-first century, but they didn't get on to the winning list. One was James Cameron's *Avatar*, which (in an accompanying note) he calls 'a brilliant synthesis of mythic tropes'.

I first voted in 1972 when I was in my late thirties. My ten films included *Citizen Kane*, *La Règle du jeu* and *Battleship Potemkin*, which all made the top ten list that year, unlike my other choices, which were Buster Keaton's *The General*, Francesco Rosi's *Salvatore Giuliano*, Kurosawa's *Ikiru*, Hitchcock's *The Lady Vanishes*, Ford's *Stagecoach*, Kelly and Donen's *Singin' in the Rain* and Bergman's *Winter Light*. This year (which even an apprentice actuary would tell you is likely to be my last) I decided to make a defiantly different choice of current favourites. They are (in alphabetical order) *Au revoir les enfants*, *La Grande illusion*, *Kind Hearts and Coronets*, *The Leopard*, *Meet Me in St Louis*, *Pather Panchali*, *Seven Samurai*, *Stagecoach*, *Vertigo*, *Wild Strawberries*. Only *Stagecoach* was on my 1972 list, and only *Vertigo* also appears in the latest top ten. On reflection, I find it much easier to list my hundred favourite westerns or ten best films featuring dogs than to pick the ten all-time best pictures.

Lawrence of Arabia (re-release) (David Lean)

The Observer, 25 November 2012

It's astonishing to think that Lean's stately masterpiece was made half a century ago, a mere twenty-seven years after the death of T.E. Lawrence, and that following the initial showing in 1962 the film was cut, making it necessary for the restorers to have Charles Gray dub the voice of the late Jack Hawkins. There are no intelligent epics like this today and, because of computer-generated effects, it's unlikely that there ever will be again. To appreciate the film fully, *Lawrence* must be seen in a cinema, in 70 mm on the widescreen and in stereophonic sound, and the present theatrical revival is not to be missed. I spent a year in the desert doing my national service and read *The Seven Pillars of Wisdom* there, but when I think of sand it's Freddie Young's images from *Lawrence* that I remember.

I'll never forget seeing the film for the first time at the Odeon, Leicester Square, a few weeks before Christmas 1962, and meeting my old university friend, Christopher Lambert, during the interval. Kit was a flamboyant gay, later co-manager of the Who before going to an early grave. 'This is the first queer epic,' he proclaimed to anyone in the foyer within hearing distance, and rhapsodised over the romantic encounters of a dune kind between Peter O'Toole and Omar Sharif.

If you can't get to a cinema or want to have a souvenir, there's a handsomely produced fiftieth anniversary special edition, which contains three Blu-ray discs that include the film itself, some first-rate documentaries, various interviews, deleted scenes (introduced by the great Anne V. Coates who won an Oscar as editor) and a frame from the 70 mm print. It's accompanied by an attractively produced book about the production and a CD of the score.

Django Unchained (Quentin Tarantino)

The Observer, 20 January 2013

The Italian western appeared in the mid-1960s, its aim both to compensate for the reduced number of American westerns and their lack of action. Shot in Spain by directors usually adopting American pseudonyms, they rapidly became known for ultra-violence, sadism, operatic staging, sharp colours, enormous close-ups and emphatic music. In the dubbed and heavily cut versions that reached the English-speaking world they had a crude quality that offended the few critics who saw them.

They did, however, have a vigour and a broad Marxist thrust in their attitude towards capitalism and third world exploitation. They made a considerable impact on the Hollywood western in its last days (especially on those featuring Clint Eastwood, the only American actor to become a star through working in Italy), though the name of only one Italian director, Sergio Leone, has become widely known outside the world of the genre's aficionados.

This sub-genre, known derisively as spaghetti westerns, more or less ended in 1978 with *China 9, Liberty 37*, a Spanish-Italian production that can be seen as a fable about moviemaking itself. Appropriately enough it was directed by Monte Hellman, the cult American maverick who co-produced Quentin Tarantino's directorial debut *Reservoir Dogs* in 1992. Because not only is Tarantino's first western, *Django Unchained*, a brilliant revival of the genre, it's an admiring and adroit harnessing of the spaghetti western to his own aims and purposes.

The name Django was frequently used in the 1960s for remorseless revenge heroes in Italian westerns, most especially the masochistic protagonist played by Franco Nero in Sergio Corbucci's *Django*, a 1966 picture banned in Britain for twenty-five years because of its extreme violence. Nero drags a coffin containing a machine gun around a corrupt post-Civil War town on the Mexican border and clashes with the Ku Klux Klan. In Tarantino's picture (in which Nero has a cameo role) Django is a fugitive slave (Jamie Foxx) in the Deep South two years before the civil war, who forms a curious alliance with an itinerant German, Dr King Schultz.

In an extremely funny sequence Django and Schultz challenge a raid by a hooded gang of proto-Klansmen. Schultz, a dentist-turned-bounty hunter, is evidently inspired by that frontier outsider, the dentist-turned-professional gambler Doc Holliday. He's seductively played by Christoph Waltz as the good side of the suave, silver-tongued SS Colonel Hans Landa in Tarantino's *Inglourious Basterds*. Waltz's wit and composure lend a lightness of tone to an incandescently angry film.

Teaching in the form of the experienced passing on their knowledge has always been a major theme of the western, and *Django Unchained* is the story of Schultz freeing Django and transforming him into an individual person, Django Freeman. It's also about how the cynical Schultz, who affects to believe that bringing in criminals dead or alive as a bounty hunter is 'a flesh for cash business' much like slave-trading, gets in touch with his own innate decency.

Schultz and Django first meet outside civilisation when the bounty hunter sees the slave chained to four others being led to market by brutal traders out west. After a lethal fracas they go on together to a primitive Texas township where the confident Schultz demonstrates his superiority to the crooked sheriff, the dim federal marshal and the prejudiced settlers. Django assists Schultz in tracking down three vicious criminals with prices on their heads. He in turn is helped in his search for his lost, humiliated wife and fellow slave, Broomhilda (Kerry Washington). Discovering that Broomhilda has learned German from an immigrant mistress, Schultz finds a role that appeals to his romantic German soul in reuniting the married couple.

In a wholly unpatronising way Schultz gives Django a sense of his own independence, channelling his anger against his exploiters but without tempering it with mercy. He learns practical matters such as handling guns and reading, and more complicated ones such as role-playing and biding his time.

The journey takes them ultimately to the world of Calvin Candie (Leonard DiCaprio), the charming Mississippi aristocrat and committed racial supremacist. His vicious personal fiefdom of Candyland becomes a symbol for the sadism, oppression, theft of identity, false assertion of enduring superiority and the corruption of the human spirit that lie behind slavery. He represents the self-deception and cruelty underlying the South's much vaunted hospitality and chivalry that has for so long been the subject of sentimental celebration, not least by Hollywood movies.

Tarantino's fascination with language comes to the fore in the terrifying verbal conflict between DiCaprio, the ornately loquacious villain, and Schultz, the eloquent democrat. They provide the prelude to the film's violent climax the way the debates over abolition were the curtain-raiser for the Civil War. *Django Unchained* is a long, powerful film, its dramatic brush strokes broad and colourful, its psychological points made with considerable subtlety and wit. In a sense it can be seen as a companion piece to Steven Spielberg's *Lincoln*, and it certainly places Tarantino among the most impressive filmmakers at work today.

A Late Quartet (Yaron Silberman)

The Observer, 7 April 2013

Musical groups, coming together, working harmoniously, splitting up, reuniting, provide one of the great metaphors for human activity. In the cinema we encounter them in such different forms as the real-life bandleaders Jimmy and Tommy Dorsey feuding and going their different ways in *The Fabulous Dorseys*; Bing Crosby's inner city priest reforming delinquents as a choir in *Going My Way*; Fellini's allegorical *Orchestra Rehearsal* presenting Italy as a musical rabble that can only function when submitting to a firm conductor; or Dustin Hoffman's recent *Quartet,* which sees elderly singers burying old differences to recreate their celebrated quartet from *Rigoletto*.

A Late Quartet, written and directed by the American documentarian Yaron Silberman, is a major contribution to this continuing cycle. A subtle, intelligent picture with a suitably resonant title, it quietly observes the internal dynamics of the Fugue String Quartet, an internationally acclaimed musical group founded and based in New York that has been playing around the world for twenty-five years. We encounter them as an entity, working together thoughtfully, a trifle self-regarding perhaps, and then we get to know them as individuals.

Their founder, the cellist Peter Mitchell (Christopher Walken in an uncharacteristically pensive role), is a quiet, paternalistic figure, whose wife, a well-known concert singer, has recently died. The second violin, the impetuous, overweight Robert Gelbart (Philip Seymour Hoffman), is married to the quartet's graceful, composed viola player, Juliette (Catherine Keener), whom he met as a student at Juilliard. Both are in their forties and have a daughter, Alex (Imogen Poots), herself a student of the violin. The fourth member is the first violinist, Daniel Lerner (Mark Ivanir), an intense central European immigrant of great technical brilliance, who makes bows, rebuilds violins and is a highly demanding teacher, one of whose pupils is Alex.

We sense the tensions between them but appreciate that they have been subsumed into their quarter of a century of playing together. They have found satisfaction not in discarding their individuality but in unselfishly contributing to a collaborative endeavour. Their unity is expressed in the music and also in the joint filmed interview that illustrates, a little too demonstratively perhaps, the face they present to the world. But all this is to be disrupted, the quartet challenged both singly and as a group.

Early on, the somewhat melancholy Peter introduces his student class to Beethoven's Op 131, the String Quartet No 14 in C sharp minor, which is to figure centrally in the film, and he precedes it by delivering the first ten lines of *Burnt Norton*, the first of T.S. Eliot's *Four Quartets*. But he speaks the lines in a conversational manner quite unlike Eliot's sepulchral, Anglican-pulpit style. He's talking of time in music and life, of continuity, circularity, eternity. And he goes on to point out that this late quartet has seven movements instead of the customary four, and that Beethoven demanded that it be played *attacca*, that is without any pause between movements. Both Op 131 and *attacca* become key elements in the film's dramatic structure.

Peter has been having trouble fingering the strings of his cello, and a sympathetic doctor (a gentle performance by Madhur Jaffrey) diagnoses early signs of Parkinson's Disease, and while he accepts this with resigned equanimity the quartet is thrown into confusion. In facing an uncertain future, they begin to consider their own careers as musicians and individuals, and Peter himself is involved in seeking to find a cellist who'll replace him and assure continuity. Fissures occur, fears are released. The first violin seeks equality. Robert and Juliette's marriage is threatened. Their daughter turns against them and embarks on an affair with Daniel, the first violinist. Although a punch is thrown and bitter words exchanged, this is about a buried turbulence that registers forcefully on the civilised seismographs of the characters' minds and hearts.

The film is set during a bitter but deeply romantic New York winter. Central Park is covered in snow. The warm, welcoming interiors contrast with the outside world, reflecting the feelings of the leading figures and the futures they face. There's a particularly expressive scene at night when Juliette, Daniel and Robert leave a meeting with the isolated, stoical Peter, knowing that his Parkinson's will soon take him from the quartet. They stand in the street, the snow falling in the night, talking reservedly of what lies around the corner. As the rotund Robert gets a little too frank about his intentions, his wife and Daniel draw away from him in moral disgust and each walks off in a different direction. He's left alone, bewildered, frozen out in the enveloping dark.

The cinematographer Frederick Elmes, a frequent collaborator of both David Lynch and Ang Lee, has made a wonderful job of locating the characters in their domestic environments – the plain wood of Peter's spacious brownstone apartment, the seedy hotel where Robert finds temporary refuge when his marriage is threatened, the messy student bedsitter where the rebellious young Alex has a confrontation with her judgmental mother. There are also lovingly staged scenes in the concert hall at the Metropolitan Museum, at a Sotheby's musical instrument auction, a visit to the Frick Collection, where Peter communes with a late Rembrandt self-portrait, and a drive into the countryside for Daniel to buy horse hair for the bows he crafts.

A Late Quartet is visually and musically rich. But above all there are the performances, individually and as an ensemble, and they're pitch perfect. It's a minor moment, but there's one scene that particularly sticks in my mind. It's when Philip Seymour Hoffman pulls himself together for a crucial concert by shaving off his unkempt beard. In that simple act of looking in the mirror, putting on the soap and wielding his razor you witness a life being rethought.

The Lone Ranger (Gore Verbinski)

The Observer, 11 August 2013

As soon as the western genre was established in the second decade of the last century, comedians headed to the frontier. From Chaplin and Keaton via the Marx Brothers to Abbott and Costello, the comic stars got their laughs by appearing far from home on the range among humourless tough guys riding tall in the saddle. As the B-western developed, its poker-faced, straight-shooting heroes had to be accompanied by comic sidekicks such as the ubiquitous George 'Gabby' Hayes or Fuzzy Knight. At the same time there developed the comedy western, a relaxed, easy-going affair – James Stewart as the peaceful new sheriff refusing to carry a gun in *Destry Rides Again*, for instance, or shy cowpoke Gary Cooper being mistaken for a gunslinger in *Along Came Jones*.

In the 1960s, the comedy western took on a sharper, darker, more ambivalent character. There were attempts at genuine satire, broadly farcical in *Blazing Saddles*, rather subtler in *Cat Ballou*. *Butch Cassidy and the Sundance Kid* mocked conventional morality, and Arthur Penn's brilliant, picaresque *Little Big Man* poured comic scorn on manifest destiny and dared using the word 'genocide' to describe the treatment of Native Americans.

The Lone Ranger (principally inspired by Zorro, the masked avenger of early nineteenth-century Spanish colonial California, but with some borrowings from a real-life Texas ranger) began life as a kids' radio programme in the 1930s, which spawned a cheap movie serial. World fame came through a long-running postwar TV series, which had two low-budget film spin-offs. In 1981 big money was invested in a widescreen treatment called *The Legend of the Lone Ranger* that rapidly vanished, and even more was spent on this new movie, a Disney company production, which is very consciously in the insouciant 1960s *Butch Cassidy* mode.

Like the current tales of superheroes such as Batman, Superman and Spider-Man, the new *Lone Ranger* sets out to provide the foundation story for John Reid (Armie Hammer), the Texas lawyer who became a legendary defender of justice as the masked Lone Ranger, and his devoted Indian partner, Tonto (Johnny Depp). It begins, like *Little Big Man* and *Young Guns II*, with the discovery way into the twentieth century of a famous frontier figure in old age, who tells a story that may well be at best a wild exaggeration.

In 1933 San Francisco, with the Golden Gate bridge magnificently incomplete in the background, a little boy wearing a white Stetson and a black domino mask enters a museum about the American West, passing dioramas about the great buffalo and the mighty grizzly bear before stopping before 'The Noble Savage in His Natural Habitat'. He's an ancient Native American, his face covered in cracked war paint. Suddenly his eyes swivel and transfix the little boy. It's Tonto, a Comanche brave, and in flashback he unfolds his story and his first meetings with John Reid on a Texas train that's taking a notorious outlaw, the sadistic, cannibalistic, hare-lipped Butch Cavendish (William Fichtner), to be hanged.

What ensues is a violent, action-packed film that draws on and refers to numerous westerns but mainly Sergio Leone's *Once Upon a Time in the West*. Here, a railroad tycoon (Tom Wilkinson) in league with a ruthless outlaw is buying up the land that will link the nation coast to coast by rail and control the water supply. Leone's film also has a subplot about a search for vengeance on behalf of persecuted minorities, and on top of this *The Lone Ranger* piles the extermination of the Indians, the stealing of mineral resources, the corruption of the law and the subversion of the military. In this it resembles the indictment of unreconstructed capitalism that Michael Cimino proposed in *Heaven's Gate*.

In this revisionist account of how the West was won, Tonto is no longer the sidekick. He's the wise, witty narrator, the tragic victim of progress and racial oppression, who shapes the character and demeanour of the naïve, upright Reid and, ultimately, turns him into an avenger. In putting the mask over his eyes, he makes Reid see. Hammer doesn't have much to do beyond looking handsome, baffled and surprised at the wickedness of the invading palefaces. Johnny Depp, however, gives a splendidly rich, sly performance that makes up for the increasing self-indulgence of his Captain Jack Sparrow in the *Pirates of the Caribbean* franchise.

The Lone Ranger is Depp's third western. In Jim Jarmusch's bleak, monochrome *Dead Man* (1995), he played a sad clerk with a striking resemblance to Buster Keaton who travels west to seek his fortune at a small-town engineering factory and accidentally becomes a wanted man. Adopted by sympathetic Native Americans, he ends up receiving an Indian funeral.

Depp followed this pessimistic, postmodernist film with the brilliant animated western *Rango*, directed by Gore Verbinski, who made the *Pirates of the Caribbean* pictures and *The Lone Ranger*. All the characters are animals and reptiles and Depp provides the voice of the lizard Rango, a would-be gunslinger who becomes involved in a story that conflates *Once Upon a Time in the West* and *Chinatown*. The music for *Rango* is by Hans Zimmer who draws on Morricone and a variety of others, as he does in his elegant pastiche score for *The Lone Ranger*.

This film is not the miserable disaster that American critics (much influenced by reports of its troubled production) have claimed it to be. Nor is it exactly a triumph. A trifle overlong and marred by a certain narrative confusion, it begins and ends with spectacular train chases worthy of Keaton's *The General* and is overall a handsome, exciting, affectionate movie. Sit through the final credits and you'll see a brief, really touching shot of Tonto making his journey home across the Old West.

Bonjour Tristesse (Otto Preminger) & **Plein Soleil** (René Clément)

The Observer, 1 September 2013

What goes around comes around. Or 'This is where we came in!', the words we'd whisper back in the days of continuous movie performances, before heading for the exit when we reached the point at which we'd entered the cinema. Appropriately in the week I write my final film column, two classic movies, *Bonjour Tristesse* (1958) and *Plein Soleil* (a.k.a. *Purple Noon,* 1959), are re-released from that period at the end of the 1950s when I was embarking on a career as a professional writer. Both appear in beautiful new prints that do full justice to the Mediterranean sun which dictates their mood of dangerous eroticism, and both are closely associated with what was popularly known as the French Nouvelle Vague. In the first of them an English-speaking cast play French people; in the latter a French cast play Americans.

Based on the 1954 novella by the precocious eighteen-year-old Françoise Sagan, *Bonjour Tristesse* centres on Cécile (played by Jean Seberg, shortly to become a New Wave icon). A wilful, spoilt seventeen-year-old in a semi-incestuous relationship with her rich, philandering widowed father (David Niven), she schemes disastrously to prevent him marrying his sensible middle-aged fiancee (Deborah Kerr). The cinematographer is Georges Périnal, whose credits range from *The Four Feathers* to *The Fallen Idol.* The sequences in an existentialism-lite Paris milieu are shot in low-key monochrome; the flashbacks to the previous summer on the lotus-eating Côte d'Azur are in glowing colour.

Eric Rohmer, in *Cahiers du Cinéma,* called it 'the most beautiful film ever shot in CinemaScope'. François Truffaut, like all *Cahiers* critics an admirer of Otto Preminger for his objectivity and evenness of sympathies (as represented in the framing of his actors), lauded the movie for the auteur-director's handling of Seberg. He even went as far as to suggest that Sagan might have lifted the plot and central relationships from Preminger's *Angel Face.* As with all Preminger and Hitchcock movies of that time, Saul Bass designed the exquisitely evocative titles, a series of Picasso-esque images that play on middle-class Americans' expectations of postwar France.

Jean-Luc Godard chose *Bonjour Tristesse* as one of the best films of 1958, and later, in a celebrated 1962 special Nouvelle Vague edition of *Cahiers*, he said: 'The character played by Jean Seberg in [*Breathless*] was a continuation of her role in *Bonjour Tristesse*. I could have taken the last shot of Preminger's film and started after dissolving to a title 'Three Years Later'.' At that time Preminger wasn't regarded in the English-speaking world as more than an accomplished journeyman. But the critic-directors of *Cahiers* and their brilliant American exponent Andrew Sarris argued persuasively that he was so much more than the provocative gadfly that critics in London and New York took him to be. They saw Preminger's work as a coherently developing oeuvre.

Plein Soleil was the last great movie of René Clément, an established moviemaker whose work was being sneered at in the late 1950s by the *Cahiers* critics, Truffaut prominent among them, as *le cinéma de papa*. A great director, his artistic career was to decline in the 1960s, though for a while his polished international thrillers prospered. *Plein Soleil* is an early example of what was called *noir en couleur*. An amoral psychological thriller, it made the twenty-four-year-old Alain Delon a star as the charismatic psychopath Tom Ripley. The anti-hero of Patricia Highsmith's novel *The Talented Mr Ripley*, he suddenly murders his tor-mentor, the rich playboy Philippe Greenleaf (Maurice Ronet), and takes over his identity, virtually turning into him. The innovative cinematog-rapher Henri Decaë shot two films for Louis Malle before collaborating with Truffaut on his feature debut, *Les Quatre cents coups*.

This links *Plein Soleil* to the New Wave, as does Paul Gégauff, Clément's co-screenwriter, a frequent collaborator of Claude Chabrol. The film is a masterwork that made the beautiful, sexually ambivalent Delon a dashing, romantic, yet strangely withdrawn figure in movies by Visconti, Antonioni and Melville. His much-publicised activities in the French jetset and demi-monde added a dangerous edge to his cinematic reputation.

Plein Soleil led to a string of movies across Europe featuring Tom Ripley: Dennis Hopper in Wim Wenders's *The American Friend*, Matt Damon in Anthony Minghella's *The Talented Mr Ripley*, John Malkovich in Liliana Cavani's *Ripley's Game*. Delon remains the Ripley that comes first to mind, but no doubt there's a definitive Ripley to come.

As a lifeguard stalking the cinematic coastline this past half-century (beware of a nostalgist saying half a century rather than fifty years), I've observed filmmakers surfing on *nouvelles vagues* on to our shores: the French, the Germans, the Czechs, the Australians, the New Zealanders have all had their new waves. Some were spontaneous (usually influenced from France), some government-sponsored. Every new country has aimed to create a national airline, and then a national cinema. I now feel it's time to descend from my *Baywatch* observation tower, check in my towel and surfboard and hand over the responsibilities for patrolling the beach to my young, experienced successor Mark Kermode and settle down inland.

Mark is a devotee of the thriving genre of horror flicks as I have been an assiduous proponent of the dying genre of westerns, and the job is in good hands. This chair is significant in a newspaper that has consistently taken film seriously from the moment the great cinéaste Ivor Montagu became the *Observer*'s first movie critic.

I have on the whole had an easy pass through life. An important part of this has been due to working for a paper I've always loved and which has been for me, as Holmes says about Watson, 'the one fixed point in a changing world'. I'd like to thank its editors for their sympathy and its readers for their attention. As my longest-serving predecessor C.A. Lejeune (her watch extended from the coming of sound to the shock of *Psycho*) said in the title of her autobiography: 'Thank You For Having Me'.

Index of Film Titles